Advance Praise for Held in Love

Here in many voices, forms, and stories we encounter afresh the mystery at the core of our existence—the mystery we belong to and essentially are. This beautiful, humble, and amazing book sings my heart and mind awake. ~**Joanna Macy**, *author of World as Lover, World as Self.*

We are all nourished by stories, particularly by those that inspire and empower us. This book offers a rich feast of just such stories, affirming over and over that we are indeed loved and we are never alone. Reading them was a delight, like hearing once again love letters from the soul in each of us. I recommend it. ~**David Spangler**, *spiritual teacher, Lorian Association.*

This book is a gift from the heart—to the reader's heart. Personal stories, amplified by poetry and photography, awaken us to the power of love, and the experience of numinous powers beyond the individual ego. In an era of cataclysmic change, this book offers insight, wisdom, and hope for each of us, and for healing our planet. It is a resource rich in soul. ~**Meg Wilbur**, *Jungian analyst, Vice President of the CG Jung Study Center of Southern California, teacher with internationally known Jungian analyst Marion Woodman.*

This is a most wonderful book and so needed at this time! The selections generate such a strong "field" of faith that we are indeed held in a loving Universe, no matter the circumstances, and that we can awaken to this fact and live it. I am very grateful to be part of this community of writers who testify with their experience and creativity to the omnipresence of love within, between, and around us and the process of awakening to it. ~**Thomas Yeomans, Ph.D.**, *writer and artist.*

This is a book you will not want to put down, and a contribution to the betterment of humankind. If you are in despair over the lack of love you see around you and within you, here are stories filled with divine hope. If you are in despair over the immediate threats to Mother Earth and her myriad creatures and peoples, here are stories of possibility and inspiration. If you are in despair over the lack of community and human kindness in our world, here are stories of our interconnectedness and common joy. Come to this well of flowing water, drink your fill, and be held in Love. ~**Rev. Emily Haight, Ph.D.**, *Clinical Psychologist, Diplomate, American Association of Pastoral Counselors.*

We are each uniquely who we are by virtue of our relationships to everything else, including to the mysterious totality that holds everything. Not only are we not alone, we are in an intimate dance with all things, a dance that defines us and supports us. In this wonderful collection, Molly and Carolyn have gathered from a host of colleagues poignant stories and poems describing how people discover, often unexpectedly and astonishingly, their full belonging to Earth, Universe, Mystery, Community, or Self. ~**Bill Plotkin**, *Ph.D., author of Soulcraft and Nature and the Human Soul.*

Held In Love is a tribute to the power of heartfelt stories and poetry to help each of us understand our relationships to each other and to our planet. ~ *Jenny Clad, Executive Director, The Climate Project.*

Thank you for doing this book. It is a goodhearted, wholehearted one. ~**Bill McKibben**, *educator, environmentalist, author of The End of Nature and Deep Economy.*

Contributors to this volume share significant, loving snatches—little bits of life—that come to them as their lives are marked with openness. I come away believing that all of life holds these bright, deep "bits" ready for us to discover and share as we experience life-altering shifts in what and how we see and feel. Gifts like these are right there waiting for us in our own lives. ~**Emma Justes, Ph.D.**, *Distinguished Professor of Pastoral Care and Counseling, United Theological Seminary, author of Hearing Beyond the Words.*

This book is a beautiful gift of inspirational stories that will encourage all seekers to open their hearts to the awareness of love's presence in our lives. ~**Frances Vaughan, Ph.D.**, *Psychologist, author of Shadows of the Sacred.*

To Allison,
with many blessings,

Molly Y Brown

Held in Love:

Life Stories to Inspire Us
Through Times of Change

Edited by Molly Young Brown
and Carolyn Wilbur Treadway

HELD IN LOVE: Life Stories To Inspire Us Through Times of Change.

ISBN 978-0-9611444-6-3
Library of Congress Control Number: 2009935780

Front cover art: "Cherishing the Earth" by America Worden

Back cover art: "Life Becoming" by Cindy Caldwell

Cover design by Ted Slawski

Technical Editor Ted Slawski. Set in Adobe™ Minion Pro.

∗∗∗

Psychosynthesis Press publishes books that further the full flowering of the human potential in harmony with the interdependent web of life. Psychosynthesis is a transpersonal psychology based on the work of Roberto Assagioli, M.D. (1888-1974) that seeks to integrate all the dimensions of life: physical, emotional, mental, interpersonal, social, ecological, and spiritual. Our books are based in this inclusive, holistic perspective. For information and to order books, visit our web site: www.PsychosynthesisPress.com.

Psychosynthesis Press

P.O. Box 1301, Mt Shasta CA 96067 • 530-926-0986

Table of Contents

On a Vision Quest ten years ago, Carol experienced a safety she had never known before. She came to realizations about her life's challenge and purpose, and felt a love that will be with her forever.

At a weekend retreat with other therapists, Carol suddenly found herself in an altered state of consciousness, in union with all that is, knowing that Oneness is Love.

Two amazing dreams teach Anne about the healing power of love.

On a visit to a nearby lake, Abigail struggles with her loneliness and learns acceptance and trust as she swims.

Lyn writes of a transformative experience at a rock concert years ago, giving her deep knowing of peace, unity, and love.

Jill vividly describes experiences she has had in the Yukon territory, feeling held in a timeless embrace and held by the force of her love of wild nature and all of life.

Paloma shares a numinous experience of waking up in the web of life, which has shaped her life and work ever since. The first story in a series of three.

Part Two – Awakening in Relationship

Linda was a midwife for thirty years, and was wearing down. She attended an home birth for the first time in many years, and felt held in love. She knows she still belongs with women as they give birth in this time of the Great Turning.

After hearing her mother's terminal diagnosis, Jen receives a massage and has a spiritual transformation that enables her to accept her mother's illness while caring for her with love.

Barbara tells of her mother's youth, and of her own. But now all is changed. Mother, tiny and silent on an oxygen pump, slips away to go dancing with the stars.

Ellise tells of a young man with AIDS who was first her client, then her friend, whose spirit remained unbroken through illness and death.

The suicide attempt of Carolyn's therapy client brought them both to the emergency room. Carolyn's spontaneous responses changed the client's view of herself and her world. The client later used this experience to hold a dying family member with compassion and love.

At a group meeting, Catherine acts out in anger and falls into a pit of self-loathing. Then to her surprise, she feels embraced by a sustaining love.

For America, both as a child and as an adult, the image of lighting a flame within herself has connected her with others who are also on fire with love for the world.

Carl fondly remembers his third-grade teacher who drew his attention to the wonders of nature and the universe, helping him feel a deep sense of belonging and connectedness.

Paloma recounts how she and her comrade Anne Herbert created the phrase: "Practice Random Kindness and Senseless Acts of Beauty" and launched a movement. The second story in a series of three.

On Barbara's flight to be with her ill father, her seatmate turned out to be an "angel" who prayed with her, giving her calmness, gratitude and strength that carried her through her father's dying and beyond.

Part Three: Awakening in Community

year old open hearted self and came to realize that all of us share One Heart. The joy of our inter-being can hold us all in rough times now and ahead.

Acknowledgments

We, the editors, would like to express our profound appreciation to our courageous contributors for their willingness to share their lives and souls through their stories, poems, and artwork. In doing so, they have gifted our world. We also deeply appreciate other heart-felt contributions sent to us; while they did not fit for our book, they were beautiful nonetheless.

Ted Slawski's expertise in book design has been invaluable; we appreciate his steadfastly working with us while we made up our collective mind. Many people have helped in various ways to bring *Held in Love* to fruition. Some suggested contributors whom we did not know ourselves, others advised us about publication, and so much more. For their marvelous support, we wish to thank Joanna Macy, Paloma Pavel, Dennis Rivers, China Galland, Mariellen Gilpin, Karen Latvala, Marty Walton and Linda Lyman, and Marika Foltz.

Throughout life and throughout the creation of this book, our families and our close friends have held us in love, thus enabling us to edit a book about Love. Our husbands, Jim Brown and Roy Treadway, have been unfailingly supportive and patient through our year and a half of e-mails, lengthy phone calls, and endless computer time. We also want to express our appreciation for each other. Through the shared journey of co-creating this book, we have discovered a depth of soul-friendship and connection that is all the more remarkable because, in person, we have never met!

We dedicate this book
to the memory of
Francis Underhill Macy (1927-2009),
compassionate giant across cultures
and a beloved wise elder to both of us;
and to our grandchildren:
Benjamin Brown Rousseau, Summer Luan Rousseau,
and Oliver Ross Stratton Treadway.
May they inherit a far more peaceful and healthy world.

Introduction

We live in times of change and tumult, times that challenge us mentally, emotionally, and spiritually. The chaotic effects of global climate change are impacting life around the Earth, and it now seems we may have waited too long to take action to prevent it. Much suffering will no doubt accompany these changes. We may have to endure years and years of intermingled catastrophes, one after another, as our oil-dependent economy unravels, natural disasters and epidemics sweep through the land, and civil society struggles to survive. Where can we find the spiritual strength we need to face these challenges?

Spiritual traditions throughout the world teach people to seek out a Source of healing, support, and guidance in difficult times. Some teach that we can find this Source within ourselves, through meditation and contemplation. Others urge us to pray to a Deity beyond ourselves, a Divine Companion who can carry us through. Whatever their religious beliefs, people are sometimes blessed with direct, spontaneous experiences of this Loving Presence—especially in times of heightened awareness and in times of despair. In this book, over seventy people share their stories, poems, photos, and paintings of such experiences, offering inspiration, wisdom, and hope.

We Western humans must move from over-emphasis on the mind (intellect) to more emphasis on the heart (love). It is vital to our survival to do so; we can't solve all the problems we face with reason alone. We must call upon the intelligence of the heart—which is holistic and encompassing—to guide us through the hard times that are already upon us. The stories in *Held in Love* provide evidence of this possibility and can help us make this shift.

Additionally, *Held in Love* can be used as a kind of guidebook for the ways love can guide and sustain us though the challenges that lie ahead. The descriptions in the Table of Contents will help readers find stories relevant to various situations. If someone is alone, sick, and scared, she can read "I Am Held in Love," which may remind her to call upon her own Higher Power. If someone is part of a group in which there is conflict, he can read "Wrestling with Truth/Love" for ideas on how to build community. Someone trying to understand an encounter with a non-ordinary state of consciousness might read "Not in Kansas Anymore" or "A Noetic Experience." Someone grieving the loss of a loved one might read "Healing Across the Veils" or "Siblings."

Gifts from Times of Darkness

Many of these stories and poems illustrate the gifts we can receive from dark times. On her web site, eco-philosopher and activist Joanna Macy mentions three of such gifts in her year-end letter for 2007 (www.joannamacy.net/html/letters.html#dec07). The first is the gift of uncertainty. When we look honestly and directly at the challenges we face, we see both the peril and the promise inherent in them all, with no way of knowing how things will unfold. We all would prefer a happy ending, but we have no such guarantees. We are like people who live with a diagnosis of a terminal disease; we know full well we may die of it, and yet we can still hold the possibility that we might be healed.

However, when we let go of our attachment to "a happy ending," something wonderful happens: we become more alive in the moment, more open to the wonder and beauty of the world. Uncertainty can also bring forth our creativity and ingenuity in responding to change. Life self-organizes in amazing and unpredictable ways. When we know what will happen, we tend to get into ruts of behavior and perception. In times of uncertainty, all bets are off, and we can come alive in creative new ways. One story that illustrates this gift is Demaris Wehr's "A Decision Made From Deep Within."

The second gift Macy describes is intention. This is something we can count on—not the outcome, but the motivation we bring, the vision we hold, the path we choose to follow. Firm resolve can save us from getting lost in fear or grief or despair. We can choose to live our lives according to our deepest spiritual values, no matter what the circumstances—and that choice can carry us through the most difficult of times. Our intention can be to bring love and healing to bear in every situation. As Gandhi said, "You must be the change you want in the world." Kevin Kamps illustrates this gift in "Defending Mother Earth."

And then Macy speaks of the gift of devotion. Our love for one another and for the Earth and all its life forms nourishes and illuminates our intention. In times of uncertainty and peril, we are impelled to reach into the wellsprings of our devotion, whatever that may be, to both sustain and guide us. Dark times invite us to go within and find the light, so it can illuminate our inner path—and often our outer path as well. Ruthann Johansen's "The Hammock of Love" speaks to the gift of devotion.

We can add two more gifts to this list: the gift of service, and the gift of community. The changes that lie ahead will call upon each of us to serve one another in ways we may never have thought possible. Such service will prove to be the most fulfilling experience many of us will ever have in our lives, deeply meaningful and rewarding to our souls, as Linda Seeley describes in her story "Birth, Rebirth." We may be called upon to listen to and support people going through trauma, strangers as well as friends—and we may never know in advance when we will be needed. We will be called to serve in our neighborhoods, on the street, in our work places. At other times, we ourselves may need help, receiving the same kind of support we have given. We are all in this together.

This leads us to the gift of community. In the hard times ahead, we cannot survive alone, individual by individual, family by family. We can only survive by helping each other, bringing our varied skills and gifts to bear, sharing what we have, and planning together to meet our common needs. Our neighborhoods and towns can be transformed in the process into more friendly, vibrant, sustainable communities. Carolyn Treadway describes a thirty-day taste of this kind of community in her story "WE."

At this pivotal time in human history, we walk into the unknown together, as into an initiation, a collective encounter with the human soul. We in the industrialized world have reached the end of our collective adolescence; it is time now to grow up, to move fully into true adulthood, with a broader, more encompassing sense of responsibility to the Earth, all its peoples, and all its life forms.

Global climate change can be a rite of passage for humanity, an opportunity for spiritual growth. We can do more than endure the dark times ahead; we can actively embrace them, armed with the gifts of uncertainty, intention, devotion, service, and community, held and sustained by Love.

At the end of Thomas Yeomans' novella, "Walden Water," the protagonist writes a letter to his family and friends about the awakening he has experienced during the winter and spring. His words speak profoundly and precisely to the basic premise of *Held in Love*:

> What is this? What is this that stirs us, prods us, wakes us from the sleep of our living? Last Fall I was asleep, though I had everything a man could want. And now I am more awake, yes, this is true, and the awakening is to this preciousness, this amazement, this realization of how loved I am, and how grateful I am for this love. You can say it is God's love, but that can be too abstract and distant, and leaves out the ordinary, everyday exchanges like the one with this man today. My experience is that this love comes from all directions all the time, from places and people you least expect, and that it is we who choose the degree to which we are open to it. It literally pours through the universe, uniting all creation. It is inexorable and gentle at the same time, insistent and full of truth and peace…Everywhere surrounded in love, and I, like a fool, missing this in my preoccupations!
>
> Not that there isn't suffering, my God, what suffering there is, and I have known it more, not less, as I have begun to realize this fact of love. The pain is bone-deep in all of us. Yet somehow the love is more than capable of holding this, and, as we are willing to touch the pain directly, we awaken to the love. And then they are both there, and there is such an aliveness in this, and thanksgiving.
>
> My dear ones, it may sound crazy, but I'm coming to think there is no death. Rather there is this death in life, in not living, and we are all struggling to awaken from this death to the Life which surrounds and holds us in this love.

May the stories and poems in this book help us all awaken to the Life that surrounds us and holds us in Love.

---

* Thomas Yeomans, 2000. *On Earth Alive.* Concord, Mass: Morning Star Press, pp. 146-147.

Part One

Awakening Within

Unfurling Rose – Carolyn W. Treadway

I Am Held in Love
By Molly Y. Brown

Between the mid 1980's and the end of the Soviet era in 1991, many Americans visited the Soviet Union as "citizen diplomats," attempting to build bridges of friendship and understanding between the American and Soviet peoples. I felt called to do what I could to heal the insane separation between the two "superpowers" of the Cold War and joined in this effort, co-leading groups of helping professionals to the Soviet Union from 1988 through 1990. We visited various cities and countries to offer training workshops to psychologists and mental health professionals. During one year's journey, we visited Vilnius, Lithuania, and were housed in a University dormitory, our trip occurring during a break between semesters.

We had a floor to ourselves in the large, poorly heated dormitory—and no hot water. We shared this inconvenience with a good part of the city, because under the Soviet system hot water and heat were all centralized.

I became quite ill one evening and someone drove me back to the dormitory, while my companions continued the evening's training program. I found myself completely alone in a cavernous building in a strange Soviet city—no concierge to call upon and no phone, even if I had known how to use it or whom to call.

As the hours dragged on, I felt sicker and sicker, plagued by stomach cramps, sore throat, vomiting, diarrhea, and high fever. Somewhat delirious and more and more frightened, I could think of no way to summon help. I tossed and turned on the narrow bed, crying and moaning to myself, when I wasn't staggering to and from the bathroom.

Then suddenly, without any forewarning, a palpable Presence flowed into the room and encircled me with a warm motherly blanket of love, without words or explanations. Wrapped in that love, I *knew* in the depths of my being that I was not alone, and never had been. I was loved, cherished, and safe, no matter what pain and fear I was going through. The love did not magically heal me, or interfere with the process of my illness; it simply held me as I struggled with the pain, nausea, and fear.

I began to sing a little song to myself. "I am held in love; I am held in love. Even when I suffer, I am held in love." Singing this eased my fear and discomfort, so I sang some more, with other phrases such as "Even when I doubt it" and "Even when I'm frightened."

By the time my friends returned to the dorm an hour or so later, I was in bliss. All twelve of them crowded into my little room to hear my story and my song. I think they all joined in singing it with me, although I can't remember now for sure.

I have never forgotten the experience of being held so strongly in love and have recalled it many times when in distress. I have also told the story numerous times to others. I can never doubt for long that I am held in love—and believe in my heart that we are all held in love, always.

I Have Been Held
By Carolyn W. Treadway

I have been held in love
even if I didn't know it
even if I didn't experience it
even if I doubted it, mistrusted it.
Love has brought me safely thus far
through thick and thin--
lots of thick and thin.
The angels have watched over me,
not visible to me,
but not banished by my unknowing.
My invisible guides have guided me
along an oft barren path,
which, nonetheless, has bestowed
countless riches upon me.
Spirit has expressed Herself through me;
countless people have told me so,
but how would I know?
Ahh…
"By your fruits ye shall be known."
The fruits of my life
could only have come
through Spirit.
Praise be!

Discovering Grace*
By Carolyn W. Treadway

Several years ago, early in my training to become a personal life coach, we trainees were guided through a "future self" visualization. Usually guided imagery does not take me anywhere, but this one was different, powerful, and beautiful. When I entered this visualization, I never dreamed it would be a profound spiritual experience. But it was.

Guided from present time and place into interstellar space, and back down to somewhere on Earth twenty years hence, I became acquainted with my future self--myself twenty years from now. After "seeing" the beautiful surroundings and the home of my dreams in which she lived, I "saw" my future self clearly, and began to get acquainted with her. She was beautiful—erect, silver haired, graceful, flowing, calm, smiling, spacious, connected, generous, and compassionate. I loved her immediately! A wise woman and respected elder indeed, she touched my heart deeply and opened my vision of who I might eventually be able to become.

At the close of the visualization, we were to ask future self her name. What came through to me were two names, Graceful and Gracious—I did not know which. Processing this exercise with a partner, we were both moved when I named my future self "Grace," the common denominator of both names I had been given for her. But Grace was still an abstraction, very much my *future* self, far into the distant future, and as far from me as if she and I were on opposite sides of the Grand Canyon. We were instructed to use our future self as a resource for our coaching. It sounded like a good idea, but I did not know how to do so.

Later that day a training colleague young enough to be my son coached me in a twelve-minute practice session. Soon he called upon Grace (my future self) to offer her suggestions. I (Carolyn) shared my ideas, but they were abstract and lifeless. He asked to speak to *Grace*. I replied that she was not here; she was "way over there" in space and distant time. He asked me to show him Grace, here and now. What would she be doing right now if she were present? Dancing! The word fell out of my mouth. My young coach rose, pulled me to my feet, and started dancing with me, around and around the room. It was amazing! I moved ever more freely and spiritedly. During this dance, I realized that Grace *was already* present, right here and now! *She was me and I was her!*

In those moments, something shifted in the ground of my being. The Grand Canyon gap between Grace and me just disappeared. It truly was a moment of Grace--a time of discovering Grace, when she welcomed me as part of Her. These moments for me were perhaps similar to Helen Keller's "waaah moments," the moments when Helen comprehended that Teacher Annie's motions, signing into her hand, actually meant something--meant the "waaaater" from the pump gushing over their hands. From that moment on, a whole new world opened up for Helen. My world also changed, by my knowing that Grace was *already* within me and I was *already* within Her. Inexplicably, we were already one. Of course I have long known the fundamental tenet of my Quaker faith: there is "that of God" in everyone. But this was a visceral knowing, not a head knowing. Truly, I was gifted by Grace in these vibrant moments.

Grace's gifts have not left me since that day. Moment by moment, I can tune in to Grace's presence or absence in me, or to whether or not Grace is being expressed through me. Once awakened, I can no longer *not* know when I am in, or not in, a state of Grace. Day by day, I am very often *not* Grace, not gracious, not even graceful. Still, Grace guides me, and constantly invites me into a state of being that I glimpsed so profoundly in my own future self twenty years hence. That vision draws me toward her. Would that I could fully become her! Would that I could truly and continuously express Grace here and now!

Quakers might call my future self-visualization an experience of being in the Light, or having the Inner Light illuminated by Grace. Many have had such experiences. For me, there is now a vision, and an understanding, of what it looks like and feels like to be in a state of Grace (or in the Light). This guides my days and illuminates my path. Now I am so aware of when I do, and do not, act as Grace. My coaching colleagues call me Coach Grace. It takes only hearing that name to invite me back into the state of being I experienced in that training exercise: the state of Grace, and the state of being graced by Grace. From the place of Grace so much more is possible, even in the most mundane dimensions of ordinary daily life. For the opportunities to learn this, I am most grateful. Grace invited me, and continues to invite me, to live up to the Light I have. I now believe that as I do, more *will* be granted me. May Grace gift you too!

*Previously published as "Birthed into Grace" in *What Canst Thou Say?* 50: May 2006

The Reckoning
By Judy Young Smith

I closed my eyes as I lay dying,
Not in surrender, but denying
That which essayed an end to life.

And in that darkness, I affirmed
The light, the fire that in me burned
And would not be extinguished.

The rage to live within my soul
Would not allow death to control
The limit of my Being.

I closed my eyes, I saw the flame
Strong, eternal, it spoke my name
And I came back to answer.

Eternal Flame – Carolyn W. Treadway

Held in the Great Vastness
By Anne Yeomans

Iwas walking to school. I was the oldest of four in a very unhappy family. I was probably ten or eleven, maybe in the 6th grade. I remember exactly where I was on the sidewalk. Not on my block but the one after it, just where the road turns to go down the hill toward the busy street that led to the school. It was the stretch of sidewalk where we used to play, " step on a crack and you will break your mother's back", as we walked. I always felt kind of disloyal when I played that game, and tried hard not to step on any cracks.

I was just walking along and suddenly into my mind came the realization that there were planets and stars around us, and that the world was so much bigger than the unhappy house I lived in, than the arguments of my parents, than the uninspired school I was attending, than my shyness, than my pre-adolescent awkwardness, so much bigger than the job I had given myself as the oldest to be good and to work hard to make the people in my family happy and safe.

It is as if the sky opened up in my mind.

It just happened. I wasn't thinking about it. All of a sudden I knew that we were very small, that my unhappy life that I was taking so seriously was also small, and that we were all living in this very big, big space. I was still Anne Eastman, a sixth grader walking to school, but everything was different

I am not sure I have words that adequately describe how that made me feel. I know on some level it was deeply comforting. Instantly I felt relief in knowing that my life as I had experienced it up to now, and my place in the family, which I took so seriously, was not all there was. It made feel me freer, and allowed me to exist within something much larger than what I had been existing in before.

As I look back at it now, I think that moment actually changed my life forever. Though I didn't understand that at the time.

On my way home from school either that day or the next, I went to my friend Nancy's house. She was both my friend and also mean like sixth grade girls can be to each other. I tried to tell her and her mother what had happened to me on my way to school, and what I understood now. I remember mumbling something about the planets. It was definitely hard to put into words, but it didn't take long for me to decide that they didn't understand what I was talking about. So I never said anything again about it to anyone for a long, long, long time.

But I know that everything was different from then on. I knew that I belonged to my family still, but I also belonged to that vastness.

Lilacs
By Coleen O'Connell

Spring has arrived once again in this northern climate. I eagerly await the beauty and smell of the lilac—a constant throughout my life—whether in Minnesota, South Dakota and in recent years, Maine. I can count on it like the moon growing big through the month then disappearing again. Most people love lilacs, yet there is something so deeply personal about this smell and sight of lilacs blooming.

In a busy household packed with five children, two parents, and one bedroom, as a young child I discovered that the lilac bushes nestled against the outside of our house held possibilities for privacy. During the course of several weeks at the age of four, I spent hours breaking off shoots and branches on the inside of the bushes slowly hollowing out two small round "rooms" in the middle. When my mother discovered what I was doing, she helped cut the stubs of the shoots with her scissors. Her permission to be so industrious in this way fueled my nest building.

Once I had the two rooms cleared, I began what was to become a daily ritual. I would grab the rugs from the porch and place them on the floor of my rooms. I then hauled out my doll bed, the dolls, a picture to hang on the "wall" and any other treasures my mother allowed me to borrow—blankets, a pillow, baskets, books, toys, etc. The china tea set I had received at Christmas from my godmothers inspired my daily tea party. Back and forth, back and forth I went. Often the entire morning was taken up retrieving and placing the items in my house. One room was a bedroom—the other the living/dining room. Into each I would place the appropriate items often experimenting in the function of the rooms and changing and rearranging all morning.

Once I had everything settled, my mother would often bring my lunch to me on a tray. It was there that I would sit and eat with pleasure in my own home. Often the afternoon brought a nap snuggled into the blankets on the rug. My mother, busy with two younger children, knew always where she could find me in the heat of the Minnesota summer. My older sisters, busy with their friends, only rarely showed interest in my little hideaway—all the better for me as I preferred the privacy. I did on occasion allow my little brother to visit or more importantly, a neighbor boy who was my best friend. He loved playing in his sand box so we often traded out sandbox time for lilac bush time.

My favorite picture that sits by my bedside is the photo of my first wedding—taken in front of my lilac bush home with that little boy and myself the day we got married at age five. I announced to my mother that we were marrying and sought permission to put on my favorite dress with my little blue wool coat with the pink rosebud on the collar, and my dress shoes. Rusty in his little corduroy jacket and baseball cap is as cute a husband as anyone will ever find. Officiating at the wedding, my mother laughed her way through our ceremony. In the photo, we are both grinning broadly as my mother snapped the picture to consummate the marriage.

I was held in love by both a wonderful mother and by those lilac bushes. The day the robin came to build her nest above me amidst the branches, I was a bit distraught. Complaining to my mom, she invited me to view it as a blessing—a sign that the bird felt so safe she could build her nest and lay her eggs and I would be there to protect them from harm. With that inflated understanding, I made peace with the robin and sat eagerly while she incubated her eggs. It seemed to take forever but my mom reminded me that it would be much quicker than the baby she was incubating. This was how I found out that another sibling would enter my world.

The days of summer passed. The birds grew and fledged. Somehow the smell of lilacs is about babies, love, home, safety, contentment, independence, joy, and ownership. Each afternoon before supper my mother made me bring all my furnishings inside lest it rain in the night. I tried to get by with leaving them but I soon learned that if I did not do it in a timely way, I would be out there in the dark before bedtime hauling everything in. That was a bit too scary for me. And so each day brought with it the back and forth ritual that filled my small world with such industry and mission.

The winter months were hard ones for me as I longingly looked at the naked branches and the empty spaces so visible to everyone who came to our house. My long-standing present to my mother each Christmas was a cheap bottle of lilac perfume from the Five and Dime Store. It was the smell of contentment.

Those lilac bushes held me in love for many years—maybe until I was 9 when being at the park with my friends became more important than playing with dolls in the lush green of bushes. Eventually we moved from that place and the house was torn down and with it the lilac bushes. What I have now is a deep connection to earth as home, a wedding photo by my bed, and a large patch of lilac bushes growing tall and thick by my house in Maine. What I lack is a four year old to begin the process anew.

Bathroom Grace
By Paula D.

Almost thirty years ago now, I was in deep despair. My marriage was in tatters—all I wanted to do was get out, but I had a baby boy. I felt as though I was losing my self and didn't think I could survive staying in the marriage to raise my child. At the same time, I was terrified of leaving the marriage; I didn't think I could raise the child on my own. Late one evening after yet another senseless argument with my husband, I took refuge in the bathroom. I stood with my back to the door facing the bathtub and from the bottom of my soul I cried, "help!" And whatever power there is in this world responded. It was as though someone was placing healing hands on either side of my head and from those hands peace washed over my whole body and I knew absolutely that I had the strength to do whatever I decided I needed to do.

I haven't needed to call on that healing love since then. I've been close a few times, but each time I remind myself that the healing love is there and that I can do what I need to do without asking for reaffirmation. I have no idea what "it" is, except to know that "it" exists absolutely—that amazing affirmation of spirit.

Not everyone has a bathtub for an altar.

The Fall
By Anne Yeomans

Walking a path
I had been on hundreds of times before
A long branch like a snake
Hidden in the last leaves of fall,
Brought me to the ground.
It was night.
Two cars stopped.
"Are you alright?" they asked.
"I don't know," I answered.

A fracture—hairline, but
Nonetheless a break.
The x-ray technician in the
Emergency room was named Tara.
I wondered at the time if she knew
She bore the name of a Goddess.

Grounded in my life
By a stick in the road,
I stopped.
No traveling somewhere else to find
Something more or better.
For days I sat in a long green
Chair in the living room.
I watched the sun move round the house.
My breath deepened.
Rest came.
The richness grew and grew
I was nowhere else but here.

Om Tare Tuttare Ture Svaha*

*This line when spoken or chanted evokes the presence of the Goddess Tara. It can be translated as:
"Praise to Tara, Praise to the Great Mother, who liberates from suffering, who grants all successes."

The Promise
By Dorothy H. L. Carroll

I am sitting in meeting for worship in my beloved Friends Meeting, looking out the window at the tall pine tree, trying to get centered down but not being able to get there…the clock on the wall shows twenty minutes has already ticked away, and still I sit, not able to center down…

There is so much on my mind: the Dean's letter, which has been traveling back and forth in my briefcase for a week, waiting to be filled out and handed in; my mother's nurse's tantrum about the practical nurse who did not sign her log the right way and "obviously never will"; no time to have a cup of afternoon tea with my mother again this week; the course I am teaching that is not going just the way I want it to; my student so nervous over the final exam that she cannot think of anything else; the research we three professors are doing that is shoddy and yet we are too tight for time to do it right; and this week's visit from my department head reminding me that I will be up for tenure next year—I ought to have a book "in the oven", some new research being published, speaking engagements planned, an extra faculty committees I should serve on…

College teaching, I had thought, would be the zenith of my teaching career. It would be a place where we could exchange exciting ideas about our profession; a time to be with other educators trying out new theories, testing them with each other's thinking; sharing new books on learning, new articles in journals. "What do you think of this idea?" Stuff like that. Time to have lunch with other educators who were in the fore-front in their fields…personal moments with good friends in the faculty lounge…rich conferences with students eager to learn, to exchange ideas, to learn from me and with me…

While a few of my hopes and expectations have become a reality, very few have. There seems to be no time in our frantic, fast-paced, overworked schedules to do these things, no time to nourish each other and share our minds. No time to be with my mother. And no time for myself, to live a different kind of life, a quieter life, a centered life…

As I sit here, I wonder if I left this college, would it be any different at another college? Today there are very few academic jobs for anyone, especially a sixty-year-old woman like me. No, the question I am facing is whether to give up my job and my profession to have the kind of life I really want.

Months of attempts to make this decision have not worked. I have spent hours making pro and con lists, praying, co-counseling, consulting friends, family and colleagues. I have tried everything I can think of, and still I cannot decide.

I am used to listening to God in meeting for worship and in many other places and times in my life. So maybe if I actually can get centered down, and ask God what I should do, God will speak to me. Again I try to get really still inside, to clear my mind and listen.

Slowly the static in my mind diminishes. The calm creeps in. I am unaware of everything and everyone else in the meeting room. No sound disturbs this exquisite quiet. I am intensely alert.

And then I hear the Voice, clear and distinct.

"IF YOU LEAVE YOUR JOB, YOU CAN HAVE YOUR CALM CENTER ALL THE TIME."

I was being held in such divine love it took my breath away. What a promise God was offering me—my calm center—*all* the time?

I left the job. I spent precious time with my Mother. I was with her during her illness and her recovery. And I was with her, loving her, when she finally died, holding her hand and being so very grateful that I had had this precious woman in my life, and this time with her.

Now, twenty-six years later, I am still holding close the promise God made to me, that I could have my calm center all the time. I think my life is still a work in progress: I have my calm center some of the time, and am doing some important work to get there all the time.

Understanding myself and where I have strayed from the path of my life's journey, and what I have learned from this, is an important part of getting rid of the flotsam and jetsam in my life, clearing the way for my calm center all the time…living up to God's promise for me.

For instance: looking back on my struggle to get my doctoral degree, to get a college professorship, I wonder why I did that. Surely I made up a story of what it would be like to be a college professor…a story, which turned out to be a fairy tale! Was I after what I call my 'fame and fortune' pattern? That I thought I would be top of the heap if I became a college professor? Probably. Fortunately I could afford, financially, to learn this lesson. What I did learn is that the life I really want has nothing to do with status and position, but has to do with my calm center.

Reading Thomas Kelly's *A Testament of Devotion* has meant a lot to me. He understands where I am wanting to go as he writes: "…if only we could slip over into that Center…we have seen such lives, integrated, unworried by the tangles of close decisions, unhurried, cheery, fresh, positive…with quiet joy and springing step…"

And what is my calm center? I am learning that it is the everyday love of God and the everyday love of people, the everyday beauty of the landscape and God's world. It has to do with being in this world, being in my calm center…being, not doing. Being all I can be, the highest and the best of all that I am. All the time.

*Thomas Kelly, 1941. *A Testament of Devotion,* New York, NY: Harper and Brothers, pp. 115-116.

Marble Meadows
By Maggie Ziegler

Water tumbles down from the ice fields below Morrison Spire and the long ridge out to Mount McBride. Four friends climbing, four body rhythms falling into one silent breath as we move through fields of limestone set into volcanic rock towards the spire, stopping just below the ridge to drink greedily from the waterfall pouring cold into our cupped hands, splashing sweating faces thrust into the spray. If water is safe anywhere, it is here and we leave the filter pump buried in a backpack. My body falls into almost forgotten memories of drinking freely from mountain streams, into ancient species memory. Who are we without this?

On the spire we watch anise swallowtail butterflies fall through space, drift up on wind currents. To the east the abrasive fossilized stone of wide Limestone Cap; the limestone formed over two hundred and sixty million years ago in a south Pacific sea-bed, carried eastward a hundred million years later, finally pushed five thousand feet above sea level to create the mountain backbone of Vancouver Island. The spreading cap filled with fossilized remains of dense meadows of waving crinoids—ancient starfish ancestors—and scattered broken shells of brachiopods that resemble bivalve mollusks. Feeling my age: energy formed and dissolved and reformed through endless time, connecting me to the old beings locked in limestone. Wildness flows into me, light exposure on the shadows.

We begin a lazy descent to where the waterfall pools quietly and the late afternoon sun slants onto the luminous green mosses creeping to the water's edge. We walk silently across the plateau towards the next ridge and the drop to our camp on the other side. Caring blasts through the loosening boundaries of my body towards these friends with whom I am quietly attuned. When we stop to rest, friendliness fills the space between my still body and two fritillary butterflies motionless on yellow flowers, golden wings spread wide. The possibility of relationship glints off the glossy black coats of bear and cub across the pass, the small one rising on hind legs to place forepaws on mama's shoulder to peer curiously at us from this place of safety. Mother bear walks unhurriedly away from us, the cub a protected shadow at her side.

There is grace in this rising kindness, a sweet peace, despite knowing things are not quite right, that the melted snow pack we drank from carries air borne toxins, that the land is too dry, that in these times loss and grief temper joy. I dig a ball of snow from an icy patch near the trail, push it under my hat. Ice water drips into sun stressed eyes, rolls over hot skin, sits on the end of my nose, forms blotches on my glasses. The earth crying, I think, as the ice tears fuse with a sudden hot wetness rising from within. I walk slowly, blurred vision, no separation between the earth's grief and my own.

On the ridge we stare back at the spire and the dark slopes pierced with multiple thrusts of white fossilized limestone, thinking about the shifting tectonic plates, volcanic outpourings and—most recently—almost a million years of glaciers spreading and retreating. We look into space and time, seeing all we are and all we have been and all we could be, then turn, descend through meadows of paintbrush and monkey flower along a small mossy brook. When we reach our tents we wrap our arms sweetly around each other.

Last morning, thermal mug full of scalding tea, walking back and forth on an outcropping that follows a mountain stream. Walking on old rock, feeling gratitude for the enormous dawn silence (the absence of insects, the absence of grief). Gratitude to the earth visionaries, who protected this pulsing place, for mountain air, the freezing tarn water shocking every sense into urgent life, the sweet heady smell of vetch, the white anemone flowers growing at snow melt. Gratitude for this body that can carry a house on its back, pick a way across loose rock, kick to solidness on slushy snow fields, climb to where wild snow peaks stretch full circle. I walk back and forth on my rock, along the stream banked with mosses and small yellow flowers catching the first sun, catching my heart smiling.

We hike across the meadows, past Limestone Lake, to a hillside covered with intoxicating purple lupines. Caution has returned and we pump water from a small tarn into our canteens for the descent. We take pictures of each other in the lupines, careful not to crush them. Half way down the mountain we stop for lunch where dozens of white pine butterflies dance in filtered sunlight between Douglas fir trees. One rests on my arm, white wings with black markings. A light touch, a magic blessing. Re-enchanted, I am willing to go on to the place where I live most of the time.

Holding the Stars
By Sara Wolcott

While the human mind has the capacity to hold almost anything, for some reason, my mind is particularly good at holding onto worries, fears, anxieties, 'what I should have done,' 'I'm not good enough,' and other such voices that encourage separation and suffering. But sometimes my mind clears, and I can be in the present moment, and open myself to the incredible grace of the world that is always there, waiting.

That night, we had made a campfire on the beach, myself and several other new-found friends at a month long retreat. I was far from the arms of my partner, and filled with recent memories of feeling lost, confused, and uncertain about where to turn next. The sky was darkening, and one of the men suggested we wait for the moon to rise. Knowing little about the cycles of the moon, we all thought it was a great idea.

After several hours, and the moon still had not risen, we heard shrieks and laughter from the far end of the beach. Not long after, another cohort of friends came running to our campfire, bare feet red. The phosphorescence, they exclaimed! The sand is phosphorescent and it sparkles when you stomp on it! It is so beautiful! Curious, and still waiting for the moon, we set out, into the dark and the cold.

The four of us—three men and me, a young woman, all in our jeans and boots—walked across the sands. I don't recall the conversation. I remember laughing, and the biting wind, and how the waves were luminous in the starlight. In the depth of the night, with comforting crash of the waves, my mind was quiet, and peaceful, not rushing to the next thing. The waves did enough repetitive motion; I could just watch and love.

And then we found the spot, by accident, when one of the men kicked his boot on the sand and the sand flew and it looked like shooting stars. We laughed and jumped up and down. As we landed, the tiny phosphorescent bits leaped about. We tried walking, arm in arm, in sync, and watched tiny sparkles of light radiate out from where we walked. It was as if we were creator-gods and the stars rose to meet our feet where we walked.

Then, after playing for a while, and standing close for warmth, someone pointed upwards. Ah, the stars! Here, far away from the campsite, the stars shone fiercely, daring us to love enough to reach them. Below our feet, the tiny bits of phosphorous shone like the Milky Way. Above us, the stars of our closest neighbors winked their greetings. And here, between the two, we held one another, these strong men embracing one another and me, no fear, just the power of an intimate mystery. It was as if the stars held us, from above and below, filling our very selves with the essence of dancing light.

Or was it we who held the stars?

And look—there—a glowing ember on the horizon over the Pacific Ocean—is it— yes it must be—yes, yes it is—the moon! A mere sliver of silver, she rose slowly from the horizon, and we laughed, delighted and exhausted, to be so well held in love.

Held in Her Love
By Janine Canan

Were you bathed in her beam,
entranced by her glance?
Intoxicated in her scent,
thrilled by her chant?

Were you waked by her cry,
tossed in her dance?
Dashed in her storm,
buoyed on her wave?

Were you cooked in her flame,
seared by her light?
Freed in her bliss,
purified in her peace?

Were you held by her love,
humbled by her grace?
Home in her embrace,
saved on her lap?

Song to My Mother
By Janine Canan

The Earth is my Mother,
the wind my Mother's breath.
Trees, flowers, birds and animals—
all are my beloved Mother.

The waves are my Mother's cheeks,
the stones my Mother's feet.
Trees, flowers, birds and animals—
all are my beloved Mother.

The stars are my Mother's crown,
the sun and moon her eyes.
Trees, flowers, birds and animals—
all are my beloved Mother.

Mother Spirit – Janaia Donaldson

My Guardian Angel
By Ulla Neurath

It was a cold Christmas Eve in 1965. I was 11 years old sitting in my grandmother's kitchen. Oh, dear grandmother, poor woman, who had survived two World Wars and whose heart was frozen to ice! But I could feel a glimpse of warmth in her nice cooking of tasty food.

It was evening and she told me that it was out of the question that I could stay overnight. I must go home where I belong, to my mother, she said. After all it is Christmas Eve. I could not understand why she was so heartless to turn her back on me and send me home.

What home? Home was hell, and she knew that! I was very disappointed, and frightened of the kind of situation I was going to meet when coming home. Nevertheless, my grandmother told me to leave her as she was old and tired and had to go to bed.

There I stood outside her house in the middle of the street. It took about 20 minutes for me to walk home. It was cold and snowing. I was afraid, my heart was beating, and I hoped that no one could hear it. As I approached the building where I lived, my heart beat harder. I took out my key out of my pocket, opened the front door, and went up the stone stairs, one heavy step after another until I stood in front of the entrance door.

I could hear loud radio music. I took out my key for the second time but it stuck, because my mother had locked the door from the inside. I rang the bell—no answer, so I rang it again and again. Still no answer, but the music became louder now. I knocked with both hands and with all my power on the door—that is, all the power an 11-year-old girl could have.

Then the music was turned off and my mother shouted, "Who is there?"

I answered: "It's me, Pussi, your daughter," and I asked her to open the door.

She said, "No, I won't let you in, because you left me alone this afternoon on Christmas Eve to visit your grandmother; if she is more important to you than I am, you can go back to her."

I could neither go back to my grandmother nor call her, as she had no phone. I asked my mother again to let me in, but she refused. I heard her steps going away from the front door and then she turned up the music. There I stood, frozen, sad, frightened. No one to turn to.

I lived alone with my mother in a small town in Germany at that time. Being a child of an alcoholic I didn't have friends because I was so ashamed of my family situation. So I did not knock on the neighbours' doors, either.

One last time I rang the bell, but I just heard the loud music and my mother saying, "Go away!" I was tired, frightened and felt totally abandoned. I sat on the cold stone stairs outside the front door crying. "Is there no help, nothing, must I stay here all night?" I thought. I cried and cried in despair and trembling, pleading inside: Please, please help me; what shall I do?

I don't remember if I fell asleep at last, and I don't remember when, but suddenly I felt a kind of warmth inside me, some soft sense of safety. I became calm and then I was given an idea from somewhere deep in my heart. A soft voice said: "Pussi, I will help you; don't be afraid. Just follow my advice: Go downstairs outside the house and look for the closest phone box. Go inside, pick up the phone, dial your home number and tell your mom the following words: 'Mom this is Pussi. If you don't open the door within 10 minutes, I will call the police.'"

I thought, "This is impossible. She is drunk and she won't pick up the phone. I don't have money for the phone." The voice continued, "Pussi, everything is fine. Please trust me; I am here for you and I will guide you."

I went down the stairs out into the cold winter night looking for a phone box. An elderly couple passing by wondered what a little girl was doing out so late alone in the middle of the night. I asked them if they could show me to the closest phone box and they did. "Here, you have some coins," they said and asked me if they could help. I answered, "No, thank you. I must phone someone." The couple walked away.

I did exactly as the voice told me. I felt very calm and safe. I dialed my home number and waited and waited for many rings. Then my mother picked up the phone. "Hello, who is there?"

I answered very calmly: "Mom, this is Pussi. If you don't open the door within 10 minutes, I will call the police." It was quiet on the other end; I heard her breathing. "Do you hear me, Mom? Do you hear what I am saying?" and I repeated the words. Suddenly she started crying and hung up the phone.

I went back to the house and the voice inside me said, "Go on; the door is open now." I went up the stairs until I stood in front of the door. I grasped the knob and the door opened.

My mother stood in front of me still crying like a child and staring at me. "I am so sorry," she said, drunk, with a choked voice. Then she said, "I am very tired. I must go to bed now."

I was awake a long time that night, wondering and astonished about what had happened, until I finally fell asleep.

Today I know that it was my guardian angel—the power of my higher Self—that helped me that Christmas Eve. I knew from then on that whatever distressing situations would be in my life (and there were a lot to follow), I would survive with my guardian angel inside me.

Amazing Grace
By Tom Nylund

I grew up in a family with a predominantly atheistic culture in which religious and spiritual experience was seldom discussed. We traveled widely in the United States and abroad, camping wherever we went, and so we met and had fun with a wide range of people from around the world. We loved animals and the outdoors and had a deep appreciation for the wonders and beauty of nature. As best we could, we lived by accepted moral and ethical standards, and we did our best to treat others the way we thought they would like to have been treated. I guess in retrospect, I was at home in my family, in my world, and with my values, but I was shy and unsure of myself. My relationship to myself tended to vacillate between self-criticism and sadness for my perceived shortcomings. I was woefully ignorant of the beauty, inner strength and power of renewal within myself and others. I was just not very aware of the deeper dimensions of life.

In my 30's, challenges started to present themselves, which I was unequipped to handle; I was successful at work (by my supervisor's standards) but I felt inadequate. When I was promoted to a supervisory role, I felt dissatisfied with my ability to inspire and support those whom I supervised. Also, as I began to see the havoc that our materialistic culture was reaping on the natural world, my work goals (to create a product in support of the advertising industry) seemed hollow and contradictory to the direction I felt humanity should be taking to protect the earth and its inhabitants. In my personal life, I struggled with intimacy and created problems for my wife and our marriage. Inwardly I was dying, but I had no idea how to find relief.

Eventually I developed the strongest urge to do something which was not about me. I noticed in the local newspaper an opportunity to train to become a volunteer, short-term counselor to help troubled teenage girls. The only training session for the next year conflicted with a previous commitment, but inexplicably I felt compelled to do the training. In retrospect, this decision signaled the moment in my life when I started to seek my deeper, spiritual self. I remember one day, when I observed a professional counselor listening to the grief and emotional pain of an adolescent girl struggling with her circumstances. I was awe struck by her trust, vulnerability and courage, and by the compassion and kindness of the counselor. For me it was as if some very dry part of my soul had just received water for the first time.

Over the next few years, during every free moment, I was either reaching out to others challenged in their lives, or I was focusing on my own challenges through reading, self-help groups, spiritual and psychological workshops, and counseling. Paradoxically, as I began to feel more and more alive within myself, the structure of my life began to disintegrate: I left my research and development career at Eastman Kodak, my marriage ended, and eventually I left Rochester NY, moving halfway across the country to Illinois in hopes of pursuing a relationship with a woman I had met at a workshop in Idaho.

Living in Illinois, unemployed, and not knowing what to do next presented a challenge, but also an opportunity. Each morning I would get up and do whatever called me in the moment. I trusted that with time and awareness of my feelings, some kind of direction would present itself. I documented my dreams each night, and found comfort and inspiration. I continued with workshops, counseling, and self-help groups. One morning in August 1990, after about a year without employment, while on a walk, it occurred to me that I would like to spend the rest of my life helping people with their dreams so they could discover their deepest desires. With that thought, I felt such an intense, energetic reaction in my body that I knew I needed to pursue the possibility. I immediately called the Jung Institute in Chicago to determine the requirements needed to become a Jungian Analyst. Discovering that I needed a degree in psychology, I went to the library and looked up the admission requirements to the local colleges. Finally, I went to Illinois State University, and by the end of that week, I was enrolled as a graduate student at large with four courses in psychology. In May 1993, I got my Masters Degree in Counseling Psychology. During those three years other opportunities presented themselves, and so I never pursued becoming a Jungian Analyst, but instead became a counselor and assessment specialist for children and adults. Dream-work continues, however, to be my favorite way of helping people search out their personal truths.

Even as my sense of comfort with myself and my life increased, I continued to have difficulty reconciling my spiritual life and my doubt about the existence a divine being responsible for creating the world. I so wanted a belief structure about God that made sense and felt right. On October 28, 1992 I had a dream that brought an end to this struggle. In the dream I was climbing a steep snow slope to the top of a mountain. As I approached the summit, the snow gave away and I found myself being hurled down the mountain. The roar of the avalanche was deafening. I tried to make swimming motions with my arms to try to stay on the surface of the falling snow. I knew I was about to die. I woke up in shock, eyes open, but the sound and the vibration of the avalanche continued to shake my body for another half minute or so. I lay in bed wondering: if I were to relive that dream, what I could do to save myself? Then it occurred to me that I could pray. A peace came over me and I fell asleep again.

As I slept, I dreamt again that I was at the same mountain. Now everything was peaceful, and I saw myself as a baby, floating in the air with the massive slopes of the mountain in the background. God was above the mountain, I sensed, as in invisible presence. As I watched, the baby began to shrink, until it was a speck and disappeared. It occurred to me that I had just watched my own death, but it wasn't awful. I had felt loved, held, and cared for. Everything was all right. When I awoke, I felt sure I would never fear death again. I realized that a living God was the essence of who I was deep within myself, and that God within every person gives each of us the capacity to be OK in whatever circumstance we will ever face, from birth to death and beyond.

Since the dream, I have come to trust in life, in the wisdom of life, and in the small part given to me to do each day. When I look back over the past 20 years or so, I notice that my life has been ordinary. I have not accomplished any great things. I have done a lot of little things that, hopefully, have been helpful to others. I remarried in 1995 and continue to have a loving family, wife, and stepdaughters. Clearly, I have been blessed and my journey has been guided down some inexplicable, kindly path. As I age, I think more about death as a friend (who will come some day, hopefully with a minimum of pain). I do not really trust beliefs that much anymore, and rely more on my experiences and what seems to be true. I let my goals flow out of my experiences and inclinations each day. I try to keep my head out of the way as much as possible and just let life happen. And you know, if I think too hard about God, I notice that I am still pretty much an atheist, but this does not seem to matter anymore.

The Breath of God
By Pollianna Townsend

(This is a story I wrote twenty years ago, at a time of profound change in my life. My old self was dying, and my new self emerging.)

A darkness has come upon me from whence I do not know. It hovers as an enemy watching my every move, waiting that it might consume my soul. My days grow longer as the day turns to night and the nights turn to hell. I look to the sky in search of an answer, in search of a divine revelation from a kind and merciful God. Instead, I am met by the face of the dark as it leers and laughs at my pitiful cry for help.

I know that I am dying and feel my time to be short, yet I still seek out the very old and wise. As they speak of great mystical healing, I am left with the knowledge that even the wisest of the wise do not have the key to the lock that bars my soul. The fight has been fought as I stand in utter defeat. With back bowed I hear the knock of death at the door of my soul. I succumb to my plight as I make my way home.

I travel back to an old and familiar place and watch the foam covered waves caress the sandy shore. The once beautiful woods appear through a dark foggy haze. The air is thick and stale, the wind is still, the sea is calm, the spirit has ceased. All is lost, all is gone. Too weak to move I loose myself to the infinity of the sea, and surrender to imminent death.

In that still moment, I watch in amazement as the fog begins to make way for a gentle wind. Sweeping in from the distance, a sweet breeze fills my nostrils as the fog clears.

With tears rolling down my cheeks, I look to the sun and see its brilliance. I look to the trees and hear their welcome. I join the sea in its peaceful rhythmic motion. And in this sacred moment, I give thanks, for I know I have been graced by the very breath of God.

Peace Vigil
By Molly Y. Brown

Have I known this all my life
And held it buried out of sight?
This aching grief
This great sadness
For a world gone so far awry?
When it finds its way
Through the well-built walls around my heart
I am frightened and annoyed:
I have no room for this!

Yet feeling this
May be the path to peace.

Restoration
By Molly Y. Brown

I came here cross
Prickly and petulant
Closed off from beauty,
Irritated by ants

But in time the sun gentled me
As I napped in the warm tender breeze.
Now peaceful again
I've returned home to my heart.

Undulate
by Rebekah Hart
Undulate: Rising and falling; building up and breaking down.

Today my mind
filled itself up
with dreams and thoughts
and preoccupations
longings
worries
fantasies

and underneath
the bothered sense
of being somewhere
I didn't want to be.

It was not the outer place
but the inner one that bit at me,
gnawing away like an
endless itch.

Of course, it was the child
living out the fear and sadness
of her days.

I kept telling her,

Look!
The world is here around you

The trees and water
call your name

The wind and fiery sun are dancing
in your lungs,
on your shoulders...

She only glimpsed and turned away.

A tenacious, spoiled child
addicted to fairy tales and temper tantrums

What could I do?

I tried painting
swimming
making her wash dishes

Nothing worked.

Until finally
I lay down next to her
closed my eyes
and held my arms out
resting open

I know you are here,
I said,
and I am happy.

The child quieted.

Spoke to me in
pressing sensations
the size of my thumb
rising and falling
in the space
between my lungs.

Breathe in,
she said,
and I did.

Breathe in again.

On The Edge
by Rebekah Hart

Why am I waiting
for all of this to end?

Tying knots in the web of the world
tumbling towards death
a final destiny.

We kill so mindlessly
the threshold of life
held precariously
between our fingers

a mosquito slap

the ant I accidentally drowned
in the bathroom
sink.

And still the stars appear each night
The world turns in its usual way
Babies are born
Husbands leave their aching wives
The spider weaves her magic web
only to have me
walk through it
again
in the fresh new morning

Goddess
I know you are here

And who
can I imagine myself to be

in the face of this
delicate dance
this filling up
and draining out
the endless resurrection of the world?

Here in this sacred place I walk barefoot.
Rough soles touching holy ground
the pulse of a body
much older and larger
than this small life
holding me
as I move between her crevices

I imagine myself in a large womb

I am in the Goddess
The Goddess is in me

My will and my body
are just a small wish
standing on the edge of a love that never ends

Another Kind of Therapist
By Mariellen Gilpin

My recovery from mental illness has been stepwise, and this is a story about one of those steps. In January 1994 I had been ill for sixteen years—doctors, pills, hospitals, therapists—all had worked to help me manage the illness, but none of them was making me really well. I often thought I needed a different kind of therapy, another kind of therapist. I took my pills faithfully, and worked hard to control the hallucinations myself. As a result of a spiritual experience I understood I was to give up all praying. Because of that decision I was able to remove one medication entirely, and managed my illness on just one pill a day. I was stronger, yes, but the illness had a life of its own. It was now six years since I'd made that decision.

The night of January 7, I prayed a prayer that came from the bottom of my soul: "Jesus, I know you are with me every step of the way in this journey without prayer. I try hard to put my love for you into action. I pray with my life, not with words. But one of the pleasures of my life is telling my husband I love him. I do for him, and I do for you, and I know that doing love is far more important than saying love. But I love telling my husband I love him. Please, make it possible for me to tell you I love you without hallucinating because of it."

With that Spirit-led prayer began my exorcism. (The story of my exorcism appears in *God's Healing Grace: Reflections on a Journey with Mental and Spiritual Illness*, Pamphlet #394, Pendle Hill, Wallingford, PA: 2008.) Over the next five months I released eight demons. No human assisted me; I knew no spiritual helper whose character I really trusted. God was my exorcist, as I grappled with my own shadow. In early May the eighth demon left me, and suddenly I was enabled to pray without hallucinating. I was still mentally ill, but praying no longer triggered the illness. I gave thanks daily for the gift of prayer, doubly given: first at birth, and now restored to me.

Then suddenly on June 6, I became very, very sick—sicker than ever before in all my years of mental illness. *Something* wanted me sick. All night, every night, night after night, I hallucinated. I was unusual in my experience in being attracted to the hallucinatory world. Since the hallucinations were attractive, I chose them over and over—and hated myself for my choice. I had been trying so hard to get well, and now this. On a Sunday morning in mid-June I walked three miles to worship praying every step of the way: should I try to blot out this craziness with heavy, heavy medication? Medication had made me a zombie before; I hated to do that again. Was it the way to sanity this time?

Quakers worship in silence, and when I arrived at the meetinghouse I went into silence at once. I'd said it all to God already during my walk, and I simply fell into a deep inner silence. Near the end of the hour I came out of my wordless state and asked God my question again. Often the solution to a dilemma had come to me as a result of silent worship; I had often entered the silence crazy, but I had always left worship saner.

What came to me in worship that day was the greatest challenge of my life: *Don't increase the medication. Use your mind to think it through, with My help. Walk into your inner darkness. Face your shadow, and overcome it with My help. I brought you safely through the exorcism. You are now able to pray. I want you completely well. Take my hand, and we will walk into your darkness together. I will be your therapist.*

I reflected on the dangers I had faced during the exorcism. I had clung to God throughout, and God didn't fail me. I might still be horribly ill, but since the exorcism I could pray without causing hallucinations. So I put my hand in God's hand. I would not increase the meds. I would do my best to learn what I needed to learn about my shadow, and God was promising to be with me.

The next fifteen months were hard, hard—and lonely. The mental health professionals never dealt with the content of my hallucinations nor helped me think it through.

The theory seemed to be "Just take your pills and never mind the talk," and when I finally insisted I needed to talk, the therapist discouraged talking about what was actually happening to me. She also discouraged my writing about my illness. I told her, "I write my way to sanity." With that she reluctantly stopped dissuading me, although she never approved. She was a fine lady, helpful in many ways, but not somebody with any understanding My illness was quite complex, but one important strand was my relationship to power. My family of origin taught me powerlessness; I was terminally nice, compassionate of others to the exclusion of having compassion for myself. I was also terribly afraid of anger, easily bullied by others. Like most terminally nice people I was out of touch with my own anger, stifled as it was, and my shadow self erupted in self-destructive choices: I chose power by healing others with the laying on of hands, making myself crazy every time. I hallucinated because I didn't know my anger, and had never processed it. Other cultures are full of stories of selfish healers coming to a bad end; my own medical culture failed me, as I co-opted God's healing power to meet my own unexpressed need for a more authentic self.

God brought me face to face with my anger and then helped me find ways to take care of myself, respecting the bully's essential worthiness while asserting firmly for my needs. Slowly, painfully, one bullying friend at a time, I developed power of my own, power I had earned by speaking up. I didn't need healing power—God's power to heal—because I had self-respect I had earned by facing my fears and doing the right thing anyway. I gave up all healing that involved my direct participation. (I am free to ask *God* to heal someone, but I personally am supposed to stay entirely out of the process. As a matter of fact, I focus my prayers for others' healing almost wholly on their spiritual healing. That seems to me to be much safer.) When I stopped choosing to heal others, I stopped choosing insanity as well.

When I pray about a problem, I sometimes have thoughts that are not my own. Sometimes my thinking gets into a deep rut, and God presents me with a more objective thought. Needless to say, it is a trick to know which thoughts come from me and which come from God. God's suggestions are always, always helpful, sensible ones—challenging me to think things through more deeply, challenging me to use my own good sense. Sometimes the suggestions are seeds for thought, and I have to work for my insights.

So many times during that fifteen months, I prayed about a problem and received helpful guidance. Each time I faced a new terrible dilemma, God helped me see my pattern, think it through and make different choices, asserting for my needs. If I ever had any doubts about the wisdom of walking directly into my inner darkness, my shadow world, I had only to reflect on God's clear presence in every decision for sanity I made in those fifteen months. I have never been so frightened as I was then, but I knew as never before that God held me in Love, challenging me, teaching me, keeping me in Divine care while I learned what I needed to learn in order to change my ways.

Nowadays I very seldom hallucinate—maybe twice a year. I still take a little medication, but I have a stable, happy life surrounded by friends and filled with meaning. I recently completed my third year as clerk of my Quaker meeting—a "clerk" is a combination of spiritual and temporal leader, a servant leader of the community. My shadow and I have become friends, taking care of each other and learning what each knows. We work together now. I may still be mentally ill sometimes, but I am saner than most people, most of the time. God challenged me to choose life, and has made it available with great abundance. Praise God!

Birth and Grace[*]
By Carolyn W. Treadway

In November 1972, I was nine months pregnant with our second child. All was well within me and without. This baby was planned and much wanted. The pregnancy had gone well, we were quite prepared for natural childbirth, and both my husband and I were eagerly anticipating the forthcoming childbirth and new family life that the birth would bring. About a week before my due date, obstetrical exam revealed that I was ready to go into labor. New life was imminently forthcoming for my family and me. I knew that we were poised and on the brink of change and newness from which there was no escaping and no going back. Regardless of the outcome of my labor, whether our baby was perfect or stillborn, my life was about to change, forevermore. I would never be the same again, nor would our marriage or our family. Time shifted—the future was intersecting the now.

Many such feelings grew within me, each connecting with another and then another until I felt involved in the interconnectedness of the universe. This week of my life was truly incredible, phenomenal, mysterious, inexplicable, and extremely powerful. I shall never forget it. I hope I can express some of it for you also to share and claim your own such experiences and how they have changed your life forevermore.

This week was not of my doing; it was far beyond "me," encompassing me and carrying me along tenderly yet with unbelievable strength. I came more and more to know that whatever the next days' imminent changes would bring, I would be able to handle it and handle it well. I was deeply aware of my own energy and strength. As I looked at my huge abdomen so bursting with life, I felt like Mother Earth or some goddess of fertility, giving myself and others vibrations of positive energy. I was radiant, aglow; maybe the light within was showing through. All of this is hard to put into words eight years later. Perhaps it can simply be said that I was more fully alive than I had ever been before. I knew it; others knew it. Everything I did that week was full of meaning and power. What came somehow from within me went outward on and on like ripples in a pond affecting others who affected others who in turn affected others. This occurred whether I was cleaning my house, playing with our toddler, practicing childbirth exercises, talking with a neighbor or meditating. The new life I felt within was without, everywhere in life.

When I did give birth, the experience was magnificent for me and my husband and gave us a lovely, healthy nine-pound daughter. My body and my spirit had never been so powerful as in those hours when I was helping her down my birth canal. Never before had I been so able to take control while yielding control…going along with what was clearly so far beyond "me." I viewed this birthing as a peak experience and realized the week before had been equally as much so. The week and the birthing itself complemented each other to make a whole greater than the sum of the parts. The richness of this new life burst forth from the verdant soil within and around me at particular points, but this life was and is growing within me and you all of the time. Sometimes we are open to it and sometimes we are not. When we do experience that bursting through of new life within us, it seems miraculous, even though the seeds for such growth are there all along.

Years later, after spiritual journeying and theological study, I found words to name this experience in another way. Now I would call that week in 1972 a time of "walking in the Light." Many of us know, or have experienced, what it means to be in the Light, to be filled with the presence and power of God, which does make all things anew. Some of us will resonate with this more than others and all of us will have difficulty describing what being in the Light, or experiencing Grace means, for it is a beyond words experience. Once experienced, however, it has become a part of my reality, reminding me like a beacon that what is, is, and what can happen once can happen again. Since 1972, I have experienced being in the Light several times. Fortunately, it does not take giving birth to be there, but the birthing led me to see what had been there all along. For that particular miracle of Grace, I am profoundly grateful.

Birthing, growing, aging, dying are all parts of a cosmic whole. The process in the Light that I went though in giving birth is equally available to us throughout the life cycle and even in our dying. May we all be open to the Light as we traverse our roads of precious life, and realize that as we travel, we are all deeply linked together by the Something beyond any of us, supporting and empowering us all.

*Reprinted from *The Friendly Woman 5:2*, Spring 1981, and from *What Canst Thou Say?* 38: May 2003.

Childlike Wonder
By Lynn Clemens

I was about 28 years old the first time I went camping by myself. I dismissed the nay-sayers who didn't think it was a good idea for a young female to spend a week camping alone. I had just finished a full load of classes while working full-time to support myself and pay for my education and I needed a break—from everyone and everything. My itinerary included a couple of days in Yosemite and then a few days in Emerald Bay, which is on the south side of Lake Tahoe. While spending a week alone in Yosemite and South Lake Tahoe is an incredible experience in itself, I had an unforgettable experience on the drive from Yosemite to Lake Tahoe.

The highway between my two destinations meanders through the Sierra Nevada Mountains with mile after mile of tall pines. It's almost mesmerizing. Somewhere along this highway I spotted a clearing, or should I say, it spotted me. There was a gigantic log lying in the middle of this small clearing with some interesting boulders and various flora and fauna around. It was the log that caught my attention while I was driving by at 60 mph and I just had to stop. I didn't question why I had to experience this clearing, I just did. I pulled the car to the side of the road, walked into the clearing, and sat on the friendly log.

I sat still on that log for no longer than twelve or fifteen minutes. But I wasn't just sitting on a log in the forest. I was given a ticket to witness, and to be part of nature at work. I could almost hear the plants growing to the songs of the birds and bugs around me. I didn't see any squirrels or badgers, but I knew they were there, too. I felt like a kid who snuck into Santa's Workshop to watch how the toys were made. In this case, however, God brought me into his workshop to be a part of the beautiful orchestra that plays to perfection twenty four hours a day. It was an amazing experience. I can't say that I was cognizant of everything that was going on around me, but I was part of it, and it was part of me, for that brief period of time.

Oh yeah, the camping was cool, too.

Held by Love in the Wyoming Desert
By Carol Clarke

I had begun work with a new therapist who encouraged me to explore Native American teachings. I was looking for spiritual direction and support after crawling out of an emotional abyss in which I had recovered abuse memories from my early childhood and had struggled with suicidal urges. The ad for the week-long Vision Quest workshop in Wyoming not only caught my eye, it called to me. My therapist actually knew somebody who had done a similar workshop with the same people, and knew that this was a safe, well-led offering. It felt like destiny to me. I signed up.

The workshop was based on a Lakota rite of passage. When a Lakota boy turned fourteen, he would go alone into nature, choose a sacred space, and stay there inside a circle of stones for three days and three nights, taking neither food nor water, praying to the Great Spirit for knowledge of his 'Medicine' helpers in the natural/Spirit world, his role in the tribe, his purpose, and the direction of his life's path. During the last night, he would stand vigil, keeping a fire going, awake for the visions and messages sent to him from Spirit. During this sacred time, everything that he experienced, both awake and sleeping, was a message from Spirit that he would carry with him forever.

A small group of us gathered at the Antelope Retreat Center in the town of Savery, Wyoming, population 486. We passed a talking stick as we shared our intentions and feelings about the vision quest we were each about to undertake. I spoke of fear. What I was most afraid of was inside my mind and soul. I was afraid there might be more pain and darkness from my childhood that would reveal itself and I was afraid of being tormented by the memories I had already surfaced.

We had a full day of group exercises to open our attention and become attuned to the natural world. I remember vividly walking blindfolded, holding hands in a line, as we were led on a barefoot walk outside, and being delighted to discover the different textures under my feet as we crossed grass, sun-warmed dirt, and straw and I found that with each step I felt less fragile and afraid of what might be underfoot. That night we began our spiritual journey with a sweat lodge where we shared songs and prayers for purification and connection to Spirit and our Earth Mother.

The next day we each filled four gallon bottles of water, and took our camping gear into the desert. I thought we were already remote, but we drove three hours, away from all settlement. On the way we saw wild ponies, hawks, eagles, and antelopes. We arrived in the midst of a natural outcropping of hills and exposed stone, sparsely covered with cedar and sagebrush. Once there, we were sent off alone to find our sacred space for the quest.

I was immediately attracted to the west, and found my feet drawn in a particular direction as if I was being pulled by a magnet. After crossing a flat meadow I passed a low wall of exposed rock and turned right. This led to what felt like a gate formed by two upright boulders, and I continued on. It felt like I was entering a yard with a garden full of small rock pedestals made by fairies. Along the right side of the path, the ground dropped away, and on the left was a big outcropping of rock up a cedar and sage-covered hill that formed the garden. The path led toward a couple of huge upright rock formations next to a flat, sandy table on the left.

The rock formations were on the edge of a bank that dropped away on the right and in front of me. I walked to the middle of the circle of soft, fine sand, and I knew I was home. There was no place to go from here except up the hill to the base of the big outcropping of rock. From the edge of the sandy circle I looked east, west and north, out over miles of empty, rocky desert. To the south was the small hill topped by the outcropping of rock. From the center of the sandy circle, this rock resembled the head of Mary Poppins wearing a dowdy flat-topped hat. As I looked up at this silly, dowdy head my body tingled with recognition and excitement and my eyes filled with tears. This space was my space, and this rock was my Mother, my protector and my anchor.

The next morning we stood in a circle at daybreak for prayers and smudging. As the sun appeared we each left the circle and headed toward our personal sacred space. I arrived at the sandy circle at the foot of the hill with the rock that felt like Mother, put up my tent, and felt a sense of safety I had never known before. I spread out my sleeping bag inside the tent, and with the release of months of tension, fear, anticipation and anxiety I settled into a deep, restful sleep.

When I awoke, I felt like a child in a new place of perfect safety. I climbed up the hill to take a close look at Mother, and she invited me to sit under her chin. In the shade of her chin, I smelled the cedar and sage around me, noticing how much cooler the air was here, and how the breeze played on my skin. I made friends with the clouds and I looked for and greeted the other beings that shared my Mother's shelter, mainly ants and a few flies. I familiarized myself with the land and rock formations that spread out below me in every direction. I noticed my hunger and wondered eagerly what Spirit would send me over the next three days.

The next day I was full of energy and felt relaxed and peaceful at the same time. From the center of the sandy circle, where I slept, I looked up at my Mother and felt completely protected and safe. This was a feeling that was unfamiliar! I found a rock that was large and shaped like a duck's head, which felt like a talisman. I examined the walls of the rock formations across the bowl to the west, and found a face that felt like my spiritual Father, also standing guard for me.

The day went by very slowly, and I paid full attention to how long a day is with no tasks to perform and no diversions. At my Mother's urging, I wandered down the slope among the rock pedestals that seemed to be fairy-made. I felt like a child playing in my Mother's garden. I was disappointed that the cairns didn't speak to me, but then laughed at my silly expectations, and enjoyed the carefree spirit that made me feel light and playful. I wondered how many decades or centuries the rocks had stood there being washed by the rain and bleached by the sun, taking on the forms that stood before me in my brief time with them. So many above-ground stalagmites—it was like a colony of rock children, all so much older than me!

For a long time I pondered a scrubby cedar tree growing out of the side of the hill below where I sat under my Mother's chin. It had a long, curved trunk near the ground and two-thirds of its branches were dead, but still it grew and clung to life on this barren, sandy hillside. It seemed old and wise, and not at all unhappy; it carried its dead wood proudly as testament to years of vitality and survival, and was content with the limited growth in the part still green. I felt its joy in the warmth of the sun and the cool of the breeze sliding across and through its needles.

Late that day, as the shadows grew longer and the air cooled off I saw three coyotes walking away from the base camp where our leaders kept vigil for us and prayed for our quests. The coyotes looked huge and gray from a long way away, and I was glad they were headed away from both the camp and me. I felt very small, but also very alive, and I was happy that my Mother was showing me some of my fellow creatures of this place.

The next day I felt like I was 10 feet tall, hollow, and made of light. When I moved too quickly, I saw stars and had to hold still for a moment. With great attention and care I made my way down the slope into the shallow bowl to the east to gather firewood for my last night's vigil. I found an intact, bleached antelope skull in this bowl, and brought it back with me; my Mother had given me an ally. I also found some feathers—small and red at the center, also clearly meant for me.

As I sat under my Mother's chin that afternoon, I prayed for direction and knowledge of my future role. An answer came. An unmistakable word suddenly filled my consciousness, and stunned me with its certainty and unexpectedness: healer. I have never felt any call to the medical profession, yet my mind was filled with images of people on cots in big spaces and along underground passageways, with attendants crouching over them or moving about them. When I prayed for more information there was nothing more. When I asked if I should leave my current work and investigate going to school for nursing, my Mother was silent, but in a way that let me know this was not the right path. The answer, I felt, was that only time would reveal how this role would come to me, and that I was still a child and needed only to enjoy my safety and play.

My Mother let me know that my biological mother was a part of my being in this lifetime, but was only a player to help me fulfill the role that I chose for this incarnation. My spirit extended both way back, before the physical existence of anybody now alive in this time, and also far into the future, well beyond my ability to imagine where I will go and who I will be. The pain and concerns of my childhood in this one lifetime are an essential part of my spiritual journey. Accepting that I have already survived this pain, and that it will serve me by widening my perceptions and enabling me to connect, support, and assuage the pain of others, is my lifetime challenge and purpose. Standing up through the pain, staying awake through the pain, and using the pain to help others who are suffering is the path I chose for this life. This is a path of strength and grace and, yes, healing. But I am not doing this alone. I am doing this with the support and protection and love of my spiritual Mother. She is always with me, whether I know it or not.

That night I built a big fire, which I fed all night. Through the night I heard the chanting of male voices, in a song that never paused, whose words I didn't understand. The chanting honored me, my fire, and my pain. As I fed the fire I felt the small, frightened child inside me as a small flame that created bright colors in my soul and somehow managed to play games of invention and escape through the worst of the abuse. I had tended the small flame that was my inner child all my life, and kept it going inside me while I had shut down on the outside. I fed the fire all night remembering how I had found ways to fight against injustice in my youth which kept my inner fire going, I had found my way to the twelve-steps that led me out of self-destructive behavior, behavior that was deadening my soul as it deadened the pain. As I fed the fire, I saw that my spirit has always been tending my soul's flame, and a fire spirit told me I am 'Firetender'. The song of the ancient fathers was loud in my ears and I still had no understanding of the words, but I know now it was a song about the importance and honor of tending fire.

The sky began to lighten long before I had run out of wood. I watched the daylight grow, and my soul sang with triumph, but also some disappointment. I didn't want the night to end! I wanted to keep my big beautiful bonfire going as long as I could! However, the sun was coming despite my supply of wood and desire to tend this fire. I had to put out this physical, outer fire and leave my sacred space, but the fire inside me has never gone out, and my sacred space was burned into my inner world forever.

I did this Wyoming fast more than ten years ago, and over time my ability to put myself back into this sacred space has grown. My Mother is there, ready to bring peace to my heart and comfort to my soul anytime I choose to be there with her. I brought a small, broken, lichen-covered stone from the top of my Mother's head away with me; it stays with me wherever I go. When I look at this small bit of Her, I am back in the desert, smelling the cedar and sage and feeling the ease and delight of this time. When I am filled with dread or my mind is agitated, I put myself back in this sandy circle, and look up at that silly, dowdy head, drawing again on the safest feeling I have ever experienced. My gratitude to the Universe and my Spiritual Mother, and all the people who supported my Vision Quest is boundless. In the desert I felt for the first time my true Mother's love, and this love will be with me forever.

She Carries Me*
By Jennifer Berezan

She is a boat, She is a light
High on a hill, in dark of night
She is a wave, She is the deep
She is the dark where angels sleep
When all is still, and peace abides
She carries me to the other side
She carries me, She carries me
She carries me to the other side

And though I walk through valleys deep
And shadows chase me in my sleep
On rocky cliffs I stand alone
I have no name, I have no home
With broken wings, I reach to fly
She carries me to the other side
She carries me, She carries me
She carries me to the other side

A thousand arms, a thousand eyes
 A thousand ears to hear my cries
She is the gate, She is the door
She leads me through and back once more
When day has dawned, and death is nigh
She'll carry me to the other side
She carries me, She carries me
She carries me to the other side

She is the first, She is the last
She is the future and the past
Mother of all, of earth and sky
She carries me to the other side
She carries me, She carries me
She carries me to the other side

*Song from CD, *She Carries Me,* available at www.edgeofwonder.com.

A Noetic Experience
By Carol Hwoschinsky

"OK, God. If we are all equal in your eyes—if we are all your sons and daughters—and Moses got a burning bush, I want a sign too." I had held that wager for many years. I had started on this quest for meaning in my early teens. It was a life and death issue for my whole sense of identity was tenuous as I had the idea I was unloved by God. My earlier beliefs had held that God was the judgment figure depicted in the Old Testament and would wipe me out with his fury because I was such a despicable human being.

On the one hand, I believed in a very judgmental God who was constantly judging my very being. In order to be loved, it was necessary for me to follow what I thought were the teachings of Jesus: chastity, poverty and obedience. On the other hand, I sensed these absolutes couldn't be so, for God was Love and this approach didn't seem very loving. I obsessed a lot over this conflict, but fortunately, life went on and I put it in the background while I continued my education. But it never left me.

When I again had some time to read books of choice, I started with determination to resolve this conflict. Paul Tillich was my first venture into the spiritual realm. I felt joy and relief to realize God as a "Ground of Being." No longer was there a demon God external to my Self who was sitting in judgment. The yoke of that thought system had pretty well cracked, but reading Tillich, Buber, and then Teilhard de Chardin confirmed my fragile belief.

Through my search for meaning, I had concluded that God is the All—the One. God is Love and it is love that unifies. Later, I started reading about Quantum Physics and

Field Theory. The impetus to that was the exposure to David Bohm's book: *Wholeness and the Implicate Order,* which was further confirmation of this unity. Science and Spirituality were beginning to merge. Bohm, a physicist, described the Universe as unfolding. We know more and more about the nature of the Universe, but it is impossible to know the implicate order—the full meaning or the full story. What we do know is the explicate order and it continues to unfold.

My personal evolution has continued to unfold, and from what I have been learning more recently, it parallels the story of the Universe itself. All life is interconnected, it is held together through Love, which is the unifying principle. We, as a species, began with the 15 billion year old story: we are made of star stuff. Our emergence marks a continuous unfolding of life beginning with our planet, which is perfectly evolved to not only support life but to be living itself. This part of the story has become explicate in the quite recent past with newer and newer information coming from astronomers and cosmologists. It excites me beyond measure. I read voraciously. I talked with ministers. I wrote about it. I dreamed about it. I had many conversations with my God/Self and I continued to long for a sign.

At the time, I was one of a group of therapists who had a counseling practice in the first holistic health clinic in the country. We were excited to be on the cutting edge of healing. My three colleagues and I had decided to rent a house at the beach for a weekend retreat to discuss our vision, goals, and plans for the future. Friday evening we simply relaxed and enjoyed being together by sharing a bottle of wine and talking late into the night. The next morning we started our agenda anticipating a full day to work through it.

After breaking for lunch we continued a discussion—the subject I can't really remember. I do remember having an idea I wanted to contribute. I opened my mouth to offer my thoughts and I found I couldn't formulate the ideas into a meaningful sentence. I stopped, took a few moments and tried again with the same result. I knew what I wanted to communicate, but I couldn't put the idea together in a string of words. What I wanted to say seemed really important, yet I couldn't catch it—it was bigger than the container of my mind. Actually, it seemed quite frightening to me. I thought perhaps I was losing my mind. My colleagues, all transpersonal therapists, realized something unusual was occurring and encouraged me to lie down on the rug and to stay with whatever was happening.

What began to unfold was a Gestalt—everything at once. It is difficult to describe in words what was a totally nonverbal experience. What appeared before my eyes were beautiful clouds, embedded with every thought, idea, conversation, dream I had ever had in my whole life. Everything was familiar and I knew it all from a deep, cellular level. I couldn't follow one cryptogram to its completion because they came to me as a Gestalt—all at once. The complete meaning was embedded in the totality and could not be separated into a string of words or ideas. At one point, I stopped trying to catch them and just let the whole thing unfold. I recognized dreams, conversations, thoughts. It was absolutely amazing to see my whole life float by and to feel so comfortable with the familiarity.

I had no concept of time and place—just pure awareness. I have used the word "see" but I didn't see with my eyes. I just knew. As I recall, with what seemed like a continuation, the clouds of knowing dispersed and all that remained was blackness. This blackness also had a sense of familiarity and comfort and as I floated in it, I began to feel a sense of complete peace. In retrospect, I came to realize that this blackness was beyond duality: there was no thing to set against another: no right or wrong, yes or no. There was no-thing but there was everything. No thoughts were available to me: I sensed this, I felt it, I knew it with every cell of my body and it was completely familiar. I knew it to be the Oneness before duality manifested.

The joy I felt was indescribable. I remember sobbing with ecstasy and floating without the encumbrance of my body. At some point, I distinctly heard a booming voice say "You know, Carol, there is nothing but Love." I knew that the Oneness is love. Love is the Unity of All. Love exists beyond all division and separation and it is the so-called glue that holds all duality together in one coherent whole. Love simply is. I floated with this realization. It was not as I think of it now: it was a complete experience and deep sense of Knowing. Yet there was no "I" who knows. I was the knowing.

It was already dusk when I returned to this reality. This experience had lasted over three hours. I have such gratitude for my colleagues for having stayed with me for that period of time. They claimed I had reported to them some of my experience as I went along. I don't recall that.

Why did this happen? Why then? Why there? I must have chosen the moment on some unconscious level for I can't imagine any more supportive environment in which this could have happened. My colleagues provided safety and support for this experience to unfold.

I had researched Near Death Experiences (NDE) prior to this and as I thought about it later and discussed it with Ken Ring, a psychologist who had researched the phenomena from a scientific perspective and written a number of books on the subject; my experience actually fit many of the identified criteria of an NDE. Ken thinks the near death part of the label is unfortunate for one does not have to be dying a physical death in order to call it that. In this case, it was the death of doubt—the part that seems dependent upon my linear thinking. Though I am still using my rational mind and respect the ability, this experience enabled larger knowing.

Did I change as a result of this? Yes. I have total trust in the goodness of the universe. Do I remember this all the time? No. But I can come back to the awareness and memory at will.

I am not special. Many people have similar experiences. It is not unlike what many of the mystics describe. It is a peek into reality that is available to every one. It was the answer to the many years of supplication to please know the essence of God. I had pursued this search with focus and intensity and I was rewarded with this great gift.

Passionate Flower – Carolyn W. Treadway

Circle of Love
By Anne Scott

I paid little attention to my dreams until the age of thirty-six. I was on a rare trip to Hawaii with my parents, my brothers, nieces and nephews, my husband and children. The hotel was brightly lit with tinsel-covered artificial Christmas trees for the tourists. I felt hollow and filled with sorrow. There were strained relationships among many in the larger family, and I went to bed crying on Christmas night.

The next morning I awoke when it was still dark. We were going to leave the next day, and I felt a need for something that I couldn't even identify. Compelled by a barely articulate desire, I walked down the long hotel road to a little path I had seen each day. It frightened me a little, this path into the lava beds, and each day I had avoided it, walking instead on the other side of the road. This morning, however, I had to go in.

Turning off the main road, I left behind the soft glow of the street lamps. I followed the narrow path for at least a half hour. The sun had not yet risen, but there was just enough diffuse light in the east to discern the path. It felt good to be walking alone, and my mind became very calm and peaceful.

At some point, I decided it was time to go back to the hotel, and turned around. But instead of the single path that had taken me to where I was standing, I saw that there were many paths, and the lava formations were so high that I couldn't see how to get out. I couldn't see the hotel, or the main road, and for some reason, it felt darker than when I had started.

A feeling of panic began to take hold of me. I realized I didn't even know if it was safe to walk here alone. I tried a path but it forked several times, and then I knew I was completely lost. The lava field extended for acres, and the only recourse was to wait until the sun rose. I sat on a rock and closed my eyes. I had recently learned to meditate, and knew that it would help to calm me. I relaxed and the panic subsided. Another half hour had gone by when I felt the rays of the sun rising over the hills, touching my face.

As I opened my eyes, ready to find my way out, I saw that I was sitting in the midst of hundreds of petroglyphs etched into the lava. I was sitting on top of them, surrounded by symbols that I couldn't understand. The most beautiful was a circle with a dot in the center. It was repeated many times, and I bent down, touching it with my fingers, astonished at the fact that I had been sitting in some sacred spot. I explored this area until the sun became hot, and it was time to find my way back. In the bright daylight I could easily see the narrow path that led to the main road.

I spent the day with all of the family, and when I went to bed that night I knew that I had finally seen beyond the outer appearances of my life, and had been touched by something deeper and real. But still, the sorrow about my relationship to my family remained. That night I had the first dream I ever remembered.

It was direct and simple. I was shown a circle with the dot in the center, the very symbol I had seen that morning. I then heard a voice say, "This dot in the center of the circle is Love. If you would be this dot in the center, the problems you have with your family would not exist." I was pulled into the dot in the circle, and waves upon waves of love poured through me, through my entire body. I woke up in awe of what had just taken place.

This dream changed the course of my life. It awakened a longing to return to the experience of love, to live from the center of myself, although I had no idea what that even meant, or how I would go about doing it. I only knew that I could no longer live my life as I had done before. For the next three years I stumbled along. I tried to improve my life but it only seemed to get worse. I even forgot the dream.

One night, during a crisis with a loved one, I went to bed, exhausted. I felt the weight of total despair. Curled under the covers and hopeless, I began to say a phrase that I had recently read in a book about a man's journey in the Sufi tradition. I hung on tightly to these words, crying, while silently repeating *La illaha illa'llah*. It means "There is no God but God."

Suddenly I saw my despair from a distance, no longer feeling it, but witnessing it as far below me. I 'saw' only blackness, but it was vibrant and somehow also illuminated, and filled me with joy. I realized that I was being held, as was my whole family, by this love; I was resting on a vast hand of love that held every part of me. As my mind began to question, "What *is* this?" the experience began to dissolve, and I fell asleep.

The next morning, I woke up with a sense of wonder at what had happened. It was as if a secret had been revealed, one that I could carry with me in the day-to-day tasks, in the midst of difficulties, a secret that I could no longer afford to forget. Yet over the years, sometimes my own darkness could veil this light. Then, at such times, I would have only the memory of this sweetness.

As in the experience with the dot in the center of the circle, I found that love, this mystical love, appears in the most ordinary of times of need. To remember this love requires a simple orientation of the heart in the midst of daily life and in the difficulties and beauty of our world.

A Perfect Day
By Abigail DeSoto

It was late August, but I could feel the kiss of fall in the air. Today was Sunday, and I was alone with no plans. I had been again struggling with solitude and feelings of heavy, oppressive loneliness.

I decided to take advantage of the last Sunday morning when the grocery store would be open, since at the end of the summer vacation, in *"la France profonde,"* once the tourists left, Sundays would return to their "sacred" quietness, the one day a week *no one* worked except mornings, in bakeries and outdoor food markets. (Food is sacred in France, and consequently, exceptions can be made in work legislation).

The day was crisp, partially sunny, but promising to be dry, with that incisive edge of clarity fall brings. I knew it would be good for me to swim, though I wondered what the water would be like at the lake; it had been getting cooler, and quite chilly at night; even today only registered about 25° C.

I arrived at the lake, where only a young couple with a very cute and happy little dog played on the makeshift beach. I watched the little dog repeatedly, yet with great joy, jump into the water in search of the little stick its masters mechanically threw to it. While they seemed rather blasé and rigid in their actions, the little dog was *totally* in the moment, joyous, barking, and aware only of his stick, the water, and the joy he had from retrieving that stick for his beloved masters.

I realized for a moment that life really is only made of moments. Each moment comes and goes, brings us so much to see, and enjoy, if only we can be present to it...*really present to it,* instead of preoccupied with worries or plans for the future, and regrets or analysis of the past.

I settled myself at a new spot, a place I had never sat before, despite my many years frequenting this lake. The spot was like a mown lawn and led easily down to the water. It was very sunny and quiet, except for the sounds of happy barking to my left.

Brownie went to the water's edge to have a drink, wet his feet, and then proceeded to demonstrate *his* joy by running crazily around me in circles, rolling over repeatedly like a circus dog, and throwing his own stick in the air. Decidedly, there was joy and happiness in the air!

I lay in the sun; it was warm, and quiet. The place and weather were absolutely beautiful. Still I was unable to totally enjoy that beauty—I was lonely and tired of being alone, all the time. I lived alone and was looking for work, now that I felt strong enough (both emotionally and physically), and though I loved my quiet little house in the woods, I was isolated. I felt I would have to leave it. For several months I had stopped fighting to *"get out there"* and be with people (anyone to avoid the loneliness), so consequently, I found myself more and more alone.

To be honest, I was proud of how well I was doing. The quiet and regular aloneness was not as bad as I had anticipated, and often (again to be honest), I enjoyed the quiet, and knew it was my only door to communion with my true Self, or with the Divine.

But lately, I felt impatient, like I had done my "cloistering"; it was time to get out, serve, *do* something, work, meet people! Why did no one call me, contact me? Why did I live in such isolation? My heart ached from feeling abandoned, and my chest felt heavy and oppressed, a memory of recent pericarditis.

I went for a swim. No one was around—the young couple had left, and it was still early for the average Frenchman to be out, given the long, traditional family Sunday lunch. Brownie sat with my clothes and towel, and I swam, back and forth in the middle of the lake. The water, though cool at first, felt fresh, clean, and lovely. My body moved effortlessly, with strength; my breathing was easy. Up and down I swam, staying in the middle of the lake. I felt no fear, only the easiness of my movements, and the sure support of the water.

I wondered briefly, if anyone could see me, would they not liken me to a dolphin or other water creature playing in its element?

I realized how lucky I was to be so totally at ease in water. I am, thanks to all those swimming lessons my grandmother forced down my throat years ago in Chicago when I was eight years old. Water has also been my element—cleansing, calming, and taking care of me. I have never felt fear in water—I adore it, and am drawn to it.

When I had had enough, I swam back to Brownie, and got out to dry in the sun. I no longer felt lonesome, just refreshed, cleansed, anchored. As I sat on my mat, the warm sun beating down on me, I watched the water move. Sometimes the wind would gently whip up the surface and push the water into fast moving wave ripples; at other times it seemed to twinkle in the sun while moving happily in the direction of the current. I was aware it did not say *"no,"* or in any way resist, or counter the flow of "what came."

I noticed the tall grasses growing at the edge of the water where I sat—they also moved with the wind, when it blew. I looked up at the blue sky with big, billowy clouds that passed now in front of the sun. The sky did not seem to shout angrily at the clouds to get out of the way—*"You're covering up my blueness!!!"* I remembered how things change, how big, angry storms brew, and the sky turns grey and becomes full of dark, menacing cloud.

Nature does not resist, question, or fight. It just *is,* and *does.* Storms come and go; the wind blows, then dies down…grasses lie flat, and then stand tall again in the sun. The surface of the lake is pushed by the wind, and then becomes calm, quiet, and pancake-like.

Why was I resisting "what is"? Why not go with the flow? People come and go—they always have in my life. There is no reason to think I will always be alone, and if I am to be so today, resisting, or pushing to maneuver company will not bring me serenity.

Equanimity and serenity were qualities I wanted to cultivate; nature responds with equanimity—why not me? Whether I like it or not, as Thich Nhat Hanh teaches: "I am of the nature to grow old; I am of the nature to become ill; I am of the nature to die; and everything in my life that is dear to me, (or not so) are of the nature to change."*

Life is impermanent. How many times had I heard *that* in Buddhist retreats or teachings? Today, in my life I was in transition, change, and flux. Why resist, or find it unusual? Life is change; that is one thing we can count on, that, and that death will come to this body we inhabit.

Nothing else is certain, yet we continually live as if nothing will, or should change in our lives. We resist a change in situation (new job, or lose of one); lose of a life partner (divorce, death, or mere change of mind), change of abode (or the need to), due to an internal call or other impetus.

Today I was alone, and how I fought it, as if it were a flaw in the script. It was OK for a few months, while I was "healing" from my past pain, but not for such a long time: "I am ready to have someone in my life…enough already!" But, no matter how much I anguished, complained, felt sad, "out of sync", or whatever, I was in no way able to change "what is".

Life is a series of moments; they come and they go, like the clouds in the sky, like our breath. We can be aware of them, and live them, as they come…or we cannot. But come they will, nonetheless. As my sister had said to me on the phone, just the day before, "We *think* we are in the driver's seat, but we aren't really."

This perfect day, I had been given another lesson in faith and support—why did I fight so? In many ways, God is like the water that supports me every time I go swimming. I don't question each time: "Is this water/pool/sea/lake going to support me?" I *know* it, and in I go without fear or anxiety. What would happen if I approached every situation with that faith and knowing, as if every day were indeed "a perfect day"?

* These come from the Buddhist "Five Remembrances," translated by Thich Nhat Hanh in the "Plum Village Chanting Book," and recalled before meals on Sundays and other days at Plum Village in France. Cited in Molly Young Brown, 2009, *Growing Whole*, Mt Shasta CA: Psychosynthesis Press.

Not in Kansas Anymore
By Lyn Goldberg

Twenty-five, confused and desperately wanting a man in my life, I was asked by a male hunk to go to a Pink Floyd Concert. It was 1975 and for me it was the 60's. Throughout my childhood and teen years, I lived in a little rural community in Kansas. Unlike Dorothy with the red slippers, I wanted out and with the first opportunity I headed to the big city. By 25 I had lived on my own for 8 years, traveled Europe and had my M.A. Even with independence, childhood patterning dies hard, if at all, and to be single, with no prospects was a crushing blow to my ego. I had left Kansas, but had Kansas left me? I was always on the prowl, looking, wanting and actively seeking my husband. It consumed my every thought. So, when a tall dark man looked my way and asked me to Pink Floyd, there wasn't a moment's hesitation. Never mind the fact I didn't like rock and I didn't have a clue who Pink Floyd was. There was a man interested and therefore, so was I.

The day before the concert I ran into my wanna-be lover and he said, "Just want you to know we will all be doing acid at the concert. You okay with that?" Please understand dear reader, I wanted more than anything in the world to be accepted, and he was a hunk. My response was, "Oh, of course."

My date's crash pad was the meeting place for a pre-concert party. A whole slew of Pink Floyd groupies had honed in on his pad. This was helpful for me because I was able to mimic how to actually take acid. Along with being desperate I was also always curious. I had smoked marijuana and knew the voices of the establishment were not telling the whole truth. Ram Dass was one I held in high esteem and, in his earlier life as Richard Alpert, acid had been at least interesting to him. And it hadn't killed him. So down the hatch with the acid and off to the concert we went.

Groupies of any band pride themselves on the seats they score and these followers were not to be put to shame. Our seats were front and center. I could see the strings on the guitars, the glint in the band's eyes and ever more important, the sound. My choice of music is actually classical and loud noise has never been easy for me. Here I was right in the middle of several eight-foot booming speakers. It is not the way of a Kansas Native to proclaim anything amiss and I held true in character, saying to myself, "Just go with it."

And go with it I did. The music enwrapped my soul. I was resonating with the moment. At this concert Pink Floyd had a large disc on stage showing in the beginning beautiful scenes; a babbling brook, birds, people happy together. As the evening drew on the scenes became more disturbing, the brook filled with garbage, nature was disrupted and people were at war. Then at the climax, when we were all standing, swaying in harmony, a missile came from the back of the auditorium and exploded the disc that had held my unwavering focus. For me, the entire auditorium blew up and as fire consumed the disc—I died. I left my body and looked down at myself and the crowd. I experienced the death of that 25-year-old body and embraced it.

The part that I know as ME was looking over my body as it collapsed in the chair. I watched, hovering above. I connected with a peace I had never before experienced. I was now aware of a larger Universe, spacious, unconditional in its giving of love. I breathed in the vibrations of this ever enlarging freshness and I watched as the body below opened to this new energy. An awakening Soul in this body breathed in the love that was holding me in space. It took several minutes for this breath to flow into my cells and when it had reached each and every cell, I returned to my body. I felt more connected and more at peace than ever before. Now, I wanted to be alive in this body.

The energy that reentered my body was not the naïve, troubled and desperate young woman who went to a Pink Floyd concert in an attempt to once again give herself away. I remember being quiet for several days, not quite sure who I now was. The only thing

I knew for sure, I was different.

The day after the concert I read these words and they were imprinted on my soul. They came from a Sufi book that slipped through my hands years ago.

> There are those who are asleep and know not they are asleep.
>
> There are those who are awake and know not that they have awakened.
>
> And there are those who are awake and know they are awake, blessed are
>
> they, for there is no turning back.

Cold shivers consumed me because I knew that in my dying I had awakened and there was no turning back.

I write these words thirty-three years after this event. Just in case you are wondering—I was no longer desperate to find my mate. I knew I was ok and thriving without a man in my life. There have been many times when I have said, "Oh, for the bliss of being asleep again." And yet, most of my life has been one of gratitude in knowing that I am One with the Source and the Source is One within me. It was the gift I received that night as I was held in the space of love.

I never did acid again. There was no need.

Shaman's Death*
By Beth Beurkens

I'm an empty vessel
a tabula rasa
a begging bowl
One breath in
but mostly I'm breathing out

Finding meaning
from pleasing others
convincing
struggling
pushing
Structures that were my mainsail
are dissolving
I'm allowing
abetting it

I sense the aura
the soft wing
of a new life paradigm
It feels like
snow falling
full moon rising
foam-white waves
rolling to shore

an abiding presence

steady
unfailing
like Kuan Yin
pouring her
never-emptying jar
of healing waters
over me

The Healing Drum**
By Beth Beurkens

Flying on the drum
I glimpse the wonder
of creation
Whirling, swirling
stars and illumination
Spinning, turning
One heart beating
Pulsing love into being

I am your hands
your eyes
your heart
the mouth of your songs
Trying to hold your mirror
with my goodness
So small to your vastness
Bearing witness to your
immeasurable majesty

Flying on the drum
electrified in unity
no me
no you
only a sea of love

* Shamans ritually undergo initiatory experiences that deepen their connections with their helping spirits. These spiritual deaths, dismemberments and resurrections create an annihilation of the secular personality and help transform the shaman into a "hollow bone" so she can better serve the spirits and her community. This poem was previously published in *Shaman's Eye*, by Beth Beurkens, Sky Ladder Press, 2009.
**Previously published in *Shaman's Eye*, by Beth Beurkens, Sky Ladder Press, 2009; and in *Shamanism*, Fall/Winter 2002, Vol. 15, No. 2.

Timeless Engistiak
By Jill Pangman

A golden eagle circles high above, spiraling upwards, until it is just a speck, in a deep blue sky. To the north sweeping rolls of tundra edge towards ocean, to the south an arc of mountains springs upwards in a ring of sedimentary folds. From south to north a river has incised a deep course through ancient sediments, before braiding out across a coastal plain and emptying into the sea.

This is a rare September day, warm and calm. A respite from the relentless winds that race across the roof of this vast continent. A respite as well from time's endless march from summer to winter, turning water to ice, rain to snow. At seventy degrees north latitude, in this far northwest corner of Canada's Yukon Territory, this is an Arctic summer's last hurrah.

I close my eyes, and lie back, pressing myself into firm tundra, my back curved slightly as it molds into angled crest of hill. I can sense the ground beneath me, sloping away in all directions, yet holding me here, suspended between earth and sky.

I picture the first peoples of this continent, some standing on this same height of land, scanning the horizon for signs of life to sustain their own. Engistiak, meaning hill in Inuvialuktun, the local Inuit dialect, was once considered one of Canada's most prized archaeological sites. Fossil records indicate that for up to thirty thousand years humans have roamed the Arctic coastal plain and mountainous terrain of western North America, having crossed over a now-submerged land bridge from Asia. These were a migratory people, following the movements of ice age mammals, and stopping to fish in rivers that teemed with life. Any who passed this way would have seen this lone hill, steep and vegetated on one side, sheer rock on the other, rising abruptly from the plain.

Arching skywards, this up thrust of metamorphosed rock defies the erosional powers of time that have leveled the immediately surrounding terrain. They would have been drawn to climb it, for the obvious view. But I wonder: did they too feel held by it, held by its raw wildness, and by something less tangible as well?

Archaeologists have unearthed a pile of stones at the base of the cliff on the south side, an ideal location for a shelter, protected from the cold prevailing north winds, yet still affording an expansive 180° view. Amongst these stones archaeologists have unearthed bones of Pleistocene mega fauna, some of which are now extinct, like the woolly mammoth and mastodon, and the short-faced bear and saber-toothed cat. Mixed with the bones were tools dated to over eight thousand years old and representing up to eight different cultures of Inuit people. Some of these tools were made with Enlistee chert. It was another reason for these early peoples to travel here—for the stone to make the tools so necessary for their survival.

Above the ancient shelter, maybe half way up the cliff, there is a narrow rock ledge. On it is a tangle of sticks, ringed at times by lemming carcasses, and spiked with downy feathers. Below the nest, and extending right to the ground, is a wide swath of orange lichen clinging to the face of the rock. This slow growing species thrives on the nitrogen in bird guano and, given its abundance, the ledge must have housed families of eagles and falcons for hundreds, if not thousands, of years.

It is this sense of antiquity that adds to the numinous quality of this place. It feels like I am walking in the footsteps of ancestors when I'm here, not my own, but those of life itself. Their imprints have been erased by time, but they have a memory that lingers. This is a place where life can flourish, and for now move unimpeded by the relentless march of human activity elsewhere on the planet.

Trails are etched deep into the tundra, created by the hooves of barren ground caribou on their annual pilgrimage to and from the Arctic coast. Often, on my journeys, it is only their trails, or what they leave behind, that I see. I know I've just missed them when I pull my boat onto a shore littered with fresh dung, and clumps of hollow hair. Yet other times, out of the silence, comes the clicking of hooves, as a herd scampers down a steep embankment and plunges into the river. Mothers and calves can get separated, and the air fills with the plaintive bleating of the young trying desperately to keep pace with the herd. Water splays off hooves in a garland of sparkling droplets, as the herd scrambles to shore, and ascends the slope. I remember watching such a group, of several thousand animals, disappear and then re-emerge some time later, high on a distant col, driven by an internal clock and their relentless urge to move. It was only through my binoculars that I could see them, filing over the pass. Once gone, the silence they leave behind seems deeper, somehow the land more empty than it was even before they came.

It's almost as if the land has its own heartbeat, and life itself is drummed into being. Into the silence are etched not only networks of trails, but other manifestations of life. Holes dug into sandy embankments where fox and wolves birth their pups; sticks piled high on rock ledges where birds of prey raise and fledge their chicks; tracks imprinted into wet sand or mud tell tale evidence of wild presence. Moose raggedly tear the willow branches they browse, snowshoe hare cleanly snip the twigs. Grizzly bears mark their territories by rubbing their backs, and claws, against tree trunks, leaving broken branches, smooth bark, and snagged hairs. Sheep paw out shallow sleeping depressions on mountain slopes. Tiny nests of twigs and leaves, held together by downy feathers and grass, lie abandoned on the tundra. And everywhere are droppings, of varying shapes, consistency and antiquity.

To have the opportunity to witness the ebb and flow of life that moves through this land is a gift of inestimable value. I have journeyed here countless times over the last two decades, on foot and by boat. But it is remote, at least an hour-long flight by bush plane from an already isolated Arctic community, and very few people are graced by this privilege each year. Through my wilderness guiding business I lead groups of adventurous souls down the Firth River, the riverine artery that connects the interior mountains of Ivvavik National Park with the sea, a hundred mile stretch of fast flowing water and challenging rapids. Each journey down this river reveals different faces of the land, in different moods. At times fierce storms have threatened to shred our tents, or blow our boats upstream; other days are tranquil, hot, a seeming impossibility for Arctic latitudes. Rain can transform the Firth's turquoise hues into muddy raging torrents. Snow can fall during any week of the summer, revealing tracks of animals that have passed unseen. Close encounters with wildlife can happen around any bend, usually when least expected. I have been face to face with grizzly and polar bear, wolves and wolverine, muskoxen, moose, caribou and sheep. I've been dive bombed by Arctic terns defending their young, peregrine falcon and rough-legged hawks screeching loudly as they swoop down over my head. I have seen the tundra churning with hooves as caribou in the thousands have swept through valleys and forded rivers with an unbelievable grace. I have been mesmerized by the ecstatic bursts of colour, as wildflowers in their millions burst through the spring ground; and have been moved by the delicate architecture of twin flower and poppy, forget-me-not and vetch.

Some experiences touch on the sublime. A couple of years ago I spent a night on Engistiak, a night like all summer "nights" in Ivvavik, where the sun simply skims along the northern horizon, casting a most exquisite golden hue across the land. On this particular day lit night, I pitched my tent on the only level spot right on top, and was lulled to sleep, cocooned in my down sleeping bag and cradled by the ancient rocks beneath me. I woke several hours later to a strong north wind buffeting the tent, and when I peeked out the open door I realized what the wind had blown in—a blanket of thick coastal fog. As I watched, the fog rolled back, bit by bit, leaving me marooned above a sea of clouds, that were lit from within by a three AM sun trying to burn its way through. Miraculously, the mist momentarily parted, a mile to the north, just enough to reveal a tiny patch of tundra and a lone bull caribou lit by a blazing shaft of sunlight. It was looking in my direction, or so it seemed, and as I watched it turned sideways, displaying a massive rack of antlers, and then it simply stepped into the fog, and disappeared. The cloud immediately closed in again, obscuring any sign of life or ground. I wondered if the bull had been revealed to me for a reason, with a message that was decipherable, but only if I knew how to interpret it.

There is a sacred quality to times like this, when I feel touched by something infinitesimally vaster than myself. Such experiences can inform and ignite me, riveting my attention to the present moment. It feels like I enter a state of grace when I allow myself to surrender to the purity, and fullness, of the moment; when I release my ego and cease to question, and just accept what is.

I realize that there is a pulse in the universe, and it is in fact, no different than my own. I just need to listen. As I witness the play of sun on water, clouds on sky, and wings on air, I understand that this pulse is nothing more, nothing less, than life simply revealing itself, one heartbeat at a time.

On another visit to Engistiak my listening propelled me to dance. Provoked by an inaudible melody, and an invisible rhythm, I felt my arms lift, suspended on currents of air. It was as if they were moving to the beat of an ancient memory, of wings soaring high above an ancient land. My legs moved to join suit, and in a slow waltz, I spiraled back and forth along the crest of the hill, feeling an intense love that simultaneously swept me skywards and rooted me down, deep into the earth.

It felt as if I had been here for eons, witnessing the eternal shifting of light that sweeps across this land, with its continually changing seasons, and fluctuating coastlines, as sea levels rose and fell with the ebb and flow of glacier ice. I felt held in a timeless embrace. An embrace that not only accommodates the slow pace of erosion, where grain by grain, resistant strata of rock, like those of Engistiak are worn down, eventually to nothing. But an embrace that can also contain the longings of my own spirit, to transcend the constraints of being human; to be able to soar on sky currents on long wings, and thunder over tundra on strong legs and splayed hooves; to be able to propel myself effortlessly through shimmering waters by the flick of a fin, and dance in the wind rooted only by the slenderest of stalks.

I long, as well, to be able to sink, deep into stillness, into silence, and to be held. Held by the force of my own love. My love for wild nature, and for the fact that it still exists. My love for all life and its longing to exist. To think that this light, this beacon of beauty and grace and is-ness, could be extinguished by human ignorance and greed is inconceivable to me. And for this possibility I grieve.

I open my eyes, from my prone perch on this ancient rock knoll, on this warm and windless September day. High above me, broad wings are still circling, spiraling ever higher, until they disappear from sight, into the boundless blue tundra sky.

Earth Hands – Janaia Donaldson

The Power Of One:
Waking Up In The Web Of Life
First Story Of "A Trilogy At 5 Am"*
By M. Paloma Pavel

It is 5 o'clock in the morning. After many weeks below zero, today the temperature is predicted to rise to 25° F. I place two logs of good oak in the cast iron wood-stove and bundle up for my morning assignment—gathering water for lauds, our dawn prayer service as a monastic community on an island off the Maine coast. I could not have known that this would be a day to change the course of whatever life would follow, a watershed moment from which would flow a different possible life.

The year is 1974, in January. I am living at the Benedictine Grange in the rural village of W. Tremont on Mount Desert Island. Our monastic community resides on the southwest side of the island where the locals live: shopkeepers, lobster fishermen, and folks who serve those from "away." It is the side of the island where food stamps are often a bridge from winter to summer, until the spring thaw brings the planting of food gardens and the tourist season starts again.

Low granite walls are abundant, hand-quarried and drilled, charting ancestral lots, and generational divides, marking the boundaries between farms, many abandoned now. Class differences, education, and culture form boundaries like the granite rock walls, upholding customs that New England tradition will rarely cross. These rocks also provided walls for turn-of-the-century monuments to prosperity built on the backs of slaves, wealth accumulated in then-new eastern seaboard settlements of Philadelphia, Boston, and New York. Whalers, some slave ships, sailing vessels, and finally steamers connected this pristine Down East rural coastland to the rising commercial city centers of early New England colonies.

But we live on the backside of the Island, at Elliott Farm, an old gable-roofed farmhouse offered to our abbot, Brother David Steindl Rast, for this brave venture in contemplative prayer and eco-spiritual reflection. Less than a dozen, we have come from throughout the United States, called to an innovative community experiment of listening to the still point of the turning world—not, as some believe, to abandon the world, but to listen to the heart beat and cry of the world more deeply, without distraction. In this world of collective "attention deficit disorder" and multitasking mania, we are attempting to slow down, to simplify, and to do only one thing whole-heartedly: to be present, to listen. Saint Benedict in the sixth century put it this way: *"ora et labora"*—work and pray. Father Thomas Merton in the twentieth century observed that individuals seek contemplative community out of love or despair.

For me it is both a kind of calling and a gnawing, relentless realization that there is no other life possible without an answer to fundamental questions. Questions about why I am here, what this life is all about, and a passionate commitment to find out if there is any glue in this universe. Are we just random molecules on an evolutionary jag, the latest mutant experiment of a cosmic joke? Also, a desire to confront and face death—my own and the recent death of loved ones—on a personal level. I had begun to sense a bigger Death looming, as already the extinction of species had reached an alarming level (the greatest in 65 million years), and many of us detected that we were beyond the carrying capacity for complex life on earth. How *do* you behave at the death of the world? Perhaps the most essential role I can play is deathbed attendant to a dying culture. I had traveled from California to coastal Maine to share this quest, and these questions, in community.

The months that followed were demanding and rich with learning. The Maine seasons provided a strong necessity to listen for cues to deeper aliveness embedded in nature—for weatherizing, wood chopping, and water carrying. Senses grew keener in the struggle to live in sub-arctic conditions. The fine craft of heating with wood: oak not aspen, dry not green. Silent candle-lit meals of potato or squash, with fresh broccoli on special occasions. Poetry, Buddhist sutras, Sufi tales, or the stories of Don Juan and Carlos Castaneda read aloud wove the hum of human bodies eating soup into a cosmic cantata of deep listening and shared contemplative attention.

As monks in training, we each took turns with the various chores that keep life possible at the edge of the earth. Weeks stretch into months as our hearts are laid bare to undergo deep healing and reweaving from the trauma of fragmented industrial culture. Minds grow clearer through chanting, breathing, ordering of days around the biological rhythms of life, the seasons, the time of day. This way of life provides a strong container for the inner drama of battling ego obstacles, then surrendering. Forged in the fire of a millennial wisdom process, we are being cooked in the soup of monastic tradition.

The cracking of a branch under the weight of January snow outside my window brings me back to my task. At 5 AM, both the dark and the cold are piercing. This week it is my turn to gather water for lauds, the morning meditation and prayer ritual. I reach onto the familiar barn shelf for the water pitcher, its white enamel-coated metal slippery in my wool mittens, and a Coleman lantern, then push open the heavy creaking door, guiding it back carefully to avoid slamming as I slip into the crisp air. Breath bites into my lungs; I pull the red scarf over my mouth as I follow the woods trail, crunching steps through the snow in the dark, taking care to balance the lantern while stumbling over tree roots and ice patches. From the main farmhouse to water's edge at Duck Cove is a quarter of a mile, but it seems much longer in the winter dark. I pick my way through the woods tracking the footpath in the dim silvery light from a moon-sliver still in the sky.

I know I am almost there when I smell the salt. I reach the water's edge and search for a safe perch on the icy granite boulders. I place the lantern on a flat rock. Slipping at first, I stoop to fill the pitcher, waiting for the moment between waves, with a familiar sound of metal clanging on granite rock. Once filled, I foist the now heavy pitcher at an angle that I can carry. This is the same path I have taken many times, the same place I have gathered water in a ritual action I have undertaken dozens, maybe hundreds, of times. But this time something is different. I stop, struck, frozen in my tracks. A moment expands into a timeless eternal space. Light is now flooding and illuminating the space. I am stunned. I look down at the pitcher full of water and notice that there is no hand holding the pitcher. My hand and arm have dissolved. The pitcher has disintegrated into a pattern of light and energy. I look down at what were once my boots, and the rock is no longer solid beneath them. There is no clear edge, but instead a rhythmic web of interconnecting patterns of energy…The rock, the water, and the trees are all gone. Only the stars are most themselves still…but now there is a merging between them in undulating, shining, interconnected pathways of light, bright patterns against the black fullness. Everything now perceptible has become a dark velvety field with interconnected networks and nodes of light. Another shift, and the entire air turns bright, like midday in summer, radiant, warm, and fragrant. There is a sound in the atmosphere. There is no "I" here now; instead a melding of sound and light, hovering, suspended.

This state of being held in a vast interconnected web of energy and light continues for an interminable time. I have merged with the ground beneath me, the trees around me, the ocean in front of me, the stars in the pre-dawn sky. Is it days or months? I awaken from this glowing humming state of sight and sound to yet another sensation. It is the taste of salt. Salt water in the form of tears is flowing out of my eyes and streaming into my mouth. First there is the taste and then an awareness of the sensation of movement. A damp rivulet on my cheek, waking me back into a solid form. The Me is back. I am startled by the salty taste in my mouth. The energy wave patterns of a moment before have re-assembled into solid objects of shoes and rock. Feet in boots are now guiding my legs and body along the stony path from the shore through the moss-covered woods back across the snowy field to the cabin at Elliott Farm.

When the large barn door is latched securely behind me, the bells are already beckoning us to the meditation room. The centuries-old rituals of Benedictine monastic life call me to re-enter and blend into the lauds service. On cue, I begin the ritual: I pour water from the enamel pitcher over the hands of each of the monks into a handmade pottery bowl, a daily small baptism.

The essential shattering that opened a new world for me that morning continued to reveal itself in the weeks that followed. That first morning and the aggregate of the experiences that followed provided answers for the questions that had brought me to the monastery—questions about the existence of a larger intelligence or purpose in this life (if not a God/Goddess, then a force or a pattern that is trustworthy.) That January morning at 5 AM became a kind of anchorage, as well as a watershed moment and a reference point for the subsequent course of my life that flowed from that moment onward.

This experience has remained a taproot to common ground that has been a resilient source of nourishment, sustaining me over a lifetime. It provided direct knowing, far beyond books, of feeling held in an expanded experience of love and profound interconnectedness with all of life. That day in the monastic community in Maine, and the experiences that continued to flow from it, have provided valuable guidance for navigating my solo life journey, and a resilient source of nourishment and grounding that has made other forms of connecting and relationship possible.

* This trilogy is composed of three stories of my own waking up to the experience of being held in love that has provided grounding for my life and for my work as an activist for sustainability and social justice. These stories represent three transformative experiences that have provided the soil out of which my life and work have grown.

Indwelling*
By Dennis Rivers

The seed of the Spiral:
I am in the loving heart of God
wide as the morning sky
I am in the radiant heart of Being
fragrant as a flowering tree
I am in the loving heart of the Universe
shining with endless Light
I am in the infinite heart of God
Whose presence caresses me like a warm wind
I am in the loving heart of Being
which sings through me with angelic voices
I am in the endless heart of the Universe
who holds me like a sleeping child

The Spiral deepens:
I am in the loving heart of God
wide as the morning sky and full of golden light
that fills the entire horizon of my life.
As I walk deeper and deeper into that light
I become filled with a deep peace.

I am in the radiant heart of Being
fragrant as a flowering tree.
I press my face into the blossoming branches
and my body fills up and overflows
with the perfume of compassion and delight.

I am in the loving heart of the Universe
shining with endless Light
I feel the warmth of this endless Light
washing through me with each breath.

I am in the infinite heart of God
which caresses me like a warm wind
the hands of the wind are full of joyous electricity
which fills me to overflowing.

I am in the loving heart of Being
full of angelic voices, singing,
I hear them, first far away,
then closer, then all around me,
then deep within me.
As their voices become clearer
I realize they are announcing
infinite forgiveness.
As their voices become clearer
I realize their voices are my own.

I am in the endless heart of the Universe
who holds me like a newborn child
and rocks me to sleep
on the front porch of eternity.
Every time I go to sleep
I go to sleep deep within
the endlessly loving,
endlessly beautiful heart of God.

*Reprinted from *Prayer Evolving*, by Dennis Rivers. Berkeley CA : Karuna Books, 2008.

Part Two

Awakening in Relationship

Partners – Carolyn W. Treadway

Birth, Rebirth
By Linda Seeley

I have been a midwife for over thirty years, and in that time I've served women and their babies in both the home and the hospital. About three years ago, feeling tired, worn out, and used up by the medical system, I stopped attending births. At first, I was heartsick with longing for the smells and sounds of birth, but as time wore on, I started to forget why I was drawn to midwifery in the first place. I was relieved at not having to get out of bed at three in the morning and not having to keep my ear tuned to the telephone in case someone needed me.

Last fall, after attending a 30-day retreat with Joanna Macy and 59 other people on the Oregon coastline, my husband and I took a journey to Israel, a trip we had been planning for several years. It was the perfect complement to the intensity of looking at what is happening to our world and feeling intense pain as well as deep gratitude for being born on Earth at this time—the time of the Great Turning. While in Jerusalem, I spent days at the Western Wall, absorbing the yearning that was embedded into the golden stone of the holy city, listening to the murmuring languages of supplicants from around the world, observing tints and hues of skin from peach to ebony, watching as folded prayers were tucked into narrow cracks between the massive stones. In my own prayers I asked for guidance, for help, for peace and reconciliation on Earth.

When I arrived home, there was a letter waiting for me. It was from a woman, Laura, whom I had seen during her first pregnancy six years ago. She wrote that she was pregnant with her third baby, and after two hospital births, she wanted a home birth. She knew that I was no longer attending births, and she knew that I hadn't been at a home birth for over fifteen years, but she extended her heart to me and asked me to be her midwife. I saw it as a sign.

On February 20, the night of the full moon and lunar eclipse, just on the cusp between Aquarius and Pisces, she went into labor. At about 3 AM, my assistant and I silently let ourselves into Laura's house. The children were sleeping cozily in their parents' bed, rain sprinkled down, a fire burned in the little heater in the living room. All was ready.

Laura was quiet. Her blazing cheeks were the only indicator that she was working hard. We quietly filled the tub where she hoped to birth her baby, we checked her and the baby, and we waited. Sometime near dawn, Laura, naked and gorgeous, walked over to me: "Linda, I can't take any more. Tell me something that will help me."

I quickly searched my brain, a brain that wasn't working too well without sleep. Then it poured out of my mouth like a fountain: "Your body knows the way…Your mother—and her mother—and her mother before her…bringing new life to be born… bringing new life to be born…" A song I had learned many years before with other midwives. A song that told her to trust herself and to trust her baby. Laura looked at me. She nodded. She lifted her foot and stepped into the warm water of the birthing pool. There, she knelt on hands and knees, and in silence, she gave birth to her son Joaquin, born in the caul, into water, on the full moon morning.

I was held in love. *We* were held in love: Laura's husband, her two sleepy-eyed children, and my assistant. As baby Joaquin squirmed and opened his eyes to new life, I knew that I belong with women as they give birth in this time of the Great Turning. Held in love.

Benjamin
By Anne Yeomans

I gave birth to my second child, Benjamin, in Goleta Valley Hospital, near Santa Barbara, California, January 29, 1972. He was born in the evening as a full moon rose.

The next morning, I woke early in my hospital room, my new baby beside my bed in a little plastic box with clear sides that I could see through. He was swaddled and peaceful, all in white, with a tiny cap. I watched him, and rested, and wondered, "Who is this child? Who will he be?"

My room looked out to a parking lot behind the hospital, and there I could see a small spindly tree, perhaps planted to give a little green around the building. It wasn't a particularly remarkable tree, but it was my tree, and my new baby's tree, and it was the only green I could see. It was my connection to the world of nature outside my window. And when I wasn't watching my baby, I was watching this tree.

I remember seeing the clear early light of the new day come to the tree, the first morning light of this boy's life. I saw the strong light of noon come to the tree, and then, the afternoon shadows and the soft evening light into the growing darkness.

With a three and a half year old at home, and a husband in graduate school, it had been a long time since I had had this kind of stillness just to be and just to look. Perhaps I had never watched the light on a tree all day before.

At one point in the day, and I cannot remember exactly when it was, I heard a voice say, " If you are absolutely quiet you will know exactly what to do for this child." It came unbidden. It was a quiet voice, but a very certain voice. And I knew it was right. It felt like a gift, and it was. It felt like it came from outside me, from beyond me. Did it? It brought a tremendous sense of peace with it. Peace and reassurance. To this day I remember the feeling.

Often I have recalled these words, as I have struggled to be the right kind of mother to this boy, now man. I haven't always been able to remember this wisdom, but whenever I have, it has always helped me.

I am so grateful to the voice that spoke. Still awed by the mystery of that moment.

And today, 36 years later as I write this, I have just remembered that the name that Ben was given at 21, when he was working as a counselor at a camp in Vermont that taught native ways, was *Sun Touches Earth*.

The mystery of that first day continues to unfold.

I bow in gratitude.

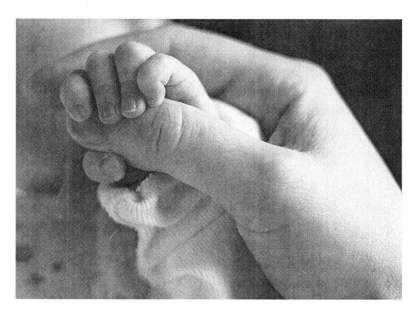

Holding Hands - Laura Treadway

Teething, Fourteen Months
By Hannah Mariah Dubé

Deep in these nights when I can hardly move an arm
        to pull this sleeping child close
        and I cry out, too
        from weeks passing this way
        the hourly rousal, his body reaching
        searching, clinging, clawing
        clamping nipple between gums
            which ache and break,
        taking my body into his, over and over
I want to roll over, lay on my other side
take back some space for me.

I want to have the stamina, the open awe
        of the first few months of this,
        when easy it was to rise and watch and calm—
        to sink down into the bliss of this
        sleep becoming secondary, something more of memory,
            something more like hope.
Instead this bed that was once so wide
        is small now
        this life of mine changed from wide open and awe-filled
        to tight, constrained
            as I ask in the night for sleep.

But—he takes his hand along my belly
        sweetly, softly, soothing my frustration
        and his voice sighs, moans, mellows
        falls into breath breath breath
this child at my breast
inviting me now to rest.

And as I sense him drift, as I hear him lift off into sleep
I know he is teaching me this:
    though disguised as struggle,
    to love like this is a gift
        a vision into myself of places
    deep and dark, but where a spark is stronger
    and brighter and lighter
than any other place.

The Eyes Have It
By Linda Gunter

Her eyes stared back at me with an overwhelming look of kindness. There was the faintest hint of a smile. Her dress was crisp and white. Her eyes were black and mesmerizing. She was beautiful. But it was the kindness that overwhelmed me. Here was a person whose heart was filled with love and compassion. Here was a person still searching for that special someone to love, and to be loved by. And yet, they were telling me now, as I stared at her photo, that the two of us would never meet.

That moment marked the beginning, not the end, of a love affair for me, a special kind of love affair that can only occur between a mother and a daughter.

I held the photo in my hand, the photo of a little girl just five months old. She was waiting far away in an orphanage in Vietnam. She had been chosen for us by representatives of an adoption agency, distant people we would never meet. She was our "match." Even if it had been made at random, there was something about their choice that felt meant to be.

We had waited four months to fetch her. But now our agency was telling us they would not complete the adoption. We should just put this child back on the shelf like a cereal box and they would find us another daughter in another country.

I looked at the photo again. If I were never to know this person, life would be unbearable. I would search for her—in my heart if nowhere else—for the rest of my life if I could not bring her home. I held the photo for a long time, and was held by her. Held in love. The fight to reach her, to hug her, to become her forever mother, intensified. She had already been abandoned once. We would not inflict that on her again. The tigress emerged, ready to walk through fire, to slay a thousand dragons, whatever it would take to keep the fairy-tale ending alive and bring closer the day my husband and I would hold her in our arms.

That day did eventually come. The kindness that shone from her baby eyes was true and remained so. As she grew we watched this unknown flower unfold and flourish. What were her talents? Who was she really? Someone else's child, but now our own, yet with a history we would never know.

As the months passed, small clues emerged. She could sing! And she did, in the morning as soon as she was awake, at night in her crib until she fell asleep. She sang everywhere, and, as soon as she could walk, she danced. There was music somewhere in the river of mystery and time that flowed back to Vietnam and to her ancestors. She swirled and swayed in perfect time to the rhythms she loved. She draped herself in scarves and veils, creating exquisite costumes out of the strands of surplus fabric that crowded the dress up box.

This magic person, whose smile lit up her whole face; who became entranced as much by Rachmaninov as by Raffi as her little hands tinkled over the piano keys; who would sing Bizet rather than baby tunes; who danced to Bollywood bangra as eagerly as to Ring-a-Roses. She was ours. And we were hers. What kinds of gods had smiled on us? Or had our stubborn refusal to surrender won us this rich reward? Maybe in the end it was some mysterious power of her own that had continued to draw us toward her, toward that smile, to be enveloped by it, comforted by it, made whole by it as we became parents for the first time. Her parents.

I have never given birth to a child. I cannot describe therefore, the bond that is born at that moment. But neither can I imagine a greater passion, a more abiding love than I feel for my daughter. I am hers and she mine without hesitation or doubt. From the day the first envelope arrived with her photo inside it, I understood motherhood completely. And I understood my own mother more completely, too.

The tigress, once released, never returns to her lair. So long as my little girl is out there, I prowl and keep vigilance, ready to hold her, to defend her, to keep her safe. And in the end nothing—no praise for work well done, no small professional or personal victory—delivers anything like the riches that she brings. I am the captive now of her love, a precious prison from which there is never once even a fleeting desire to escape.

To Be a Woman
By Molly Y. Brown

You were born of a woman's body
Into a body that would grow to be a woman's.
Why did your soul make such a choice?
Perhaps so you could more easily
Follow the ways of the Goddess
The Feminine
The Mother.
Perhaps so you would be moved
By unseen currents within you
Towards kindness
Compassion
Deep fierce love.
So you would more keenly know
The basic stuff of life:
   food, warmth,
   blood, hearth,
   endurance
So your woman's body could teach you
When the mind became insane with its own ideas
And you would sink your fingers deep into the soil
And bring forth roots
To feed the children.

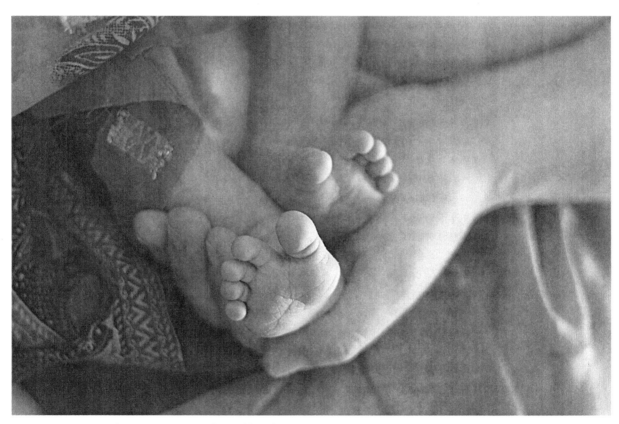

Cradled - Laura Treadway

A Love Story
By Renate Baier

I live in Austria. My daughter Teresa moved to Australia as a teenager and had lived there for eight years when she went on a world trip and an inner journey to clarify what she really wanted in life. She ended up living with me for a whole year. During this time we studied Nonviolent Communication together with a lot of enthusiasm, and also practised this "language of the heart" in our every day life in radical honesty and true compassion. Even with so much love between us, this was quite a challenge. It sometimes was a frightening process, and needed a lot of courage to look bravely at mother/daughter issues. We often went into helplessness, unsecurity and darkness, not knowing whether our loving relationship would really be strong enough to survive. This loving connection not only survived—it became deeper and deeper after every risk of being honest and truthful with each other, and not running away. There was a lot of healing for both of us. We had even started to teach Nonviolent Communication together successfully.

I had hoped so much that she would stay in Europe, and she decided to go back to Australia for better working opportunities, and also because there were so many wonderful friends waiting for her over there. Obviously she had lost her European roots.

The day before I took her to Munich Airport, I was desperately sad; I didn't want to believe what was happening. It happened that our neighbours, farmers who also have horses, were giving away a foal. Its mother was watching as the foal was taken away from the paddock and loaded on a trailer. I have never ever seen any being in so much desperation and pain as this horse mother then. She screamed, running around the paddock, writhed and rolled furiously on the grass, screaming and screaming and screaming in despair. Again and again she galloped to the fence from where her foal had disappeared, obviously hoping that it would reappear, galloping around in disappointment, when her foal just wasn't there any more. This lasted all afternoon; another horse joined in the screaming for a while. It was so hard to witness and to listen to what this animal had to go through.

And I couldn't believe how much this horse mother was in resonance with my own bleeding heart. It looked like the horse was acting out the deep suffering of both of us. I couldn't hide my tears; they just came over me. But in spite of all the honesty Teresa and I had practised together, I did not want to show my own deep, deep desperate pain in this case. I chose to respect her decision to leave, and did not want to make it harder for her by falling apart. Somewhere deep inside, I surrendered, and wanted to trust that she was following a calling from the wisdom of her soul.

In the evening I went into the stable to the still sometimes screaming horse. I went there grateful with an open heart and deep understanding. Soon I found myself hugging the grieving horse, talking softly and tenderly about how much I admired her and thanking her for the way she had gone through this painful day. Later we talked about green meadows that might wait for us once we had accepted our loss. The next day we both felt better.

Going to Munich I simply felt empty and exhausted. There were no tears any more. Inside I felt like a dry desert.

After Teresa had checked in, we still had one last hour together on the observation terrace of the airport. We sat there quietly on a bench holding hands; there was nothing more to say. So we looked down to the airfield where planes were arriving and leaving, passengers getting off and on, cars pulling up, taking luggage and bringing luggage, groups of cleaning staff, loading, catering…

I watched this coming and going. It looked almost like a dance, all these busy people. I had to think of ants working so hard, coordinated and directed by some unseen power.

Then my perception switched. I saw the whole world—mankind—fulfilling a mysterious dance, an unknown, unseen destiny, and I even had the song "in his hand he's got the whole world…" in my ears. And I felt held in this hand, secure, alive and grateful.

Even still not understanding why we had to part again, and live on opposite continents of this big, small world, I felt so embraced by this power that is wiser, stronger and so much more loving than my restricted mind. And although I had thought I couldn't bear the pain, and had been sure my heart was breaking a few hours before, in this very moment I knew we were both held by the great love that holds the universe. And I realized that this infinite power would be the connection between us, a reliable connection beyond space and time.

After she finally left, I drove home very sad, very quiet, and very touched by a deeper understanding of what love is all about.

She lives in Australia now. Our connection has even deepened through the past one and a half years, thanks to regular long Skype phone calls, and I am going to visit her soon.

***

When I shared this story with Teresa, she wrote back this letter:
> I have tears rolling, tears of joy and tears of sadness, sweet pain—it's this longing for this ultimate connection that sits so deep and is so powerful. I am so glad that we share this precious gift of bringing this longing to the surface in such a tender yet powerful way. I so much look forward to embrace you very soon and this process of saying hello and goodbye—it goes so deep, each and every time there is grief, but as you say it's not grief and loss, it's grief and tender love.

Love Poem
By Rebekah Hart

The morning we, your parents, let you go
we rose early and sat
silently and thoughtfully
in a heated room
for a long time.

Our bare red eyes looked across at each other,
and the thought of you hovered between us
and in our bodies,
though I could feel you more—
a gentle cramping of my uterus,
holding you in a pouch above my thighs.

We dreamt of you
we prayed to you
and we loved you.

We explained to you the entire situation
and I sent it to you
even through the veins through my heart,
the blood vessels in the red uteran underworld
reaching you like messages
sent through underwater telephone wires

but more intimately,
because there was touch involved
and not the touch of one to the other,
but the touch of one to oneself,
so close were you to the life of my body.

You were my body

You were
the spark of creation,
male and female collapsed into each other
          the embodiment of our love.

We loved you, and did our best
to welcome you
for the time that you came.

Comforted you with explanations,
though in fact it was our
aching hearts that needed comfort,
our eyes drawn out
and reddened from lack of sleep.

In our prayers
          it was you who whispered through us,
though we mistook the voice for our own.

There was clearly another
hovering in the space between
our pauses,
the harmonic tones beyond
the range of human talk.

In the rhythm of red blood
gliding behind each moment
infusing you with sustenance,
there was another
who whispered,

Mother, Father,
Do not be afraid.

I am with you

Closer to you
        than your shadow

I trust
your every
heartbeat

Understand you more
than you understand
yourselves.

I am an
angel in your body
angel in your blood.

I stay with you.

I fly.

Do not be afraid
        to let me go.

Oh dear one—
all this time I thought it was I
who held you
but now I see
it was you
holding me

enveloping me
with the enormity
of your forgiveness
infusing
my blood
like a warm
red wine

expanding
my heart

wide

like oxygen

A Lost Child Found
By Maurine Pyle

The name on her badge read Lorena, and it seemed to fit. An old Quaker crone, bent by time, robed in a bright red T-shirt inscribed with "The Family is Love." I watched as she approached me shyly with a question in her eyes.

She embraced me with a gentle smile across the serving table. My role as beverage server in the hot crowded dining room had kept all of my attention focused on the next thirsty person. Yet I had spotted her once or twice across the room.

Lorena smiled shyly and posed her question, "How old are you?" I answered, "Forty-seven." She looked intensely at my face and said: "I have been watching you for a long time. Forty-seven years ago I lost a baby daughter, one month old. I believe she would have looked like you."

Tears welled up in our eyes. My heart was so full of emotion. I told Lorena that I had been named for another lost child. She was the only daughter of my Aunt Chick and Uncle Johnny, who had died at a young age. I was a child of hope for them too.

I am also a lost child. My mother departed from me into the shadowy place of mental illness when I was a young girl, causing me to search for her forever after. Children never recover from these separations.

Yet here once more, a searching mother and a lost child crossed destinies in the vast universe of time and found comfort in one another.

A Decision Made from Deep Within*
By Demaris Wehr

In my experience, effective intercessory prayer is characterized by the deepest level of desire, truthfulness and intent one can muster. In my own case, it has sometimes been a prayer prayed in agony and anguish; at other times, prayer has been accompanied by an extraordinary peace. But in all cases, when it has "worked," it has been characterized by a decision made from deep within, and never from a neutral, indifferent, repetitious or bored place.

Probably my first intercessory prayer, ever, was one made on my own behalf. It was a time of great mental, emotional and spiritual suffering. I was young and desperately unhappy, feeling trapped in my first marriage. My parents had undergone an unbelievably confusing and traumatic divorce a few years earlier. This had no doubt catapulted me into my marriage as a remedy for the pain caused by the divorce.

My husband and I had recently become parents of a dear little girl who was sick a lot. My husband had a clear sense of his identity and calling. He had recently been appointed as a junior faculty member at Haverford College, while I was a "mere housewife." He worked constantly, it seemed, while my talents lay fallow as I took care of Kirsten (or so it felt to me at the time). My self-esteem was at an all-time low. The women's movement hadn't yet made its appearance. I was suffering from "battle fatigue" (by which I mean the ongoing, unresolved trauma of my parents' very difficult divorce) and from the unnameable syndrome from which many educated young mothers suffered in the 1960s. I remember walking across the sun-filled Haverford campus one afternoon in desperation. My first intercessory prayer was: "Dear God, if You exist, help me."

To my amazement, this prayer worked. Over time, though not immediately, things began showing up in my life that had not been there before. That simple prayer had the elements of what I have come to identify in effective prayer. It was heartfelt. It was honest. There was a deep intent to get better, to get out of the mess I was in, though I had absolutely no idea how. That prayer obviously had an intensity that is somewhat unusual, for I remember it still. I have prayed many prayers since, but many of them are forgotten. That one is remembered.

A few years later found me divorced, living alone in Ann Arbor with my then four-year-old daughter. The next incident of prayer changed my life. It happened this way. My daughter was prone to convulsions, which terrified me. She had spent a week in Children's Hospital in Philadelphia undergoing a battery of tests to determine their cause. The test results were inconclusive, leaving me with no recourse but Phenobarbital, baby aspirin and panic-stricken cool baths in the middle of the night if she had a fever. Unfortunately, she had fevers frequently. The doctors had said she could suffer some brain damage if she had any more convulsions.

One night, Kirsten got a high fever and showed all the signs of an approaching convulsion. A good friend, a Christian Scientist, encouraged me to call a Christian Science practitioner for prayer help for her. We had experienced some minor healings by prayer before this time, so the idea didn't seem totally foreign to me. I called the practitioner, who assured me that Kirsten was fine and in God's care. This seemed weird to me. How could she be fine? But this man was so certain, and spoke from such a depth of conviction, that he got my attention. After hanging up, rather than running for the Phenobarbital, as had been my habit, I sat down and prayed. I also read a portion of Mrs. Eddy's book, Science and Health.¨

Not long after, I went downstairs to check on Kirsten. Nothing had changed. Her breathing was rapid and shallow; her skin was hot to the touch. Normally, upon observation of symptoms such as these, my heart would start racing and I would literally run for the medicine and start running the bath. I would wake up my sleepy daughter, plunge her, protesting, into the cool water, trying to distract her with toys while she railed about, wanting out of the water. This time, however, my state of mind was entirely different. It was not exactly an altered state of consciousness, although it was certainly not my habitual state of consciousness in that situation.

What happened next was a deep moment of reckoning. I stood next to Kirsten's bed listening to her breathe. The practitioner had said she was fine. As I stood there, I asked myself: "Do I believe in God, or not?" I made myself vote. I waited, in silence, for the deepest truth of me to emerge. Finally, I answered "yes" to my question. Something sank deeper in me.

Then I asked myself: "Do I trust the practitioner or not?" Again, I stood there and made myself be absolutely honest. No fudging here. From the depths of my being arose an affirmation. "Yes, he seems honest; as people go, remarkably honest." Something sank even deeper.

Next, I stood there and addressed God—the God I hadn't even known existed in my prayer of two years earlier, and about whom I had only become sure in the preceding five minutes. "God," I said, "I'm terrified, but I leave her with you." And I turned around and walked out of her bedroom. Soon thereafter, I fell into a peaceful sleep in my own bed.

Imagine my amazement the next morning as four-year-old, golden-haired Kirsten came bounding up the stairs fully healed. I felt as though I stood on sacred ground, totally new terrain. My daughter was healed (and by the way, she never had another convulsion; never even came close). Even more importantly, my worldview had shifted to one that now included a good, loving God with actual capability of healing disease. For the first time in years, I felt safe, and joy-filled. My daughter was safe. This conviction of fundamental, existential safety under girded my prayers from that time on. And my prayers became increasingly effective as a result, I think, of my deepened faith.

Dear friends, I do not know how to conclude this article. There is a tension to hold, it seems to me, between experiences like mine above and those painful ones where prayer seems to go unanswered. I do know that when I've really gotten "down there," as I tried to describe, healings happened. However, there have been times when I couldn't get there; when I tried and tried and tried to the point of obsession with no luck. How does one find a graceful combination of surrender and hope? How does one find the ability to live with what is, if what is, is ongoing suffering? I do not know the answers to these questions. I only know that help has come my way as a result of deep prayer, and that now, prayer itself, regardless of results is, for me, a sustaining activity.

* Reprinted from *Discovering God as Companion*, Mariellen Gilpin, editor, AuthorHouse, 2007, pp. 68-70, and from *What Canst Thou Say?* 27: August 2000.
** Mary Baker Eddy, 1994. *Science and Health: With Key to the Scriptures,* Boston, MA: First Church of Christ, Scientist, The Christian Science Board of Directors.

Floating Obsession
By Barbara Heyl

Living in my bi-level mind these days,
I try to focus on the tasks at hand,
while just below the surface
butterflies arrive and flutter.

I try to focus on the tasks at hand,
picturing a little girl I've never met.
Butterflies arrive and flutter.
Can doctors or the angels rescue her?

Picturing a little girl I've never met,
her parents clothed in sterile gowns.
Can doctors or the angels rescue her?
She should be the butterfly.

Her parents clothed in sterile gowns,
they cannot touch her skin to skin.
She should be the butterfly,
but chemo stripped her fragile wings.

They cannot touch her skin to skin.
We wrap her in collective prayers.
The chemo stripped her fragile wings.
I must go back to work again.

We wrap her in collective prayers.
Students stop by, my phone rings.
I must go back to work again.
She floats in among the words.

Students stop by, my phone rings,
while just below the surface
she floats in among the words,
living in my bi-level mind these days.

The Hammock of Love
By Ruthann Knechel Johansen

Recognizing that we are "being held in love" is difficult for at least two reasons. One, we mindlessly take the elegant life supports of the planet and our human organisms for granted, or two, we are afraid. The severe traumatic brain injury of our son twenty years ago when he was a young teenager propelled me headlong into terror and, through a long journey of holding and being held, opened me toward love and gratitude. Being required to make this journey I can now describe it as a life-long apprenticeship in love. Although the apprenticeship continues, as I reflect on the past twenty years, I can clearly identify essential markings along the path.

The first marking I now identify as an involuntary call to the ineffable, to a higher power, to God, to something beyond the shock and terror the phone message that our son had been critically injured in a car crash induced in me. As we were driven by a friend the two-hour trip to the hospital, I suddenly realized, with our twelve-year-old daughter sitting close beside me, that I was silently repeating, mantra-like, poetry and music from an old hymn: "My hope is built on nothing less than Jesus Christ my righteousness...On Christ the solid rock I stand, all other ground is sinking sand." I had not played or sung that hymn for years. How had it come unbidden in this dreadful hour? The question was rhetorical, and the answer did not matter. The words rolled over and over in my mind as the tires of the car rolled over the highway to our son.

This involuntary calling to something deep within and simultaneously all around and far beyond me—what I now might call the "core of silence"—continued over the days of seemingly endless vigil in the Intensive Care waiting room, during the months and years of rehabilitation that followed, and continues to the present in daily circumstances. In silence and stillness I found some semblance of solid ground or an anchor in terrifying waters.

When we finally reached the hospital and were ushered into an emergency room cubicle to see our comatose son, I experienced immediately a second marking on the path of love. Instinctively my feelings leapt to reach behind my son's comatose form, although at the time I did not conceptualize these feelings so clearheadedly. I simply knew or believed, as perhaps most women know when new life is gestating secretly within their bodies, that my son's core silence was still present behind his closed eyes and unmoving form. Again instinctively I wondered silently to him and to God such barely formed thoughts as "Where are you?" "We are here with you." "Do not be afraid." I am surprised now, even twenty years later, by the suggestion not to fear from someone who was much of her life watchful and fearful. Frequently during the days and weeks that we waited outside of operating rooms or in waiting areas, I wondered how my fears of accidents or change or death and how the fears of our ancestors might be transmitted unwittingly to our children.

Over the months that would follow this initial meeting with profound injury and loss, I learned my third essential lesson about the relationship between fear and love. Twenty years ago at the Camden, New Jersey, Trauma Unit we were permitted to be with our son only two hours each day, one at midday and the other in the evening. In the intervening hours, my husband and I posted ourselves as guardians at the gates of the unit, just in case we might be called upon or might receive an update from a passing doctor or nurse. During the hours of waiting, my anxiety level rose, despite my efforts to meditate, to read, or to record thoughts in my journal. What was surprising and therefore constitutes my third lesson is that when I was with Erik the fear subsided. In the presence of need and love, fear has little space to prevail. I do not think that all individuals facing similar traumatic circumstances, however, would conclude that being in the presence of their injured or seriously ill loved one decreased their fear, for we met families whose anxiety and anger appeared to mount during their visiting hours.

The fourth lesson in my apprenticeship grew out of the times that we were able to be in our son's physical presence and then linked me to him during the spaces when we were not physically together. In the absence of eye contact, language, our uncertainty about whether Erik might be hearing us from within his coma, and the exchange of touch—all the ways we humans communicate from the first moments of birth until death, how could we communicate? My lesson was that holding Erik in love required images and language to become bridges to his core silence. Again without premeditation I first found myself singing childhood lullabies or songs of hope and comfort to him—"Swing Low Sweet Chariot," "Kum By Yah," "We Shall Overcome," "Sleep, My Child and Peace Attend Thee," for example. Simultaneously we began telling him stories about those who loved him and were holding him in their love and reminding him of memories from earlier years. We described the present-time weather, reported on inquiries from friends and relatives, and chronicled our comings and goings. One day I realized that I and the loving concern of others were together weaving a hammock of love in which he could swing, hovering somewhere in unconsciousness. Had that image of the hammock come unbidden from my own memory of a poem by Sufi poet Kabir of the fifteenth century?

Between the conscious and the unconscious, the mind has put up a swing:
all earth creatures, even the supernovas, sway between these two trees,
and it never winds down.
Angels, animals, humans, insects by the million, also the wheeling sun and moon;
ages go by, and it goes on.
Everything is swinging: heaven, earth, water, fire,
and the secret one slowly growing a body.
Kabir saw that for fifteen seconds, and it made him a servant for life.

—Kabir*

Other images emerged as the days of coma stretched into weeks. For example, one night as my husband and I walked through the hospital hallways back to the Ronald

McDonald House where we lodged for a month, I reported that I felt as if I were weaving a second umbilical cord to our son through which we longed to exchange life energy and spiritual nourishment.

Many weeks later, as we tried to assimilate the possible long-term consequences of a diffuse closed head injury, a friend provided the image of the injured brain as a badly tangled fine hair net. As Erik gradually regained consciousness and throughout the months of intensive rehabilitation, stories, images, and music continued to be essential resources for reconstructing his life and recollecting a sense of self.

The human capacity to make images, to turn vocalizations into meaningful sequences of words and into stories, and to see and hear both the manifest and latent dimensions of experience and story arises from and nurtures the imagination. To hold another person in love involves visualizing, feeling, imagining the beloved in wholeness. Through imagination, respect, compassion, courage, and commitment become possible.

As I was learning the preceding lessons in my apprenticeship, I daily turned into an advocate, first for the motionless and speechless child and later, throughout months of rehabilitation and readjustments, for our son who was forced to renegotiate his own and others' expectations in a hyper-stimulating world. Three examples will illustrate. Shortly after his injury, some relatives and friends referred to Erik's brain damage, even to Erik as brain damaged. I reacted immediately and strongly to that label because it categorizes and imprisons a human being in fixed ways. Some people no doubt interpreted my reaction as denial of reality. Because I think language significantly shapes the reality we experience, I preferred to describe Erik's condition as brain injury and did so in all the ways I communicated about Erik's condition. Damage connotes inalterability whereas injuries permit healing even if scars remain.

A second opportunity to advocate on Erik's behalf occurred in the rehabilitation hospital during an extremely agitated stage of his recovery. During these agitated periods, some of which occurred during the night, Erik would attempt to stand up in his bed thereby further endangering himself. The hospital wanted to restrain him in his bed.

My husband and I argued against such restraints because we sensed they would simply increase his fear and agitation. Instead, my husband, who was spending the night in the room with Erik, walked him through the quiet hallways until he was tired, the agitation had passed, and he calmly returned to his bed and sleep.

When it was time to project an educational future for Erik, we had a third opportunity to advocate for our son and, indirectly, for others who face similar conditions. The psychologist at the rehabilitation hospital advised that we plan to place Erik in a special education classroom in our public school district. At the time of the accident, Erik was a bright student in a private, college preparatory school in Princeton. Throughout the acute and rehabilitation stages, several of his teachers and his friends had remained in touch with him. To place a teenager who had been an academically high achiever, whose post-injury cognitive capacities were still unfolding and uncertain, and whose social behaviors needed guidance of healthy peers in a setting with students of limited mental abilities and often serious behavioral problems seemed irresponsible. We advocated for another approach, supported by an inordinately wise head master of the private school and a neuropsychologist who worked closely with faculty at his former school so that Erik could return for a reduced and carefully tailored and monitored program.

In this continuing apprenticeship through fear to love, I learned a sixth lesson over and over because, although it is a powerful lesson, it is paradoxically so easy to forget. Every time that I held our son through touch, image, song, story, or advocacy, fear retreated. At those moments, I found myself inexplicably held in the hammock of love myself, weaver held in the woven. On such occasions my anxious brain relaxed, my constricted chest expanded, and I was drawn to regard the miraculous in all the scenes and activities I typically take for granted: the beauty of sunrise and dusk, the bird language of song, the way a butterfly performs its love work by alighting on flowers, the way seeds die in the earth to become wheat or corn, the exquisite organization of the human brain and body, its ability to swallow nourishment and excrete waste, the surprising plasticity of the brain. When we are most truly and fully human we are makers of love, creators of hammocks that hold one another.

The journey into the belly of fear, into shattered stillness, and to silent mystery–forced upon me through our son's diffuse brain injury—has become a metaphor for what we each live on the edge of every moment but try to ignore through denial and elaborately constructed illusions and defenses. Brain injuries strike at life's animating center and make visible our vulnerability and our shared fears of disintegration, non-being, nothingness, death, and annihilation. Being forced to make the journey into fear led me gradually to awe and gratitude for how life hangs so delicately, yet tenaciously and resiliently, between unconsciousness and consciousness, between non-being and being. Through grief and anger and loss, the extremes of profound brain injury led me to emptiness where I could see dimly that the entire universe, of which we humans are one small part, is held in love.

*Robert Bly, ed. and adapter. 1971, 1977. *The Kabir Book: Forty-four of the Ecstatic Poems of Kabir,* Boston: Beacon Press.

Tenacity – Carolyn W. Treadway

God Suffers with Us
By Carole Edgerton Treadway

Our son, Eric, died March 2, 1987. The immediate cause of his death was pneumocystis carinii pneumonia (PCP), an illness associated with AIDS. He was twenty-five years old. Those are the bare facts of his last day of life and the culmination of a long story of suffering and growth.

Eric was born with hemophilia, a genetic condition in which one of the factors needed for the clotting of blood is missing or deficient. Throughout his life, from his very first week, he experienced disabling, sometimes even life-threatening episodes of bleeding. When the bleeding was in a joint, as it was more often than not, there was excruciating pain. Despite all of this, he was usually a happy little boy, always ready to test the boundaries of his limitations. Sometimes there would be long periods of weeks, even a few months, when there would be no serious "bleeds," and his life would begin to seem quite normal except for the extra caution he needed to take in everyday activities.

In his early years, treatment to stop bleeding was crude with a potential for dangerous side effects and sometimes involved hospitalization. Bleeding into his knees caused a crippling condition that resulted in a bent knee, seemingly a permanent condition, by the time he was four. Eventually we found an orthopedist who straightened the leg and recommended measures that could be taken to prevent the bleeding from being so crippling.

I knew even as a child that my maternal grandfather had been afflicted with hemophilia and that hemophilia is inherited through mothers by their sons. Since any son of a carrier mother has a fifty percent chance of being normal, we prayed that the throw of the genetic dice would be in his favor. When abnormal bleeding began within days of his birth, my heart sank with the near certainty that he had the clotting factor deficiency. I feared that I would not be able to care for Eric adequately or cope with the fear and anxiety that would accompany us every day. When that early crisis resolved and there were no more episodes for many months I told myself that the early bleeding had been a fluke and that he was normal. Tests given when he was five months old seemed to confirm that he did not have the genetic flaw. When he began to walk, his frequent bruises, I told myself, were caused by a "tendency" that was unrelated to hemophilia. By the time Eric was two years old, there had been bleeding episodes that were too serious to discount as a tendency and we had to accept that he did have hemophilia.

I feel certain that the helplessness I felt when Eric was in intense pain, and the fear that the next "bleed" might be a fatal one, drew me to religious teachings that seemed to promise healing if my faith was sufficient. In this case, "faith," meant seeing Eric whole as God saw him. For many years I sought this transformation of consciousness through meditation, reading and study. And there were times when there did seem to be recovery from episodes of bleeding that were unexpected and these kept me going on this path. But the healing seemed to be beyond my capacity for faith. Gradually, I found that a traditional understanding of Christian suffering and redemption spoke more deeply to me. I could see that healings happen and that there are many stories of Jesus healing persons who came to him or were brought to him, but the teachings I had been studying no longer seemed adequate and healing remains a mystery to me.

Eric attended Quaker meeting with his family until his mid-teens. By his late teens he was beginning to be interested in the life of the spirit and began studies and practices that he would continue until his death. He often initiated long conversations with us on these matters, which were a source of great joy to us. An important part of this journey was a struggle to find his vocation. He also sought healing of body and mind and these particular needs led him into some of the self-help teachings popular in the 1980s.

From his early twenties until his death, the specter of AIDS overshadowed his life.

Much improved treatment for bleeds became available when he was about sixteen and he quickly learned to infuse the missing factor in highly concentrated form by himself. Thus many bleeds were stopped before they could become a problem and hospitalizations became much less frequent. For him and many other people with hemophilia, the quality of life was greatly improved. Then, in January 1982, there were news reports that hemophiliacs were among three population groups who were becoming ill with and dying of a mysterious illness. We and our son were alarmed but tried not to become overanxious. A test for what was now known as a human immunodeficiency virus or HIV became available in 1984. It was known that the blood products that he and other people with hemophilia received were derived from purchased, not donated, blood and that each treatment was made from the blood of thousands of donors. The chance of exposure to HIV from contaminated blood products for Eric and others was very high. Eric was tested in the hemophilia clinic where he had been treated since he was about eight years old and he was told, as we now believe, that the test was positive. His report to us minimized the results and he considered the report to be ambiguous. We feel that this level of denial allowed him to live with the threat.

Oddly, for the years following this tentative diagnosis, Eric did not suffer any serious bleeding episodes and was not treated with blood products more than a few times. This gave him hope, perhaps an irrational hope, that he could be 'cured.' He attended college for two years, worked a full-time job, and lived on his own. But it became clear that depression and anxiety were eating away at his efforts to find direction for his life.

Eric's search for his calling went hand-in-hand with his spiritual search and he began to feel that he was drawn to service to others in the form of counseling or therapy of some kind. With our blessing, he quit his job in the spring of 1986 and went to live as a volunteer helper in a residential hospice in the foothills of the Blue Ridge Mountains. By this move he hoped to test out his leading to be of service to people who were suffering. At first, he seemed to thrive. He looked better than he had for several years and he was enjoying many aspects of his work. But by mid-summer he was beginning to lose weight and exhibit other signs of ill health. In August he left the hospice and came to live with us.

During the months he was with us, his spirits were very low. He was troubled by a cough that would not go away and which his doctor could not diagnose. He would not consider that the underlying cause might be AIDS, nor would he let us. He told his doctor, "If I have AIDS don't tell me. I don't want to know." We all avoided confronting this likelihood over the months during which his health became progressively worse in ways consistent with the effects of AIDS. We told ourselves and him that when his depression lifted, he would feel better and would be able to live on his own again. In view of the lack of a cure for AIDS or any significant treatment, the denial may have served him and us well, keeping us from falling into despair. Some time after Eric's death I read the following sentence in a novel, *Time after Time*, by Allen Appel: "And so we all lived, perched on the edge of knowing and not knowing and pretending not to know." That expresses our ambiguous state of mind.

Eric lived a monkish existence for the six months prior to his death. He seldom left the house; saw almost no one outside his family; and spent his days reading spiritual literature, writing in his journal, and practicing the spiritual disciplines of prayer and meditation. He had many discussions with his father and me concerning spiritual matters, especially with regard to healing. In the meantime, his cough was becoming worse with increasing shortness of breath. The day came, February 18, 1987, when we all knew he must see a lung specialist. It was on that day that we were forced to face the worst news: his immediate problem was an advanced case of PCP and the diagnosis of AIDS was unavoidable. The prognosis was poor. Nevertheless, we were hopeful. Eric had been through so many crises before and had always come through them. Perhaps he would again.

Our hope was short lived. Eric was admitted to the hospital immediately from the doctor's office and went straight to the intensive care unit where he was put on oxygen. Each day after his admission to the hospital, Eric's condition worsened. He was put on a ventilator to assist him with breathing. Every day we anxiously awaited the report of blood gasses and every day the report gave us less reason to hope. Eric was anxious and afraid. We stayed with him around the clock helping him as we could, praying for him, asking everyone we knew who prayed to do so for him, and we surrounded him with our love. He was astonished that so many people were concerned about him and praying for him.

After he was hooked up to the ventilator, he could no longer speak and was given a pad and paper. Although he was groggy much of the time with painkillers, his communications were profoundly significant for us, with expressions of gratitude and love. One day he wrote, "God is good." We could only surmise that at that moment, despite his fear, he was feeling the love directed to him and he recognized the source.

A few days before he died, a doctor asked us to let the staff know how much intervention they should make. This was a dreaded question and we knew it was Eric's to answer. His doctors assumed he could not communicate his wishes, but I felt that he could. I went to his room, not knowing what I would say, and praying to be given the words. As I walked into his room, he held out his pad on which he had written, "Nothing is working." I asked him how he felt about that, and he wrote, "I want to be healed or die." I knew I had the answer I needed, although the finality of it broke my heart.

In the days following, Eric became less and less responsive and was sleeping much of the time. One afternoon I went into his room while he was sleeping and was startled by the very strong impression I had that the image of Jesus on the cross was there with Eric, not instead of him, or beside him, but one with him. I shook my head, thinking that my eyes were playing tricks on me—I was very tired. But the image persisted and appeared every day after that when Eric was asleep. I was puzzled by it, since it was not an image I would be inclined to imagine. It is true that for several days I had had the comforting sense of Mary the mother of Jesus with me, but not as an image, just as a sense of presence, pouring all her love and energy into me to sustain me. On Eric's last day he slipped into a semi-coma from which he roused once or twice and mouthed the words, "Help me." His very last word to his father, shortly before he died was, "Why?" We could not help him or answer his question, only watch him and love him.

During the weeks and months and years of the hard work of grief I often remembered that image of Jesus on the cross with Eric and wondered what it meant. Over time I began to see that it signified that Eric's death was a kind of crucifixion, dying to all that separated him from the real and the ultimate. Still later I came to understand it also as the assurance that God is not indifferent to our suffering, but through Jesus, suffers with us. At length, the image opened me to a much stronger and deeper experience of God's immeasurable love, not just for Eric or me, but also for everyone and for all of creation. Faith, I learned, has much more to do with love and trust than it does with knowledge. We were born out of God's love and we die in it. Nothing separates us from it.

Hugs and Kisses*
By Elizabeth J. Buckley

Hugs and Kisses from the Loving Universe
Flow through your hands piecing together
Two-inch squares of patterned fabric:
Specs of white in black,
Swirls in deep purples, midnight blues,
Reminding me of starry nights.

When wrapped inside this quilt,
I found the courage
To relive over a thousand and one moments
Of sustained terror.

Surrounded in the energy
Of your hands stitching cloth,
Protecting me from drowning
In the tsunami of words and memories
Embedded so deeply within me.

The intonation of your voice persists,
Reminding my own hands of what they know
About weaving strands of sunsets
Into masterful tapestries.

The reign of terror is over now.
At last, this quilt can rest quietly.
Once again I can join the world of
Textured grasses shifting in the sunlight
With the wind's breath.

I know that I can return within
To find the comfort of these hugs and kisses
Whenever I awaken in the
Middle of night

To the rawness of my soul's grief
Piercing my heart.

The reign of terror is over now.
Turbulent seas of pain
Can no longer drown me.

* This poem is dedicated to my therapist, who witnessed and facilitated my internal journey of healing the trauma of childhood abuse. She loaned me the use of a quilt she had made, to help me feel safe, supported and loved and to help me find the courage within as I moved forward into EMDR work with her colleague. I would literally wrap myself in it during the EMDR sessions, and often later in my studio when I was feeling overwhelmed by waves of old emotion thawing and moving through me. When wrapped in this quilt, I felt held by a Loving Force, and no longer felt abandoned nor forgotten by the Universe. Since then, my engagement with the creative process as an artist and writer contains a heightened awareness of the Life Force moving through me and into my creative work.

On The Bus
By Joana Blaney

Something was different today. Instead of the collective conversations and bantering about politics and sports that usually began the bus ride, there was an eerie quietness. It was early Thursday morning and I was on my way to work at a popular education center in São Paulo. As usual, there were no seats and I had to stand holding the handrail. Not very comfortable, especially with the pushing and crushing all around me every time people got on or off the bus. But any thoughts of self-pity I might have been having for myself were soon dispelled by an unusual sight right in front of me. A young man was silently weeping, tears streaming down his face. I began to feel a little ill at ease. Other people must have too. A couple of people stared; many took refuge from this public spectacle of tears by turning their gaze away, looking out the window. Anywhere that provided an escape from such intimate confrontation with what is vulnerable in all of us. "Yes", I thought. "This is what disturbs us. We have no time for tears, for tenderness".

The bus trundled on.   We passed the remains of a shantytown that had been torn down weeks before. Heads turned to view the remnants of the belongings of some of the 7,000 people who had inhabited the slum on the hill. What had happened to the community garden? The lone, brilliant, violet quaresmeira tree, many of it roots completely exposed, seemed to scream out for survival. Perhaps some of the bus-riders had relatives who had lived in this inconvenient eyesore that existed in the most luxurious part of the city.

Almost all of the men on the bus were construction workers from poor neighborhoods hired to build what was called "the most ostentatious shopping center in all of

Latin America". The advertisements for its opening invited us to "Come and Experience the Universe of 'Sex and the City' at Garden City Shopping." It is another symbol for me of the great unraveling that is destroying our world—this endless industrial growth for a small minority. Perhaps some of the young man's tears were about this tragedy encompassing all of our pain for the planet.

People got on and off the bus. Many ate their breakfast of coffee and bread standing at the entrance to their work sites. This was part of the shared experience of domestic workers in the surrounding mansions and the builders of these mansions. A graffiti painting on the side of the road showed a face—one gigantic eye was a crying heart. I took a discreet look again at the young man. The tears were drying up. But what provoked them was still stamped on his face. An immense sadness, so it seemed. A suffering that was only his alone. Yet of such universal significance that it touched everyone around him, even, and maybe particularly, those who feigned indifference.

I remembered that today was the autumn equinox as well as the Jewish feast of Purim and Holy Thursday for Christians. Perhaps the presence of these energies was enfolding us in this moment of deep time that was the tender heart of this young man. I wondered about all that was going on in him and how his suffering seemed to unite us on this rickety bus. The depth of the silence seemed so beautiful and painful. The tired and empty space of our daily bus routine was torn open. If only for a few minutes, I felt that we were submerged in an in-between place that is pure gift, perhaps the loving heart that is our universe.

Eyes followed the young man as he got up to get off the bus. Two arms were put around his shoulder in a gesture of compassionate solidarity, one body tenderizing another. This was surely a gift to me on this day, if not to others.

The Guardian
By Abigail DeSoto

This morning I held my little Brownie in love…or maybe he held me. Despite his size, he is the largest container of love, acceptance and joy I have ever witnessed, (next to his "sister", Misty, who died 12 years ago). He is the incarnation of the bigger-than-life, orange 'Cuddly Dudley' toy dog I so craved when I was eight years old. Cuddly Dudley had soulful eyes and long silky ears; Brownie has dark, deep eyes filled with love, compassion, understanding and playfulness.

When I adopted him in 1998 at Christmas in Paris, he did not resemble, or even suggest, who he is today. He was skinny, almost fur-less (shaven) and ugly—he looked like he had been in a concentration camp. Despite his looks and the other 499 dogs available for adoption, he exuded a calm knowing and acceptance that caught my attention. Nine and a half years later, I have held Brownie in love and respect, and he has returned it tenfold. To be exact, he has been my 'guardian' all these years. Two weeks after I adopted him, my husband walked out…needed time, "to find himself." Although I tried to be understanding and patient, a year and a half later we decided to divorce. It was a horrible shock for me, for though I had felt for a number of years that B. was not stable and at peace, deep down I had always believed, or been confident that with understanding and time, he would "find himself" and be happy. Alas, that was not the case.

When I was a child I needed someone to play with, to love me unconditionally, protect and comfort me; it took me years to "see" how totally lost and left to my own devices I actually was as a child. My parents may have been my progenitors but they were in no way ready or able to be true guardians or parents. I was left alone, criticized or shouted at, hit, used, and abused. By the age of thirteen, luckily for me, I left 'home' and went to live far away with my grandmother. I never returned.

My first experience away from 'home' happened unexpectedly when I was eight years old. I was sent (without warning or explanation) to live with my grandparents in Chicago. They lived in a 14-room, dark, forbidding house in the inner city, at the time, a poor portion of town. Though my grandmother was extremely agile for her age (75), my grandfather was weak and in poor health. I was put into his mother's (my great grand-mother's) large, heavy, front room, a room furnished with French antiques, cactus-like plants, and a stuffiness that revealed a desire to keep things as they were, in an attempt to respect the past and those who have gone before.

I remember lying in the big double bed at night feeling alone and afraid of the shad-ows created by the cacti and the light from the street. To lessen the fear and terror I felt alone, I imagined the bed as a spaceship with a dome that would close up to protect Cuddly Dudley and me from the heaviness, loneliness, and foreboding I felt.

Today I can see that Brownie is the incarnation of that 'Cuddly Dudley' I so longed for and needed when I was eight. To be honest, I am amazed at my ability to have mani-fested in flesh and blood the living version of my 8-year-old stuffed, canine companion. Brownie has been, and is an amazing guardian and manifestation of love. He has taken care of me through the pain of my divorce, and through an even more painful separa-tion with a man I loved, just two years ago. Through Brownie I am held in love. He has always been there and has never abandoned me.

Patterns and Conditioning

When I was ten years old, I was sent back to live with my parents, and life present-ed me with incomprehensible experiences of neglect, physical, emotional, and sexual abuse. These experiences and hateful "voices" permeated my being, leaving deep scars of fear, lack of trust, a sense I did not deserve goodness, and, worse, a sense I did not deserve to exist. My father used to joke about finding me in a garbage can; whatever I did, said, or did not do, was always wrong.

I was fortunate to again return to live with my grandmother at age 12 (my grandfa-ther died when I was 10); still, life became a challenge of survival, pleasing others, and taking care of them, so indeed I could exist. I was taken care of, though love was not evident or 'visible'. You had to work hard "to deserve."

I successfully worked my way (mostly due to scholarships) through high school, college, and graduate school, but always feeling a deep sense of not belonging or somehow being fundamentally 'different' and not deserving. Something pushed me along, and even pushed me to follow a dream to go to France. I succeeded in doing graduate work in Paris, and managed to find a job with a company that "introduced" me through the official channels, making "a non European Union student into a worker", something the French immigration officials had informed me was impossible.

Life allowed me to experience professional success, and a pleasant, often fun, though unstable marriage (12 years) with B. But never did that deep down, uncomfortable sense of being a 'misfit' and the incredible anxiety I experienced when I went into completely unknown situations, disappear.

In time, two major emotional break-ups and abandonment (first my marriage, then a four-year affair with a man I adored) brought me "to my knees" and pushed me to open the cobwebbed doors and hidden recesses to confront the conditioning in my unconscious mind. The fear to look within was enormous—I so wanted to erase the pain and the past as if it had never happened (and I might add, so did everyone in the family). The denial over the years, had been and still is, enormous, if not total.

But now the personal pain was too much. With the help of a psychologist and my own discovery of Psychosynthesis, and other tools, I started to unfold and look at the destructive, criminal story of abuse and neglect. The journey has been hard, full of previously unshed tears and heart-wrenching anguish. But through it all, Brownie has been there, always knowing when to cuddle close to me, or jump into my lap. His head is wet with tears, but steadfast he remains; no pain is too great for him to hold and accompany.

 During this period of healing, people have come and gone in my life, for they also have their pain and suffering, and often want to push it down so they can "get on with life". I have also reacted in this way, but have discovered the truth in the adage: "The only way through, is through." At some point, it is time.

This time of great aloneness (other than Brownie), personal discovery, and healing has allowed me to open my eyes, and see all the love, support and caring that come my way, in ways and forms I do not suspect…. in four-footed canine companions or in the last-minute synchronistic occurrences dealing with my health, or financial situation.

A Course in Miracles tells us in several of its lessons: "God's Will for you is perfect happiness…joy is our function here…. let us try to find that joy that proves to us and all the world God's Will for us. It is your function that you find it here, and that you find it now. For this you came."

How hard it is to see at times. Then I look at Brownie, always able to remember joy, the present moment, and acceptance of what life brings, for he too is now being brought lessons of ill health and physical pain. And I realize what a teacher, and 'lover' I have.

> Unshaken does the Holy Spirit look on what you see; on sin and pain and death, on grief and separation and on loss. Yet does He know one thing must still be true; God is still Love, and this is not his Will.

The lessons in our life are not easy to understand, let alone forgive, but somehow, somewhere, if we look deeply, there is a love, a presence, "being taken care of". It's a deep feeling, often difficult to recognize, until we are ready to open our eyes to things "impossible", unexpected, and often 'last minute,' or more likely, exactly when we need them. This is being "held in love", and it comes in all forms, shapes, and sizes. It IS there, in all of our lives, if only we open our eyes to see it.

Chicken Wisdom
By Shepherd Bliss

On Valentine's Day this year I brought two chickens from my farm to serve as Teaching Assistants for the psychology class that I teach at Sonoma State University in Northern California. I took Silkies, whose name apparently comes from their feathers, which feel like silk and look like soft fur. They did indeed coo and cuddle during much of the class. These small, attractive love birds even felt so comfortable that one laid an egg—which I took as an expression of love. Chickens are givers—of beauty, warmth, joy, and precious eggs. My students were delighted by the connection they felt between these two adorable creatures.

"Do you know anyone who would like some chickens?" my former sweetheart asked about a dozen years ago. "We've got nine chickens here that I would like to find a good home for," she explained. I decided to take a risk: "I can take four of them." Her response: "They are a flock, so they need to go together." So I ended up with a family of nine chickens. "You mean you'll take care of my girls?" she squealed. "Yes," I committed myself. "Can I have visitation rights?" "Of course," I responded. We remained connected, these many years later, by the little darlings in the back yard.

My life has never been the same. It has been so much better, because of the presence of these sweet creatures. Now it is hard to imagine my life without these beautiful, playful, food-providing critters. Chickens have had a special meaning and role in recent years. They connect me to an important woman in my life, as well as to the Earth in which they take dust baths. Whereas humans use water to clean ourselves, chickens use dirt, which rids them of parasites. Chickens may seem lowly, and are looked down upon by many, but they have inspired me to deep experiences of connection and even love.

By observing simple chickens, we humans can learn a lot about the world, ourselves, and our appropriate role within Nature. Electricity had not made it to our family farm in rural Iowa by the early 1950s. For fun, we chicken-gazed by day and stargazed by night. Chickens play, go into altered states, wrestle, and make all kinds of interesting sounds. So instead of watching TV, we watched chickens and other barnyard animals and told stories about them and other creatures at night, illuminated by gas lanterns. "Once upon a time, a long, long time ago," my Uncle Dale used to begin most nighttimes. And we were off into imagination and what I have come to describe as sweet darkness, with all its mystery. Our icebox held the ice cream, essential for story telling. Chickens populated my childhood dreams and remain deep within my psyche, as they do in those from many indigenous and traditional cultures. Chickens are more entertaining than TV. They do not induce passivity; they are very alive and active and even speak back to their larger two-legged descendent. I still don't have a TV, so I enjoy engaging with chickens, as well as other animals.

Being A Chicken Man

OK. I admit it. I'm a chicken man. I think that they're beautiful, highly communicative, wise, useful, entertaining, and socially responsible. Sometimes they do dumb things, but they're not dumb animals, especially when compared to that other, taller biped. Chickens can teach us humility, being so lowly, yet able to rise. Chickens, at least the hens, do not have that human tendency to get inflated, arrogant, and prideful.

It looks easy enough, so I've tried to flap my unfeathered arms, but I never lift off the ground, even a little. However, my connections to and feelings for chickens have enabled me to soar and feel the unity of life on Earth.

Having fun is something that chickens know about, scratching and dancing about as they do, snuggling into the Earth. Watching them as a child and now as an adult enables me to be more playful. "Lighten up" seems to be a message that chickens naturally communicate, even in the face of impending death, to which they seem to surrender.

Chicken Wisdom

Over the years of living with chickens, I have come to see that they offer many things. They can teach surrender to what is, joy at the dawn, transformation of throw-aways into jewels, and love of the Earth within which chickens take their dust baths. Chickens offer incredible eggs, humor, joy, and beauty.

The words "chicken" and "wisdom" seldom appear together. In fact, chickens are usually considered stupid. As I have cared for these lively, giving birds I have come to admire, appreciate, and learn from them. When I look out back I see chickens. Even if I do not look, I know they are there, because they crow, cackle, purr, flap their wings, and make other sounds of delight, fear, and accomplishment. I know they are there because I am deeply connected to them. Their presence offers joy; they are an integral part of my family and what ecologist Aldo Leopold describes as "the community of the land." I have also learned—to paraphrase a famous phrase from Leopold—to "think like a chicken." That way I can provide them what they need—food, water, protection, furniture, and some stimulation, but not too much.

Some Of The Wisdom I Have Learned From Chickens

1) Greet every day with enthusiasm. You are alive again, and who knows what delights await you, or for how much longer you will live.

2) Enjoy the flight. Soar whenever you can, stretching your "wings" as you lift off.

3) Display, manifest, and share your beauty. Let your beauty bring joy to others. Don't be afraid of standing out.

4) Delight in simple things, like worms. Find humor in whichever of its forms it arrives, including getting very excited by some small morsel of food, such as a slug.

5) Jump for joy, as chickens do when confronted with a ripe tomato or berry.

6) Keep dancing. Dance delights chickens—alone, even on one foot, or with partners. Chickens move in circles and in all kinds of mysterious formations, sometimes as if guided by some invisible hand. Perhaps human dancing is modeled on observing chickens.

7) Recycle, as chickens constantly do. They take all kinds of refuse and transform it

into eggs.

8) Snuggle into the earth—the ground that supports and can heal us. Chickens love dust baths and gleefully dig in and nestle.

9) Cuddle at night with whoever may be closest to you.

10) Slow down. If we move too fast in chickens' presence, we trigger their flight-or-fight responses.

11) Protect and defend the helpless. Roosters will fiercely attack creatures much larger than themselves, including humans, to protect their charges. I once saw a cock fight off a hawk. Watching a hen care for her brood is a delight, as she leads them around and spreads her wings for their comfort, making motherly clucking sounds

12) Be a companion, even to those who aren't your kind. Chickens offer companionship to each other, within certain limitations, and sometimes to humans and other animals. A rabbit once showed up in the chicken yard and, after a fuss, was welcomed into the flock.

13) Persist and endure. Certain chickens will not be talked out of certain behaviors. Even negative reinforcement does not seem to work.

14) Combine vulnerability and hardiness. Desired as food by many other animals, they are very vulnerable. Yet they can simultaneously be very hardy, enduring attacks by hawks, dogs, and others.

15) Be prepared to let go, rather than clinging, even to whatever you think gives you identity. Each year chickens molt, often looking quite ugly, but are rewarded with new and sturdy feathers. Rather than hold on to what protects us, we could benefit from releasing and being rewarded with the new that replaces the departed. Humans hold on, even when faced with forces they can't resist. When the time arrives for chickens to go, they can be accepting, even stoic.

16) Show gratitude, and be willing to be blessed. My hens' enthusiastic response to my ministrations keeps me willing to get up at dawn day after day. Chickens offer us blessings, if we will listen and be open to receiving them.

Chickens evoke delight, irritation, nurturing, protectiveness, annoyance, caution.

They benefit from regular care. I must get up with the sun each day to let them out of their locked sleeping quarters and into their yard. My cock calls me to this responsibility, and insists that I complete my duties in a timely fashion. My early morning moments with them awake me with purpose to each new day. The chickens come running out to greet me with great enthusiasm for the day and life; their positive energy is contagious. Then I need to return at twilight to lock them up again to protect them from the many predators who desire them.

A day without a chicken sound, for me, is like a day without the sun. That sound awakens something within me and comforts me.

Excuse me, but I feel the call of a hen.

Dream Turtle*
By Kathleen Maia Tapp

The skin of your neck
holds a hundred wrinkles
       of story
          in leathery folds.

Your eyes are pools of space
with no edges, no end.

You carry a small turtle
on your back—
        me.

I would like to repay you.
I could make a cake—
but birthday candles in such numbers
  would set the world aflame,
So for now I'll just ride along
  the earth of your shell
        and hang on

The Queen is Near*
By Kathleen Maia Tapp

In my dream
I receive a gift—
      a bear's tongue.

I ponder this a long while,
then one night

the dream woman returns
bearing a honeycomb
that glows with light,
drips sweetness.

   She stretches out her hand:

"This is all part of the Mother."

and I am scribe
      poet
         bear
   falling
      into
       honey.

*These two poems are part of "Prayer Jewels in the Night," poems inspired by a series of dreams over a period of several years.

The Day I Met Five Angels
By Dina Emser

My "courageous act of peacemaking" was to "come from peace instead of fear at the two conferences I will present at this week, and to remember that my work is a privilege." But when I went to the first conference, and saw the room in which I was to make my presentation set up with over three hundred chairs, I felt far from peaceful!

That is when the first angel showed up. She was in place thirty minutes early, watching me from the second row, and she said, "Is this your first time?"

"Not to present," I replied, "But to present at this conference, yes."

"I did it last year," she continued. "It will be fine."

The next angel was sitting on the front row. "I love your red shoes," she said, and showed me hers, a pair just like mine only in black.

Another woman was sitting several rows back. She was angel number three. "Would you like some help with those handouts?" she asked. "That would be lovely," I gratefully replied, and she went to the door and handed each arriving person a handout.

Angel number four was sitting front row center. She stood up, held out her arms to me and said, "Hi Dina, do you remember me from the Y? When I saw your name on the list of presenters, I decided to come and sit on the front row to cheer you on."

Nervousness was now replaced with a feeling of gratitude and awe. I made my presentation with lots of help from the participants. As I was packing up my materials, angel number five approached me. She was a colleague from a distant state, someone I know slightly and like tremendously. She said, "Dina, I love your style—you are so serene." I murmured my thanks.

It was not until this morning that I realized that serene is a synonym for peaceful. Four angels had showed up to remind me of my courageous act and one showed up to help me recognize it. I guess I'm angel number six!

Gift at Midnight
By Catharine Johnson

It is Christmas Eve, 1961 and I am six years old. I am driving with my father and mother to my grandparent's house for dinner. A light snow is falling and we are riding in our new car whose make and model I have been repeating to myself over and over, in the back seat. There is something about the way it sounds that's familiar: *Buick Electra, two-twenty-five. Buick Electra, two-twenty-five* all the way across town. Finally, as we turn up my grandparent's street, it registers.

"It's like our telephone number." I blurt.

My father turns the music down as my mother turns her head, dark hair, red pill box hat, the movement stirs the air so that her perfume, Channel #5, drifts my way.

"What honey?"

Now, the backseat smells like her. "At-Water, three-six, two-two-oh." I explain pleased by having solved my little puzzle.

I am so proud of myself that I don't see my mother's confusion or my father's shoulder's shrug as their eyes meet. I am already off, thinking new thoughts, having solved the rhythm mystery of our new car's name. Now I am thinking about snow forts, sledding, my first Midnight Mass, and what Santa is bringing.

Bing Crosby sings on the radio and my father wonders aloud if the snow will stick as we turn up the long straight drive to "4400." That's how my parents refer to the large white house where my grandparents live.

"It's so pretty," my mother says, referring to the snow the way it sticks in some places and sifts away in others "like flour on a bread-board."

I watch the white flakes swirl and dance in the headlights as we park the car. I don't wait for my father to open my door. Instead I pull the handle, push it open with my foot and climb out. I am clutching my grandfather's package tightly in my hand.

While my father escorts my mother who steps carefully in her red stiletto heels, I skate towards my grandparent's back door on the slick leather soles of my patent leather shoes. My gray wool coat, unbuttoned, billows behind me like a cape and I hold my grandfather's package, a tie wrapped in gold foil paper with a green satin bow, out beside me for balance. *I am a lot to handle,* at least that is what I overhear my mother say to her sister, when they talk. When she says this she is speaking of the part of me that is always on the go: I run everywhere, roar down the street on my bike, move fast whenever I can.

Standing beside my grandparent's back porch steps is a statue of St. Francis. Snow has accumulated on his shoulders, the top of his head, as well as on the backs of the little birds that he cups in his hands. Taking the steps two at a time, I mumble a prayer like I have been taught in school for all the poor people. I add one for the birds as well, though no one has told me to do so. Then, I stop and wait for my parents.

I wait because that is what grown-ups do, they wait for one another. And tonight, I am feeling very grown up. Later, after Christmas Eve dinner with my father's family, I will go to Midnight Mass for the first time. Even though I am only in first grade, I have recently realized that the whole Christmas story takes place at night: with shepherds keeping watch over their flocks, wise men following a star, and the holy family camping out in a stable. Armed with the firm conviction that Jesus was born at night I lobbied my parents throughout advent.

"We have to go to Midnight Mass." I would plead, following my mother as she carried laundry up the stairs from the basement.

"It's when Jesus was really born, Dad." I would insist for the hundredth time as he raked leaves from beneath the oak tree in our yard. "If we wait 'til Christmas morning, it's too late."

Worn down by my persistence and zealous belief that this change in our family tradition was of great spiritual importance, my parents relented. There are few Catholics more devout than those in first grade.

"Watch it, Cay." Now my father says, his voice edged with anxiety that sounds like impatience. He has my mother by the arm so she won't slip in her high heels. My parents are beautiful to me. My mother is twenty-six, tall and slender in a red knit dress, black wool coat and red pill box hat, that emulates the style of the current first lady. I, of course think my mother is prettier than "Jackie" and my father, more handsome than "Jack". That is how my parents refer to the President and his wife, by their first names. My father is thirty, tall in a black topcoat, his black Irish blood shows in his olive complexion, his dark eyebrows and almost black hair. I am a miniature version of my parents, inheriting my mother's easygoing temperament and my father's features and looks. Tall for my age, I am a complete tomboy ready for action even though tonight, I am dressed in a green velvet skirt, white tights and blouse with a red velvet vest.

"Come on you guys," I urge, excited and anxious to go inside. My parents continue to walk slowly and carefully across the drive leaning on one another the same way they do in life.

Billy Johnson, my father, is the oldest son of Karl and Rosemary Johnson. The Johnsons are a large Irish Catholic family of some importance in our town. My father raised his sister and four of six brothers before leaving home for College at Notre Dame, the Marine Corps and Korea. When he returned from the war, he married my mother. I was born nine months later and was already two months old when my grandmother delivered her eighth and last child, my uncle Steve. I never thought it unusual that many of my uncles were close to me in age or, in Stevie's case, younger.

As my parents pass St. Francis, Uncle Stevie opens the back door. He could be my brother; we look so much alike, except that I am taller, faster and stronger.

"Our packages are real big," Stevie says in a loud whisper that means what he has to say is important. "I can show you." He curls his index finger beckoning me to follow him inside.

Since Steve and I are more like brother and sister than uncle and niece, our parents decided to give us identical presents at Christmas so we wouldn't fight or feel jealous of one another. He and I still had not caught onto the fact that this was intentional; instead we thought it funny and coincidental that we received the same things each year.

My father nods his permission for me to go on ahead.

"Make sure to say hello to Karlyboy and Rosie." He calls out as the back door slams behind Stevie and me. Everyone calls my grandparents by their nicknames including me.

After a quick examination by my grandparents, a couple of hugs and gin flavored kisses, Stevie and I are on our hands and knees crawling beneath the bottom branches of an enormous Christmas tree. It fills my grandparent's living room with the smell of pine and chemical flocking. Stevie starts to read tags on the presents. Neither of us has been reading for long and he is delighted to practice.

"To Paul, from Mike." He reads slowly. "To Greg, from Mom. To…" he pauses and looks at me grinning. A red ornament hangs in front of his head, so all I can see is a big red ball with a mouth opening and closing below it. The mouth says conspiratorially, "This one's for you." I giggle and clap my hands. *What is it?* I will have to wait though, until after dinner to find out

The evening is full: there are tasty snacks everywhere, little hard candies in dishes, cocktails and poker for the adults. Stevie's older brothers make a game of slipping by the bar when no one is looking, and pouring rum into their Coke-a-Colas. Stevie and I watch all this from under the Christmas tree. When the betting from the family room grows increasingly loud and more aggressive, I think my grandfather will intervene, but he and my father are talking business over martinis and appear not to notice. Meanwhile, my grandmother and mother sit on the living room couch, talking, where they can keep an eye on Stevie and me.

Our traditional dinner consists of turkey sandwiches, cranberries and mashed potatoes. Finally, when we push back from the table, my grandmother announces that we will open presents. I feel like I will explode when I slide off my chair and go running into the living room. The wait has been interminable. Soon Stevie and I are ripping into brightly wrapped boxes containing *Etch-a-Sketches,* coloring books and two large 50 piece soldier sets from FAO Schwartz. Santa has brought Steve the Union Army and me, the forces of the Confederacy. Each set comes with matching infantry cap. Stevie and I spend the rest of the evening lying on our stomachs in the middle of the living room, dressed in our best Christmas outfits, wearing our civil war caps and playing with our soldiers. Lost in our battles, we are oblivious to the rest of the family.

Eventually, Stevie has to go to bed; my mother insists that I lie down on the couch.

"What about Mass?" I say my lower lip starting to quiver.

"We're still going to Mass, that's why I want you to rest, so you'll be ready."

My mother kisses me on the forehead, slips my shoes off and tucks a light blanket around me. I watch the Christmas tree lights for a long time.

When I open my eyes again, I am in the back seat of our new car. Christmas carols play softly on the radio while my parents talk in low voices. I watch the red ends of their cigarettes glowing like sparklers in the dark. Outside, the snow has stopped and the sky is black and clear. From under the blanket of my backseat nest, I look at the stars, tiny white fires in the cold winter sky. Suddenly, a flashing red light moves across my view.

"Rudolph!" I yell, sitting up and pressing my face to the window.

"Honey, look." My mother points out the windshield for my father to see. "It is Rudolph." All the way to the church Mom talks about how lucky we are to have spotted Santa flying over our town. "You know," my mother says holding my hand as we walk up the church steps, "The shepherds looked up, just like you did tonight, and that's how they saw the star that they followed to baby Jesus' birth. Think how lucky they must have felt."

I try to think about how lucky the shepherds felt, but all I can feel is my own excitement, I am tingling all over. I also feel serious. Going to Mass is always serious.

Inside, the church is dimly lit. I am surprised by how many people are here, way more than on Sunday mornings. The air is thick with incense and the hushed murmurs of neighbors greeting one another. I keep thinking about what my mother has said, and thinking about Rudolph. Some part of me knows that the blinking red light was really a plane passing overhead, and yet some other part of me believes that I have also seen the most famous reindeer of all.

When the carols begin my Mother leans down and whispers in my ear, Let's go and visit baby Jesus." She takes my hand and we walk down the side aisle to the nativity scene. As we near the manger, the star above it catches my eye. It is nothing more than a piece of cardboard cut with five points and painted gold. There is a hole in the center of it through which a single white Christmas tree light shines. When I look at the manager I see that Baby Jesus is a toy doll. It's not real, none of it. I feel my face getting hot. I tug on Mom's arm and look up at her. She is crying.

Even though there are tears on mom's face; she does not look sad, instead she looks happy. I glance around the candlelit church. It is crowded and there is something I can feel beginning, maybe something special is happening. Something is happening inside me. I feel warm and full like a bathtub about to run over.

"Mom!" I whisper, "Is Baby Jesus really here?" I am thinking about the doll in the manager.

"Yes, honey, he is."

"Where?"

"He's all around us, can you feel him?"

I look around again, then down at the center of my chest. "Mom, I think he might be inside." With my freehand I point at my heart.

Mom smiles and squeezes my hand, like she does when she is proud of me "C'mon Honey, Mass is starting"

We walk to our seats, the choir begins to sing the opening hymn: Oh Come, Oh Come Emmanuel. I hold mom's hand; her skin seems extra soft. It does not matter that the nativity star is fake. It does not matter that the blinking red light in the sky might have been an airplane, passing overhead. What matters is this feeling inside of me, this hand in mine, every person and thing around me soft and glowing. I know somehow that this moment is the best gift I have ever gotten; way better than a soldier set.

Message for a Marriage
By Molly Y. Brown

After 20 years of marriage, Jim and I still experienced some tension in our rela-tionship. We sensed it resulted from some long-standing patterns that neither of us could discern, and decided to consult with a therapist with whom I had been working alone for a few months. It turned out to be the only marriage counseling ses-sion we ever had, because it was so successful.

I can no longer recall the specific issues we explored, nor much about what hap-pened in the session, except for one incident that stands out vividly in my memory. Jim was sitting on my left, talking with Larry about something; I was listening, probably with some sort of inner critique going on about what Jim was saying. Suddenly I had an image of a feminine figure to my right. I think of her now as either angelic or a goddess figure. She was beautiful and serene, of no particular age, dressed in some sort of simple robe. She spoke to me with deep authority; her words are etched in my memory forever. She said, "If you love this man, you will accept him exactly as he is."

I got it immediately. I saw how I had been trying to change Jim in subtle and not-so-subtle ways; if only he would just think a little differently, feel a little differently, and act accordingly, everything would be better. I saw clearly how that made him feel unloved and unaccepted as who he was. If I truly loved him—and I knew I did—I needed to live with the person he was, not someone I had adjusted to my personal specifications.

When Jim and Larry finished talking, they both turned to me somewhat expec-tantly. Maybe they saw a look on my face and wondered what was going on. So I told them what had just taken place. Jim's eyes filled with tears of relief, and I knew that what he most needed from me was unconditional love and acceptance. And in that moment, I could give it to him wholeheartedly.

That message from within transformed our relationship from then on. Of course there were many times when I lapsed back into wanting him to change in one way or another. But I would soon remember the woman's words: "If you love this man, you will accept him exactly as he is." My choice to love him unconditionally wins out over whatever I am complaining about in the moment.

I have found that these words not only change how I think about Jim, they also give me a new kind of empowerment and freedom. If I accept Jim as he is, I also accept myself as I am. Jim can be Jim and I can be Molly, warts and all.

Sanctuary*
By Duncan Berry

it is bounded
on all four sides

we come here
wreathed
in a mantle
of ashes
from burning brightly
in our daily rounds

it has called
us
to feed
on sleep
and nourish
the quiet spaces
in between

my limbs
arc round
the chamber of ribs
that harbor your
gently working heart

our bodies
tethered together
as we swing
in separate arcs
through dreams
eyes darting
behind closed lids
blood coursing
horizontally

through
the great fallen tree of our veins

the warmth of the other
like a night long
call and response
in the dark

the one
who spends her waking hours
giving me the gifts
love gives
offers one more

the
silent
expansive
sanctuary
of you

*Written for my sanctuary Melany

Twining Trees – Laura Treadway

Siblings
By Barbara Darling

I can, I do hear the canyon wind in all directions,
>   every direction

deeper

more every

more kissing my face with love.

The glisten on the twig

>   the bright light green of the piñon mountain

This is now. Now is Now.

Now I am not to the left and then to the right. Now I am not divided, dividing, splitting my mind into yes and no camps; death and life camps; worry and enjoy-for-a-moment-camps; feeling choked, yet managing-a-breath-camps; wondering where the hell and who the hell I am, feeling less than, confused, fearful.

After last year's "Cancer Year," I now feel privileged to have reconnected with my brother Charles, who died suddenly 50 years ago at age 17. My recent connections with him pertain to visceral feelings of being washed over with love from him, and to his ensuing messages for me.

In addition, the parallels of my emotional responses to the shock of the loss of Charles in 1958 when I was 15, and to the shock of the "Repeat Mammogram" phone call in 2007 at 64, are stunning.

There were no words for either time.

There I was out on Lake Fairlee, doing a near perfect jackknife dive from the float for my mother and grandmother on visiting day at Vermont's Camp Wyoda.

The gleaming blue water held my dream summer.

There I was at 64, healthy, active, thin, involved with family, work, friends, home.

Delight and connection were my foundations.

Both times I felt "at the top of my game." The two shocks were like cut-offs. Into the ozone. Am I dead? Am I not? Which one? Feeling vague, unsure, not in my body, in my body. Both times I was uncertain about my existence, my identity, my daily outlook.

I'm terrorized.

Scared of life or death.

Ambivalent about life.

My identity is: "My Brother Died."

My identity is: "I Had Breast Cancer."

While reflecting on these issues recently, more confusion surfaced. Somehow it came to me that maybe Charlie could help me…

"Don't worry," he said. "Enjoy."

For a few days I was flooded over with love from him. Wordless. Flooded. Held in Love.

"What about my Breast Cancer?" I said.

"That's irrelevant," he said.

"Love yourself and your life."

"You don't have to worry about death or life. Live your heart."

"Don't be on a continuum between death and life. Don't go over there with worry, concern, identification. Go over here to 'live.'"

"Don't mess up your life. Live it."

"Don't be ambivalent. Don't be tentative."

(Who could be closer to me than Charlie?)

"Death is a cut off from life. You don't have to do this. You don't have to be dead to be with me."

"Death cuts you into pieces. Death cuts into you and everything you own.

"Don't live death.

"Don't look at death.

"Take care of yourself.

"Don't do death. Do life."

"Being dead in the midst of life is no fun. Don't go back and forth. Go forward."

"Death is final. Life isn't final."

"But I was at the top of my game," I said.

He said, "I was cut off in my prime. You don't have to be. You get to live, be
      sensate. Do it. You're the only one of us left now."

Recently, half-way through a New Mexico hike with friends, on red sandstone, red
clay, earth, rocks, sinks and rises, along the Rio Grande Rift, an intercontinental rift
system (of which there are two in the world, the other being in Eastern Europe) where
the North American tectonic plate is pulling apart in the middle, evincing a magnificent
and unique landscape, I found myself with aching legs and a burning right hip. I was
slow for the first time in my life, crying at the end of the pack at my failure. I didn't know
what to do. I literally did not know what to do or how to be. Suddenly I thought to ask
Charlie about this terrible moment...

                              "Live."

It was as if the Red Sea had parted. By Grace I arrived in the very present. All worries were washed away. Yes there were aching legs, but I was living with what was and
that was what was. Everything else was cut through. "OK," I said. "I am walking, hurt-
ing, complete."

Free. Free. Clean. Good to go.

Something is integrated here. In the burning hip. In being last in line. In stepping
forward. In being Held in Love.

Held in Love

   means

      the in breath

the in breath with attention

        richness

the aware in breath

the clear mountain edge

   is mine to love, against the sky, I don't have to worry that I might not have it

   tomorrow

Held in Love is

   seeing the yellow flower,

   seeing the mountain rough edge against the sky, clearly

   I can love the mountain edge

   I can love the mountain *back.*

The gift is loving the mountain back.

The mountain canyon wind is near and far,

deep and up, all over and here, hearing my hearing,

        hearing my ear

        hearing my knowing of this living

Held in love is living--whatever it is—

    splattered yogurt, clothes not fitting,

   It is loving back, loving the mountain back, loving yourself back,

     In the glisten

     The gift is in the glisten

     The breath

     The living.

Healing Across The Veils
By Ruey Ryburn

My younger son Andy and I spent the summer trying to find our way again after loosing his sister and my daughter Mindy in May 1999. At first I seemed to float in a pink sea of prayers and love being sent from friends and family not to mention a house so filled with flowers in her honor that we could scarcely step from one room to the next. One month later with the memorial service over and extended family returned to their homes, each morning was excruciatingly painful as I realized Mindy was never coming back. Andy, trying to cheer me up, convinced me to go hiking with him in the mountains above Honolulu, saying exercise would do both of us some good. We put on our hiking boots and set out with our Australian healer dog Micah. The path up the trail was slippery from recent rain in the tropical forest above the valley housing the University of Hawaii in Honolulu. Even though the day was sunny near the ocean, back on the trail we were quickly in clouds and misty rain.

At the top of the trailhead, Andy decided to take Micah and forge his way back down the stream filled with large boulders covered in moss. I quickly opted to head back down the trail despite a slippery mossy path that appeared steeper going back down than it had on ascent. Looking over to watch Andy and Micah splashing down the stream, I lost footing and slipped, landing on my left hand to break the fall. This hand, having previously been broken and subsequently always 'tender' quickly began to bruise and swell. I iced, elevated, rested, and halfheartedly tried to do my own energy work for my hand, but with little relief.

The next morning I awoke again to searing pain, both physical and emotional as once again the reality of Mindy's death sunk in. I lifted my left hand, partially closed it gingerly, and realized that although there didn't seem to be any broken bones this time, my hand was going to take some time to heal. I placed my right hand on my heart, and raised my left hand into the air to connect energetically 'across the veil' with my daughter. My kinesthetic high sense perception allowed me to truly feel and hear her. She again told me that she was well, healed, and happy and wanting me to regain joy within my life. Tears rolled down my cheeks in recognition of her continued presence, yet sadness that I wouldn't experience physical hugs and her physical life any longer.

Then I realized that my injured hand was filling with a warm, gentle presence of love and light. The nurse scientist in me glanced at the clock. I continued to absorb the healing energy in my raised hand with tears of gratitude flowing down my face. I could 'hear' in my inner ear Mindy's loving voice telling me she was 'fixing' my hand. Twenty minutes later the energy eased out of my hand. I gingerly brought it down and cradled it in my right hand as I began to bend and flex it. My hand was now totally pain free, and it has continued to be so. Even the soreness I used to feel in the area where the fracture had been when my hand got too cold or over-stressed was gone.

It has now been nine years since my daughter's death. I miss her physical presence daily, and also know personally the chronic sorrow I feel when her friends marry, have babies, or achieve educationally or in their work worlds. But I have also continued to hear and feel Mindy's presence rather frequently and even see her radiant form with my 'third eye'. There is perhaps no greater loss in this lifetime than that of a child, but I also know deeply her soul's continued presence and love. Her death truly taught me that 'love is all there is.'

Through the Veil – Molly Y. Brown

The Girl Who Believed
By Jennifer Mathews

After a silent walk down the longest hallway of my life, the surgeon brought us into a small room with no windows. He sat us down. His slow, robotic voice echoed off the sterile walls: We can't operate. It's everywhere. Pancreatic cancer. Stage IV. Everywhere.

I had just driven into town from Vermont, intending to stay a week or so to help my mom recover from an unexpected medical procedure. At age 61 and recently retired, she lived an active life: tennis twice a week, photography, travel. In shock, I asked the unavoidable question. "Twelve weeks," replied the surgeon, "is average."

The following day, I left Buffalo General Hospital to keep an appointment I had made in advance. As I walked into the room, I started crying and laughing—Anugana's Shamanic Dream was playing, the same music I had played every night for almost a year to help me fall asleep. The session began with a welcomed massage. My body craved relaxation after the long drive home and the emotions of the past twenty-four hours. As I lay on my stomach, Trish working my back, my hands began tingling as if they were falling asleep. As I wiggled my fingers and focused on my breath, a clear internal voice began repeating to me, "You are ready. You are ready. This is what you've been waiting for since you were 13 years old. This is it." I found myself responding immediately, "Yes, I'm ready. I am ready." I felt incredibly open and willing to surrender to whatever came next. Now lying on my back, I was holding back tears. It seemed too exhausting to cry any more. "Let it go," Trish encouraged. "You're in a safe space." And so I did. I cried hard, my chest shaking with sobs and my ears filling with tears. Trish shifted the massage into a Reiki energy session, standing at my side, and then my feet.

As the session progressed, as I released and breathed heavily into my body, my palms began to buzz even more. The energy felt like electrical currents running up and down my body—my arms, feet, and upper thighs felt weighted as if they were being held down. I literally couldn't move them. My breathing became rapid and euphoric as if I was making love. The sensation in my hands intensified, like holding two electrically charged metal balls. Later I would come to learn the language of chakras, but at the time, all I knew was that I was undergoing a spiritual transformation. The energy continued racing throughout my body, allowing me to experience myself as spirit in human form. As this initiation continued, I repeated, "Thank you, thank you, thank you" in recognition of the gift I was being given. Yes, this was what I had been waiting for since I was young—an undeniable knowing that souls live on after death, just like I learned in religion class.

Through this experience, I reconnected to the 13-year-old girl in me who prayed desperately to witness miracles and make objects move across tables using only her mind. The girl who believed in reincarnation despite Catholic teachings; the girl who knew the spirit world is as real as the physical. I was being shown beyond mere faith that yes, an unseen world exists and that I can access it directly.

At first I assumed the energy I was feeling was Trish's, but she assured me that it was mine and that she was simply facilitating the process. After the session was over, she left the room and I experimented with the energy for a while. Lying on my back, I slowly extended my arms over my head, up and down my sides. I noticed that moving my hands farther away from my body created less sensation; as I brought them closer, the fire swirled in my palms again. When I finally got off the massage table, I stood up slowly. My ears popped hard, reminding me of a friend's description of his return to the earthly world after a shamanic journey.

I went back to my mom's house where I had spent my teenage years before moving to Vermont for college. I sat alone in the sunshine of the backyard, my senses heightened. Colors were brighter, the birds louder. Everything was crisp and still. It felt surreal.

I was so grateful for this deep sense of calm, needed now more than ever as I stepped into the challenges of being my mother's primary caregiver for the next sixteen weeks. Going back to the hospital the following morning, I remember feeling genuine acceptance of my mom's diagnosis. I think many people, including my family, assumed I was in denial. Wasn't I supposed to be depressed or fearful? Wasn't I supposed to be furious with God? But instead I felt more connected than ever. I even felt hopeful. Not hopeful that my mom's body would survive advanced stages of cancer, but that she–her spirit, her true Being—would.

I feel blessed to have been given the gift of knowing myself in my true form–pure positive energy. Before this time, my spiritual highs were ethereal, never so embodied. No one ever mentioned things like Reiki or Kundalini energy at St. Mary's Catholic School. But at age 31, I fully allowed myself to have a physical spiritual experience. That is what this awakening was about for me: the embodiment of the universal life force, of Love. I was ready to reconnect with that part of me that believed anything is possible, and in doing so, I realized the potential lies within me, that I am powerful beyond belief and can co-create the miraculous.

The Changeover
By Barbara Heyl

I came home each day from school to find you still as night on a cool, white sheet. No need to wake you, as you long since had the tableware laid out and each part of dinner waiting in covered dishes in the fridge to be heated up when Dad came home. Afternoon naps—from boredom when there was nothing left to do? Did becoming my mother, cooped up at home, make you lifeless?

You, who rivaled the sun all those summers at Balboa Beach, flitting up and down the boardwalk. At the top of the roller coaster on the pier you giggled, then screamed for your life all the way down, collapsing later into the sand to sun-bathe, still as a mummy, the sea gulls searching around you for signs of life.

You plotted with Phyllis—"I'm staying over at *her* house"—to slip away on the boat to Catalina Island. Two teenagers sneak in and out of the casino and dance under sparkling chandeliers with handsome strangers into the dead of night. Your mothers found you out.

You hounded the Pasadena Players at their stage door and stood on Sunset Boulevard with your bobby-soxer friends to scream for Frank Sinatra after the concert, the streetlights and marquee twinkling above you. My pre-teen nights were filled with small-town quiet, the desert sky, a canopy of lights. You dreamed up a plan of writing the New York leads who came west to play each summer season in LA. Post cards we enclosed, they returned—my tickets backstage to the Civic Light Opera after Saturday matinees. On my own, I explored the wings and climbed wrought iron staircases to ask stars and chorus girls for autographs, while you waited outside on the sidewalk. Was it then you shifted your life force to me? You asked for my stories. You are the sparkle in my stories.

I find you tiny, silent, on a white sheet, breathing in rhythm to the oxygen pump. But before sunup, you slip away, without permission, to go dancing with the stars.

Miguel*
By Ellise Rossen

He came because he was suffering from AIDS, and a state program offered funds for psychotherapy. He came with misgivings.

From behind the curtained window, I watched with curiosity and a little anxiety as he eased his way out of the small car, slowly unfolding his slender, lengthy frame. He walked unsteadily toward the house where I had a small office space; he leaned on a cane, but even so managed to convey an air of dignity to which the angle of his black beret added a certain flair.

We spent the first hour reviewing the past. He told me of his conventional family, of the older woman he said he probably should have married long ago, and of the man who was no longer his lover, but who had become his closest friend and daily confidant—until he had died recently of AIDS. "I wonder," I said, "Do you consider yourself bisexual, or homosexual or—?"

"I consider myself sexual," he replied, eyeing me sideways, with a slight grin. By the end of the hour I knew him to be an accomplished individual who had deviated widely from the accustomed patterns of the family whom he cherished; had worked, traveled, loved and suffered; and who retained, in spite of a body that found it increasingly difficult to respond to his needs and desires, a quick and sharp sense of humor.

An hour or so before the next scheduled appointment he called. "I'm not sure about this," he said. "I see no value in spending hours talking about the past."

"That was only the starting point," I replied. "We can go on from there."

"Well…" he paused for a time. "I guess I'll come. Maybe I can teach you something."

After the first few sessions it had become too difficult for him to drive to my office, so we met in the small rented house where he lived by himself, an immaculate dwelling that held more than a few objects of great beauty. Before long it was necessary for others to come to clean, and to cook for him as well, this man who had recently been a successful chef. "I had to tell her how to fix spaghetti," was his acerbic comment about the kitchen help.

In spite of his earlier hesitation he now spoke freely about his life and experience, and sometimes he told me his dreams, though he paid small heed to what I might make of them. To me they seemed to speak of his coming journey, of a land beyond this world, but he dismissed that; he was determined that he was not going to die, not yet. In an early dream he found himself arriving, by some sort of spiral path, at a lovely green meadow; both his parents were apparently living there, enjoying a happy pastoral existence. His mother said to him, "I hear you are going on to a higher level." She sounded quite proud. "Oh mother," he had replied, "you know you shouldn't gossip."

A week or so later a loud voice called out to him in his sleep, its impact not only startling him awake, but knocking him from his bed onto the floor. "You are dying!" it proclaimed. It took him a very long time, weakened as he was, just to get himself back into his bed. Recalling his struggles he said simply, "I don't want to die."

"I know. And I don't want you to die." When it was time to leave I kissed him on the forehead, wondering if it were proper, then realizing my concern was irrelevant. It was the most honest gesture I could make.

Soon after that he was hospitalized with pneumonia, then tuberculosis. All the rest of the family lived nearly a thousand miles away. His mother, so dear to him, kept in touch with daily phone calls, and now she came for a time, but it must have been just too painful to bear, maybe for both. She went home and his father came, the father who had delighted in taking his two sons hunting, something this eldest child had never enjoyed. The father who had been denying both his son's illness and his sexual nature, who had persisted in believing that everything would be fine if he would just find a nice woman and settle down.

Now the father fixed his son fresh, delicate salads and brought them to the hospital in a large basket along with other gourmet treats and tightly sealed glasses of wine. Once he arrived when I was visiting; I was uncertain about meeting him, but his loving eyes and warm smile erased my hesitation. Another time the brother visited, along with his two young sons, all three darkly handsome, glowing with health and strength. Miguel loved his nephews, beamed with pride when he spoke of them.

Then he dreamed again. Someone presented a beautiful crystalline globe that radiated pure light. He was frightened by the power of it and drew back. "It's all right," a voice said, "You may touch it." He reached toward it, gently laid his hand upon it, and it immediately shattered into an infinite number of just such perfect balls of glowing light. "And they are all there for you," the voice said.

The last time I saw him, there in the hospital, he was so thin and in such pain. He said the morphine did not help that much. Propped up with many pillows, his long legs reached past the end of the bed, and he asked me to adjust the pads that protected his ankles. It seemed an honor to do that, to touch his bare feet, to give him some small bit of relief. Then the nurse brought him a bowl of Jell-O, unstable orange cubes quivering in a small glass dish; she helped him to sit up, encouraging him to eat. In his weakness he could barely manage to control the wiggling blobs and maneuver them to his mouth. I felt embarrassed to witness his struggle, but knew I should not offer help. "You'd think they could make this a little easier," he said, looking over at me, once again with that devilish sparkle in his deep brown eyes, a vivid flash of the true person, spirit not only unbroken, but somehow able to appreciate the humor in this frustrating moment.

The next time I came, his brother and the boys were there; I didn't want to interrupt so I waited outside in the hallway for a time and had to leave without seeing him. A few days later, I checked at the nurse's station. "Oh," she said, "he's gone. He died yesterday. I'm sorry you weren't told."

That morning, as I had left my home to go to the hospital, I had seen a western tanager sitting at the top of an alder along the edge of the creek. Such a gorgeous bird, so flashy and brilliant, I had paused to admire it. As I watched, it took off and flew, not in a straight line, but rather in circles, a spiral path leading upward, higher and higher into the sky. "That's odd," I had thought. "I've never seen a bird do that before."

*"Miguel" was previously published in *In The Family*, a quarterly journal.

Reflection – Carolyn W. Treadway

Do Unto Others*
By Carolyn W. Treadway

For a dozen years, I have been privileged to be pastoral psychotherapist for Mary,** a hard working, caring, single woman now in her sixties. Our process together has been profound and also at times profoundly difficult. Mary's journey through rage, angst, self loathing, suicide attempts, recovery, and transformation has been a journey home to herself, and home to being truly a part of her community and God's world.

Mary had a difficult early life. The middle child of three born to alcoholic, abusive parents, Mary was always the sensitive one. Perhaps she was born an "old soul." She felt everything keenly, but had no outlet for her feelings, and very little support, guidance, or nurture. She grew up tough, reflecting the chaotic and sometimes brutal environment all around her. Her inherent gentleness and compassion were not called forth, yet remained inside her as vulnerability and incredible pain. Again and again over her lifetime, her family and the world mistreated her and destroyed her hope and her ability to trust. Her anger increased and her sense of her own worth remained in the cellar. An incident of intense rage toward her extended family during a holiday dinner, in which Mary splattered the dessert all over the festive table, frightened her (and her family) and precipitated her entry into therapy with me.

Mary had been in therapy many previous times over the years. But from the start, this time was different. Perhaps this time it was God's timing. From the beginning, we somehow connected and wrestled deeply with the myriad issues of her present, past, and future, especially with her pattern of self-abusive acting out in order to get attention, the attention fading away as the crisis diminished, and her rage only increasing. A dramatic incident occurred several years into therapy when, acting out of her "old" self destructive pattern, Mary attempted suicide in my office—by swallowing a bottle of pills in one giant gulp.

I accompanied Mary to the emergency room for stomach pumping and her admission to psychiatric intensive care. While in the ER, Mary told me she would not leave the hospital alive; she would definitely find some way to kill herself while there, and I most certainly would not see her alive again. I believed her. She was cold, unreachable, and determined—and she had wanted to die for many years. My instantaneous response to her announcement was to start to cry. A woman I cared deeply about was saying goodbye, albeit cruelly, and I was taking her seriously, and grieving. I knew the limits of my ability to help her, and we were past them. My tears continued to flow during much of the time we remained in the ER, as I continued advocating for her life and for God to help her make a different choice. They flowed as I told her I definitely did not want her to die at her own hand, but if she *was* going to die I was *not* going to abandon her, I was going to love her and believe in her right up to the very end.

As it turned out, my spontaneous tears helped to "save" Mary's life. They were transformative for her. She *could not believe* anyone cared enough about her to cry over her at all. Nobody ever had. Nobody ever would. Nor would anybody ever really care about her. But now, somebody did. My tears reached her at a level that my words could not. I cared. Mary *had* made a connection, after all. She *did* matter to someone: to me. These slowly dawning realizations changed Mary's view of herself and her world. Gradually, they changed her life. Many times since then, Mary has talked of this time in the ER and of my tears which "started to change everything" for her. To this day, I believe those tears were the expression of God's love for Mary. They came through me, but I was only the channel, the vessel.

Several years passed, during which Mary grew calmer, stronger, clearer, and happier. Her brother in law—one of the people who had earned her rage at that holiday dinner— became more and more ill with complications from diabetes. As "John" declined, Mary became increasingly appreciative of and loving toward him. Instead of being frequently angry and frustrated with him, often for very good reason, she became much more accepting of him. John was unaware, but Mary was not. She saw him struggling with his own life journey, just as she had struggled so long with her own. Her compassion for him grew and grew. Amazingly for one who had until recently devalued her own life so greatly, she longed to help John live his remaining life to the fullest. Beyond this, Mary wanted to help John with his dying. She wanted to be *with* him, loving and believing in him right up until the very end. Very deliberately she sought to "do unto him" as she had experienced me "doing unto her" in the emergency room. She remembered that time vividly, and used her own experience toward the healing of John, even in his dying.

Mary had a special talk with John, in which she advocated for his life and for him to take better care of himself. They expressed appreciation and caring for each other, and she told him she would be with him as he became sicker. Only a few days later, John peacefully died in his sleep. Mary was very upset she had not been with him at the time of his passing. I indicated that I thought she *was* with him in spirit, and that he *knew* she really was present for him all the way to the very end. Mary gave the eulogy at John's funeral. She talked of missing her fishing buddy, of his love of his family, and of his incredible persistence in getting through many hard times. She learned from his life, and he from hers, for with her heart and her actions in his last days, she lived out with John "doing unto him as she always had wished he (and others) would do unto her." Mary's ability to do this was to her and to me an amazing gift from life, and from God.

*Reprinted from *Discovering God as Companion*, Mariellen Gilpin, editor, AuthorHouse, 2007, pp.112-114, and from *What Canst Thou Say?* 35: August 2002.
**"Mary" is a pseudonym; she has given the author permission to share her story.

Gratitude
By Susan S. Scott

When one person never gives up on you,
no matter how many times you detour
down unlikely canyons, be thankful
that she remembers your compass,
but says nothing until you ask,
then shapes a Lotus Blossom
around you with her hands,
strengthened by lifetimes
of midwifery. You can
just relax into them.
She wants only
what is true,
like nectar,
to seep
from
you
into
the
center
of earth,
then rise
up to touch
the skies, the stars
and planets, the whole
solar system and beyond
to ignite with the source of all
light, which cannot be explained
only felt behind your eyes, in the cells
of your body as you breathe the rhythm
of the prayers you share, as you feel Lotus
Blossoms swaying along layers of lavender with
both of you resting in the center of Beauty, happy.

Falling into the Arms of Love
By Catherine Jane Larkin

Breakthroughs can come in surprising ways. When I was young the word breakthrough had a heroic ring to it—something you earned through efforts to be good or smart. Life taught me another version, tinged not with victory, but with failure. One where the bottom falls out and like Alice in Wonderland we slide down into a realm totally unexpected.

My first experience of what I've come to call 'a trapdoor to enlightenment' occurred in 1985. For two years a circle of five women had shared deeply in weekly gatherings. Our closeness had unearthed emotions and issues that became challenging to contain. Old childhood wounds were triggered. During one intense meeting my friend was standing over me, jabbing her finger in my face, expressing anger for what she perceived as a betrayal. I felt unfairly attacked, an old childhood trigger for me. Suddenly I reached out and slapped her. Immediately I felt so exposed and ashamed. My worst fear publicly revealed—that despite all the ways I tried to be good, it couldn't change the feeling of badness hidden inside. I quite literally had the sensation of falling into a dark pit.

Then, just as suddenly and uncontrollably, instead of hitting bottom, I was caught in the arms of love—arms of such total love that all fear and shame vanished. Like Alice in Wonderland, I slid into a realm so unexpected as to be unbelievable until experienced. Then you Know that this Love is the True Reality. In the room chaos continued, as friends took sides, justifying or blaming, depending on viewpoint. I was untouched, embraced by a love that freed me from being implicated by the drama unfolding in the group.

The teacher Adi Da talked about how inside each person is a pit of snakes, a place we've been trying to avoid our whole lives. We come to the spiritual path hoping it will help us avoid that pit. Instead any true spiritual teaching confronts us with it. As Carl Jung admonished his patients, you must go through the dark places, not around them. Then we get to discover what is prior to the pit, deeper and more real than the frightened perception of its darkness. As a song puts it: "In the middle of the pain, in the middle of the shame, mercy, mercy, in the middle."

My amazing, graceful breakthrough into freedom that night did not permanently erase the conditioning of separation and fear. In the years since then I've needed to continue to embrace the emotions that hide the truth. Yet the slide down the rabbit hole became a touchstone experience to help me learn to trust that "Love is the hole in the center of the universe.

Flame of Belonging*
By America Worden

I was shy when I was a little girl, and kept my troubles mostly to myself. I was forever endeavoring to be brave and right and good and not to make mistakes, which often overwhelmed my inside universe. I remember that feeling as a layered, weighty darkness that I could only hold by folding up, pulling my knees up to my chest and wrapping my arms around me. This feeling would come in between my days of playing and imagining, kindergarten, my little sister, our pets. I wanted everything to be all right. I wanted my parents to be happy, and safe. I wanted other children and all of the animals to be safe and alive. Sometimes I felt that maybe if I could *do* something *just right*, I could *make* everything be right in the world. This added a sort of panic to the heaviness.

When the longings inside of me became too much, I went into our back yard. It was overgrown with grass and calla lilies, and all of the fences were covered with ivy. Right in the middle of this wild green enclosure was a plum tree with one low branch that we could scramble up and enter into another world. There, up in the branches, smooth grey bark rippled over cracks where the brown wood shows through, and everywhere there was a canopy of leaves on their lacy maze of twigs. The breeze blew through this world and moved everything, even the light. I loved this world. For my whole childhood, the plum tree was my sanctuary.

The greatest blessing I ever received there came one awful day when I ran through the yard in tears and climbed into the plum tree, the loneliest girl in the world. I folded myself up with my back pressed against the trunk and sobbed until there were no tears left. My breathing slowed and I sat with my forehead resting on my knees, my eyes closed. I felt all alone in the world, tiny and small, except for my tree. But then a thought, or maybe a feeling, came to me very feebly. As I started to listen to it, it grew stronger.

Suddenly, I was sure that there were others, other children and maybe grown-ups who cared as much as I did. I wished that I could call out to them, let them know that I was here on planet earth, that I was part of them.

In my imagination, I lit a flame in my chest. It was dark inside me, and the little flame made a bright circle. I imagined that my flame was bright blue at its base, and orange at the tip, and I sent its glowing light into the darkness like a beacon, to look for the others.

Breathless, I waited, not knowing what I was waiting for, shining my flame. And suddenly, out in the darkness, there was another flame, like a star. Then another, and yet another. They flickered up out of the darkness and each one belonged to someone, I was sure of it! I watched the lights coming on one by one, spreading out into the dark. I felt lifted, stunned, like I had just been given the greatest secret ever told. I belonged to this whole growing expanse of tiny lights, like a great glittering web in the darkness. They had even been waiting for my flame to come. Currents of excitement and relief rushed through me as I realized that this galaxy of belonging was always there. I could close my eyes and call out with my small flame and all those other lights would be there, echoing back.

Now, so many years later, when the pain of trying to understand how to be in this world overwhelms me and brings its familiar depth and darkness, I still close my eyes and light up the small flame in my chest. The others are still shining. Sometimes when I close my eyes, they are already lit up, and I join them. Sometimes my call is the first, and they flicker on like they did that very first day. The feeling of arriving—relief and gladness—into that web is the same for me each time. Now, though, the web feels different. I have met many of the other flames, other people who are also on fire with love for the world. Their lights have names, now, and I know what they are burning for. I feel so blessed to belong in this love. Now, as on that day in my plum tree sanctuary, this knowing brings tears that are different than all other tears to my eyes. I have tried to explain them to myself. They feel like everything tears: both pain and joy, passion and despair, hope and loneliness. They are tears for being alive, tears of belonging.

* In gratitude for all the trees that hold and teach children

Connecting to the Web of Life
By Carl Anthony

I grew up in Philadelphia, a city planned by William Penn, who was known for his radical ideas about the relationships between human beings. He hated hierarchy and met with the native people in a spirit of equality. These ideas and his vision of Philadelphia as the City of Brotherly Love were deeply embedded in the stories we heard as we were growing up.

My family spent my early years in the most run-down neighborhood in West Philadelphia; much later I learned that it was called "The Bottom" because it had once been a swamp. It was a place where no one really wanted to live and therefore a place where poor people, working people, and people of color were allowed to live somewhat isolated from the rest of society. As the swamp was filled in, the area's reputation as a place for outcasts, sin, prostitution, and Holy Roller churches grew.

When I was five years old, my family moved to a new neighborhood. My father was determined to send me to an integrated elementary school. That school had about 300 students and was in a predominantly white neighborhood, six blocks from where we lived. My brother and I were among the 10 or 12 African American students, and we felt like misfits.

The first place I started to feel like I belonged was in Mrs. Aikens' third-grade class. I eagerly anticipated Monday afternoons when she conducted our weekly science class. Sixty years later I fondly recall our first assignment—to collect sample leaves from as many different trees as we could find. I remember the sensation of lying on my back and holding a leaf up toward the sun as I observed its margins and its unique and intricate veins. Each new leaf we identified was an occasion for celebration. Our next step was to venture out into the city and learn to identify trees by their bark. I still recognize many of those trees—catalpa, walnut, ash, and poplar.

We never tired of the time we spent in Mrs. Aikens' spell. She drew our attention to the sky above, taught us the names of the constellations, and took the class to the Planetarium. My brother and I would wake up in the middle of the night to gaze at the sky. We were thrilled to find Orion, Sirius Dog Star, Ursa Major and Minor. We also learned the names and functions of the different kinds of clouds and how to recognize the approach of a storm.

Mrs. Aikens explained to us how the surface of the earth was formed, describing the three kinds of rock—sedimentary, igneous, and metamorphic—and how each originated. Now, as I recall this, I'm amazed at how much I remember from my third-grade class.

She taught us about rocks, trees, sky, and creatures, starting with the dinosaurs that once roamed our hills and valleys. She took us on field trips to the Science Museum and locations where we observed the fossil record in the rocks, including a dinosaur's footprint. We gained a clear understanding of the difference between tyrannosaurus, brontosaurus, and others. In the midst of all these marvelous discoveries, we developed a sense of wonder, not only of the natural environment but also of ourselves as living participants in a vast evolutionary journey still unfolding.

One day she took us to see the Better Philadelphia Exhibition, a display of aerial photos and models showing what Philadelphia would look like in twenty-five years. Designed by the famous architect Edmund Bacon, who became Philadelphia's chief city planner, the exhibition occupied the third floor of a prestigious downtown department store and included a full-scale model of a street corner in south Philadelphia complete with trash can. I was excited by the opportunity to look into the future and deeply inspired by the aerial photos and models that gave me a God-like perspective on the city, seeing streets, houses, trees, and parks in miniature, as if I were larger than life. The experience helped shape my ambition to become an architect. I was inspired by the notion that I could help create a future in which my family, my community, and I would feel at home in the world.

As I grew older, I became increasingly aware of patterns of spatial apartheid in the city. I experienced the poignant realization that the Better Philadelphia Exhibition was the first stage in a public relations campaign designed to dismantle African-American and other working-class neighborhoods in Philadelphia. Facing the brutal realities of everyday life as a person of color, I moved away from the kind of inspiration I had experienced in Mrs. Aikens' class and became more and more committed to the struggle for social and racial justice.

Many, many years later I came across the writings of a famous Catholic theologian named Thomas Berry. His hypothesis in *The Dream of the Earth, The Great Work,* and *The Universe Story* is that to understand our proper relationship with our ecological surroundings, we need a new creation story, a story grounded in what contemporary scientists are telling us about the origin of the universe. Father Berry traced this story from the Big Bang 13.7 billion years ago through the development of the sun, the solar system, the planets, and all the amazing things that have happened in the four billion years since the earth was formed, including the rise of life made possible by our unique atmospheric conditions.

As I read this universe story, I experienced a moment of enlightenment, a very healing moment. Visualizing myself as the end product of 13.7 billion years of transformations helped me get a new perspective on my role in contemporary life. And then I realized that this was the same vision Mrs. Aikens had given me in third grade. I was very reassured to feel that I had a foundation in my early life for this transformative moment in which I and many other people around the world are coming to realize that we need to re-conceptualize our relationship to all of life on the planet as well as to each other and to the cities and neighborhoods that we inhabit.

Looking back on my heritage as an African American man, I realize how much was taken away from me and from African American people by being cut off from a sense of belonging to the universe. When our ancestors were stolen from the African continent, brought to the New World, and forced to work the land, we were robbed of our traditional knowledge of all of creation. We were denied a sense of the long history that goes back to the beginning of humankind and even to the origin of all living beings.

Thinking and learning about the universe story is helping me connect to the larger themes of the universe and to restore my childhood experience of being an observer and participant in the web of life. I love hanging out with my two-year-old grandson, Makai, who is looking out in the world, curious about everything he sees. We spend time in the garden observing and exploring—marveling at lemon flowers transforming into shiny yellow fruits, fuzzy peaches growing rosier and softer day by day, and countless other wonders.

To have an older person say "look at this" and draw our attention to things is a wonderful augmentation of our ability to see and understand the world. We look to our teachers or older family members to give us hints of what is worth noticing and thinking about. All of us should have elders who care enough about the mystery of our awakening to be responsive when we make discoveries. My experience of being held in the thrill of mutual exploration and perception in Mrs. Aikens' third grade class laid the foundation for the deep cellular sense of belonging and connectedness that I am now delightedly passing on to my grandson.

The Power of Two:
Comrades Link Arms and Launch a Movement

Second Story of "A Trilogy at 5 AM"*
By M. Paloma Pavel

It is 5 o'clock in the morning and I am waking early to meet Anne Herbert, my comrade in resistance to the Persian Gulf War. It is 1991 and this war is being sold as though it is a "Pac-man" video game: match the cross hairs, hit the targets.

Anne and I are working on a radical way to respond to the war. We feel no match for stealth missiles and depleted uranium, but we struggle for a direct and simple way to withdraw our consent. We are inventing new ways to work together, joining forces to forge a response. I teach graduate students in Organizational Development and Transformation at California Institute for Integral Studies, an East/West graduate school in the Bay Area, and work in private practice as a psychologist with individuals and organizations. Anne writes for the *Coevolutionary Quarterly* (formerly the *Whole Earth Review*). The two of us are inseparable on the social change front, a brigade of two.

I cross the Richmond Bay Bridge at dawn to meet her at the Sonapa Farms Cafe, which is open at this early morning hour. We order the usual shared omelet, borrow the waitress' pencil stub, and burrow in to work immediately. We decide our peace project needs a name, something to cohere our intent, a banner for our campaign. This morning we begin where we left off, scrawling on the paper place mat the commonly used media phrase "Random Violence and Senseless Acts of Cruelty." We continue to explore the variations of the phrase "random violence" seeking an antidote, a spell that will counter the collective insanity trance. Random goodness, Random resistance, we are searching…and then we land: "Kindness"…"Random kindness."

It is as though we are seeking the turning word that will end war, the war in Iraq but also the war that is growing at home, the collapse of our schools, our infrastructure, and our hope for civil society and the Commons.

We hear echoes of the Dalai Lama in the background: "My religion is kindness." How can he use such a common, "nice" word—"kindness"—to overturn the destruction of monasteries and torture of his people, the dissolution of his homeland? There are also echoes of the heartland from Anne's Ohio roots and my own people from Idaho and Montana. Some of the best of that authenticity and decency is held in the word "kindness". It is a plain ordinary, not fancy, word. A young man sitting at the next table overhears our conversation. He has been listening in and comments on our word crafting: "That's a great phrase!"

We want to pull our attention back from the Persian Gulf War with a positive plan for recovering our energy in directions that create change. Between my teaching days, Anne and I look for ways we can pass on radical (as from "*root like*") acts of caring for others. We do things like pay expiring parking meters and plant flowers and food in dirt lots.

Our Random Kindness Project was first noted in the *San Francisco Chronicle*, and then went viral on the Internet. It was picked up by journalists including Oprah, entered the mainstream through *Glamour* and *Reader's Digest*, and was later memorialized by Congress in National Random Kindness Week. Few knew of its beginnings as a protest of inner city and international violence.

Since writing *Random Kindness and Senseless Acts of Beauty*, Anne and I have had the opportunity to share, speak, and chant it in many gatherings. We share it here for those of you who missed it previously, or never knew where the bumper sticker came from. We began illustrating this work with heartfelt brush strokes of our own making, raw movements linking the phrases to the abstract strokes and creating a book at the corner copy shop. We sent it to family and friends as Christmas/solstice gifts that year.

Our friends received it and wanted more. We made more. They began to circulate like an underground message.

One of our favorite editions of the work is the version published by Volcano Press. It is a bright vermilion red hardback with white interconnected pages that fold out accordion style. The red and black brush stroke illustrations by Mayumi Oda are painted as one continuous mural linking all the pages, a panoramic landscape story with our prose poem accompanying it. We chose this version of *Random Kindness and Senseless Acts of Beauty* as an intentional embodiment of the main message—the power of interconnection. When we join with others in a common project, we each bring the cultural river of our own lives and ancestors to our shared work. I am grateful to my co-conspirator, Anne Herbert, for her daily courageous and radical search for sustainability and justice that is underneath this work. Our work grew out of countless daily conversations, prayers, and activist meetings. I still hear our shared voices when I read it on the page or share it in public.

Perhaps you might hear us chanting too, a spoken word persistent beat which invites you to join in and recite this aloud:

Random Kindness and Senseless Acts of Beauty
By Anne Herbert and Margaret Paloma Pavel, illustrated by Mayumi Oda
(Volcano Press, 1994)

Our leaders got confused,

So we're all leaders now.

They told us there was nothing we could do,

They were wrong.

When we tell ourselves there is nothing we can do,

We are wrong.

We never know how much and we never know how far it goes,

But always we have power.

WE HAVE POWER.

We're all making the soup we're all eating.

We're all weaving the cloth we're all wearing.

What we do can't go away,

We are all in the circle together.

Anything we do randomly and frequently

Starts to make its own sense,

And changes the world into itself.

Senseless violence makes more and more sense when vengeance and fear

Take us closer and closer to a world where everyone is dead for no reason.

But violence isn't the only thing that is senseless until it makes its own sense

Anything you want there to be more of,

Do it randomly.

Don't wait for reasons.

It will make itself be more senselessly.

Scrawl it on the wall:

"Random Kindness and Senseless Acts of Beauty"

We are right on the edge of discovering millions of new ways of being together,

Millions of new dances we can do together minute by minute.

And we're right on the edge of destroying ourselves out of life,

Because we are too scared to have that much delight.

We're right on the edge.

The steps we take now make new earth grow beneath our feet.

The steps we take now decide what kind of earth that will be.

In every moment we live we have the choice to find the fight or make delight.

We have power.

It's a circle.

Start the dance.

* This trilogy is composed of three stories of my own waking up to the experience of being held in love that has provided grounding for my life and for my work as an activist for sustainability and social justice. These stories represent three transformative experiences that have provided the soil out of which my life and work have grown.

Heart Angel – Janaia Donaldson

Uplift from Wings of an "Angel"
By Barbara Heyl

I was flying from Central Illinois, where I live, to Los Angeles on December 31st, 1995. My father at 85 years old had been hospitalized a few days earlier, with pneumonia and Chronic Obstructive Pulmonary Disease, and my mother was worried. I spoke with the doctors. Dad wasn't getting enough oxygen and had a bad infection in his lungs and his bronchial tubes. Though I had been home just a month ago at Thanksgiving, I found myself flying again and falling slowly into worry and unease myself.

Next to me sat a young woman reading spiritual literature. We were each engrossed in our own thoughts. I was writing thoughts about my family in my journal:

> In this family we want to live as though
>> living this day well,
>> doing this task well today is enough.
>
> To be true and careful and thoughtful,
>> to be righteous this day, will be enough.
>
> Then out of nowhere it seems the days
>> have added up, and we are
>> standing before some life turn
>> not ready
> because each day was absorbing,
>> and we didn't see time rushing by.

With a sense of foreboding, I felt distinctly unready for what lay ahead for me and for my family.

As the travel time at high altitude went by, the wall between the young woman and me came down. Her name was Jill, she said, and she was currently volunteering and staying at a church in Los Angeles. When I explained my purpose for flying to LA, she listened to the many details and the history of my father's disease sympathetically. Gently, she offered to pray with me. I accepted, and we held hands.

She bowed her head and prayed a prayer of gratitude.

Father God, she said, we thank you for this plane that is taking Barbara to her parents. We thank you for the air that surrounds and holds this plane, and we thank you for the pilots who with their skills are flying this plane. We thank you for the airport awaiting us in Los Angeles, and the controllers ready to pick up our path and guide us in to a safe landing.

We thank you for the doctors and hospital staff who at this very moment are caring for Barbara's father, with their skills and compassion. We thank you for the knowledge they have and can bring to support both Barbara's father and her mother.

And we thank you, Father God, for the love in this family—love that is strong and deep and connects Barbara's parents to each other and to her and to her brother—love that will comfort them and support them always.

And so Jill continued her detailed litany of gratefulness for all that was in place and would support me as I made my way to the hospital and to the side of my parents. As Jill's list of supports grew, I became calm and grateful, too, and I felt it was clear that I was on a path of support to my parents at this time in our lives.

I had earlier expressed my concerns about how I would be able to help my parents. So, as the plane was landing—safely, indeed—Jill gave me the verse from Isaiah 40:29. "He giveth power to the faint; and to them that have no might he increaseth strength."

And calmness and a sense of strength did follow me all through the next days, the last for my father on this planet. I stayed by his side, and we were all there holding him as he peacefully passed on. This calmness and strength continued after his death through the days of planning and participating in a memorial service for my Dad and of comforting my Mom. Literally out of the blue, I had been lifted up and made ready to step into this life turn. It was very real experience for me that at the same time seemed amazing. I felt grateful for this gift all through those days.

Before flying home to Illinois ten days later, I called the church in Los Angeles where Jill said she had been staying, as I wanted to thank *her*, but no one there knew of her or any one fitting her description. I was surprised, and I missed her voice, but I knew why she had been seated next to me on the plane. I had indeed been held in love, and what a difference it had made in my life and those dearest to me. I am grateful for it to this day.

The Sound of Grace*
By Catherine Johnson

"...Because inside human beings is where God learns."

—Rainer Maria Rilke**

I live in two worlds. One, which is bright and sharp, bursting with amplified sound; the other, muted, whispering and soft. Hearing aids give me days that are like oil paintings, rich in detail and definite in line, while my own unaided hearing presents me with watercolor landscapes, scenes more abstract and fluid. Most of the time, I prefer the quieter world. Released from the effort of accurate understanding, I feel free to simply listen. My other senses open like windows bringing in light, textures, and smells to accomplish what my ears alone cannot. And every once in a while, out of that softer wash of sound around me, a clear and perfect voice emerges, the voice of the divine.

On a recent trip to Paris, I paused at the top of a steep concrete stairwell that led from the street to the underground world of the city's Metro. I removed my hearing aids, anticipating the overwhelming sounds that lay ahead. Instantly, the traffic and the conversations around me blurred and receded. The iron handrail I grasped felt hot where the sun rested on it. A little breath of breeze brushed through my hair, and something savory drifted by from a cafe next door. Because it was my last afternoon in that enchanting and beautiful city, I wanted to remember everything—even the pull of people: young, old, tourist, Parisian, flowing around me, descending the steps and vanishing into the shadows below. I stood there, at the top of the stairs, listening for a few more moments, taking it all in. Then I, too, headed down to the trains.

While the tunnels of the Metro provided instant relief from the city's summer heat, they assaulted the senses in other ways. Fluorescent light glared against white-tiled walls only to be swallowed by winding miles of concrete and darkness. The place was both too bright and depressingly dim. A deep breath uncovered the fruity smell and acrid taste of axle grease, perspiration, and old urine. And every few minutes, the air swelled with the roar and vibration of an arriving train.

Shuffling forward with my ticket, I could hear the thunk, thunk of turnstiles ahead, but there was something else as well. A few errant notes of music filtered through the chatter and hum of the moving crowd. As I passed through the turnstile and headed for the train that would carry me to the Louve the crowd thinned but the music remained, growing louder and more pure. Long and soulful tones, rising and falling, reminded me of someone crying out in pure pleasure, then weeping gratefully in such pleasure's fading wake. The voice of a single violin was filling that tunnel with grace.

I do not remember walking the rest of the way to the platform that day, only how the music inhabited me. Each draw of the bow made me large, each return across the strings, small. A distance that could have only taken seconds to cover became a pilgrimage. Deep sorrow and deep gladness moved through me, as if I had been away from one I loved and had returned home at last. Finally, I reached the source of the beautiful music: a middle-aged man.

He was heavy in the belly, but sat on his stool with a straight back, as if occupying a principal chair with the symphony. His hair was pulled into a scraggly gray ponytail and his dark flannel trousers were worn, frayed at the cuff and along the seams. The sweat stains that darkened his light blue shirt belied the otherwise invisible effort with which he played. I stared, unable to look away. Not only was I hearing the music, but it poured in through my eyes. Each line shimmered brighter, the pitch building and straining, like the cries of a lover well loved. The music was so pure that the fibrous strings of my own heart began to vibrate and break. And in that moment, standing on the platform slightly apart from the crowd, I knew something of God, and God knew again the incandescent instant when suffering ceases, could feel the breaking of a grateful heart.

With tears streaming down my cheeks, I searched the musician's pale round face hoping for his gaze. In the presence of such grace, I could not bear to be alone. Surely he will understand, I thought. But, when my eyes finally found his, they were half closed and empty—the wandering white oceans of the blind. Many times since, I have thought how the voice of God spoke that afternoon to a woman hard of hearing through the hands of a man without sight.

*Previously published in *Face to Face: Women Writers on Faith, Mysticism and Awakening*, edited by Linda Hogan and Brenda Peterson, North Point Press, 2004.
**Rilke, Rainer Maria, from the poem "Just As The Winged Energy of Delight." Translated by Robert Bly in *The Rag and Bone Shop of the Heart*, Robert Bly, James Hillman and Michael Meade, eds. 1992. New York: HarperCollins, p. 236.

Part Three

Awakening in Community

Reaching Hands – Janaia Donaldson

The Beauty of Being Held in Love
By Karen Latvala

For me, nothing is as beautiful as being held in love, and holding others in that space. Since I first experienced this feeling of "being held" two years ago, it seems to have opened the door for me to not only receive this beautiful gift again and again, but to understand how to give it to others. This reservoir of love provides a calm and peaceful steadiness through the ups and downs of life.

The first time I remember *really* being held in love was during a critical illness in 2006. I had contracted hantavirus, a deadly disease which filled my lungs with fluid, caused my heart to flip-flop, and raised havoc with my blood, liver and kidneys. At age 62, I was in critical care, barely aware of my surroundings, but feeling an inner calmness about my situation.

Just a few hours earlier I had been moved to critical care in our small hospital in rural Colorado. The doctor was working to stabilize me so I could be flown by helicopter to a larger hospital. At some point I became aware of my husband Lyle's presence and the Flight-for-Life crew preparing me for transport. Although I knew I was critically ill, I also knew deep within me that I was going to be okay, as if my higher Self had committed to do whatever it takes to move to the next spiritual level.

As I lay there I was not afraid. When I opened my eyes and saw the pain in Lyle's face, these words came out of my mouth: "Don't worry; I am not going to die." I told him to repeat my favorite mantra "Peace, om shanti, salaam, shalom" ("peace" in 4 languages) and it would help him stay peaceful. He told me later how it had sustained him on that intense day.

I learned that mantra from Vessels of Peace, an organization devoted to women, peace and the Sacred Feminine. Some of the women held a special meditation called the "Darshan of Peace" by phone that morning to hold my weakened body in peace and love. I had the sense of a large reservoir of peace floating above me and I could just tap into it whenever I wanted to. I remember feeling so peaceful, so held in love, so protected by some unknown force. Now I realize that the reservoir surrounds me or whomever I am sending love to.

My health improved remarkably in that first 24 hours. They held two more Darshan calls in the next few days and I continued to gain strength. No matter how concerned my doctors and family were or how weak my body was, I knew I would be fine. In just a few days I made a remarkable recovery from a rare disease that 40% of people die from immediately

I am not saying that being held in love results in physical healing, but I certainly felt stronger and attribute much of my quick recovery to the increased feeling of peacefulness that love brought. I also felt blessed by the outpouring of e-mails from friends and family sending their love.

One thing became clear to me as I got stronger and my mind became clearer: I knew I could not go back to "life as it had been." Out of the inner peace came the clear message that this was my opportunity to change some old patterns. This quieting of my mind and support of my spirit was a wake-up call that changed me physically, emotionally, mentally, and spiritually. It slowed me down for months, forcing me to "do" less and "be" more. All the time I knew I was being held in love, a wonderful feeling of inner support and strength.

In 2008 I attended a women's peace conference in India, "Making Way for the Feminine for the Benefit of the World Community." I was excited to be called to hold the world in love, along with attendees from 45 countries. I felt strongly the support of all those at home who were sending love to support our efforts in co-creating a better world.

Toward the end of the conference I got a bad cough that sapped my energy for days, followed by severe diarrhea. Feeling weak and unable to enjoy sightseeing, I started feeling sorry for myself, forgetting that illness is always a sign of something healing within us. I could not seem to extricate myself from the feeling of darkness and isolation I was experiencing. I did not appreciate the purging that was going on inside of me.

Once more, the women of Vessels of Peace held me in love with a special meditation phone call. From my weakened state of being dehydrated to the point of fainting and having to be pushed in a wheelchair at a temple in Delhi, the love I received gave me a boost of energy by the next day, enough to honor my engagement to speak to a philosophy class at the University of Delhi. I was excited and was quite amazed at the energy I felt.

Again, I want to say that for me, being held in love so energized my spirit that my body was able to do something that felt very doubtful a few hours earlier. The infusion of energy continued the next day as I went to the airport and began my two-day journey home. I felt exhausted, but peaceful, and slept a lot on the trip.

In retrospect I realized that when I focused on my continuing illness, letting it overshadow the meaning of the conference, my ego was interfering with the flow of love and peace that was out there and available to me. When I was able to let that go a few days after I returned home, I opened up to receiving love again and was reconnected to the flow.

These examples of being held in love prepared me well for holding others in a loving space. A significant opportunity came one night a month after India when I received a late evening phone call saying that my 89 year old father in Portland was in critical condition following a brain hemorrhage. I immediately sent love (via the Darshan) to my dad and mom and prepared for a trip the next day.

The next morning's news was grim. With help from my daughter, plans were made to fly to Portland. As I made the three-hour drive to the Denver airport, I sent love to my mom and dad, and wondered what it would be like to be with my dying father. It all seemed surreal, and I knew I was doing all I could do by holding them in love.

When I arrived that evening I was surprised at how calm I actually felt, sitting by dad's bedside with my mom. He was unable to speak more than a few words. Our vigil continued for six days as his body weakened and finally let go. I knew that my gift to him was to hold him and my mom in love without judgment as he made his final journey. The whole experience felt peaceful and I knew that the reservoir of love was flowing in both directions, from me to them and back to me. The following day, after helping my mom with funeral arrangements, I got on a plane to California for our daughter's wedding. I wondered if it would be hard to switch roles, but it felt almost seamless, and I experienced the presence of peace and love again. I was aware that we were celebrating two of life's transitions—my dad leaving his body after a long life and our daughter beginning a new life with a loving partner—all in one week.

The day after the wedding, Lyle and I flew back to Portland for the funeral and to help my mom ease into her suddenly different life as an 88 year old woman alone after 68 years of marriage.

Through each of these transitions, while I was holding someone in love, I could feel that I was receiving it too, experiencing it internally as divine peace and strength, and externally as compassion from others. I could feel the support of friends and family, yet it felt like I had an anchor inside of me and the strength of love to sustain me. I really appreciated its essence keeping me steady and anchored through it all.

Being held in love unconditionally helped me learn how to hold that love within myself and be able to send it to others. It's a very powerful thing—a reservoir of strength always there to tap as needed. I am profoundly grateful for these experiences that have taught me so much and have taken me to a new level in my spiritual life.

The opportunities to hold myself and others in love seem to be coming more frequently now, and I feel bathed in that love. This feeling is available to everyone who taps into that resource of love with his or her heart. It is not unique to me. Just ask for the awareness and you will find it there.

Seen Through and Through
By Lynn Waddington

From the very beginning, my mother held me in love, gave me a little extra protection. I was the odd one out, too sharp for the kind people of that sleepy backwater, different in ways that had no name or example. I blossomed into adolescence in the 1950s with a clear attraction to girls, which threw me into turmoil. Clearly this was an unheard of aberration that would have to be carefully guarded from others. My deepest longings would have to go unanswered.

One evening I took my distress outdoors, the one place I felt I truly belonged. As I gazed out over my beloved river, everything changed in one awesome moment; the world somehow split open. I was awash with Divine Presence, more in that world than this. I was transparent, seen through as easily as a windowpane, all my dark secrets on view. I was abashed. Sweat poured off me, tears ran down my face, my whole body trembled.

And yet, this awesome Presence "gazed on me" with such acceptance, like a loving caress, that I could only soak it in. Every bit of me was loved. I have no idea how long this incredible moment lasted, but before it faded I saw an image that seemed to be a message for me. A path stretched from my feet to the far horizon. This Presence would be with me all the way.

I wish I could say that I felt accompanied from then on, and able to be wholly myself. I'm afraid I crashed around as much as anyone, trying to find a life of integrity. And yet there was an underlying sense of protection that gave me courage. At the critical junctures of my life the memory of this moment would come, as a very enigmatic answer to my questions.

***

In my 50's I met and fell in love with Margaret, another life-long Quaker. We felt so beautifully matched, and wanted to marry under the care of our Meeting. Our parents were in their 80s then, mine on the opposite side of the country, but they came. So did all our siblings, and so did the two surviving aunts of my parent's generation, and some of my favorite cousins. So did my adult daughter and her long-term boyfriend, and even two members of his family. So did old friends and Meeting members from two states away where I used to live.

After a lifetime of hiding my loves to some degree, my open and public declaration of love for Margaret left me feeling completely vulnerable. We stood together to say our vows, intimate in this very public setting, all my protection stripped away.

There were people here who knew me through some of my most difficult times, my gangly teens and bumbling twenties, my bad relationships and bad habits. They'd seen me, and here they were supporting me with their love. I watched these people from the fragmented eras of my life, laughing and talking with each other, knitting together my fractured soul.

All those years of wishing for another grand mystical experience like the one in my adolescence, and here it was, brought to me by these people who were my beloved family. They saw me and loved me, as God had done. I was defenseless and profoundly touched.

***

And now here I am fifteen years later, looking at the prospect of a premature death. Pulmonary fibrosis has left me greatly weakened and attached to supplemental oxygen. A year and a half ago my collapse was so sudden and thorough that I thought we were looking at a few months left to live. We made radical adjustments to our life, and we reached out to our broad network of family and friends for help.

Margaret put together an e-mail list to keep people posted and to ask for prayers and support. We also gathered a care committee that meets at our home once a month to help with practical matters and, much more importantly, emotional and spiritual matters. Here I could admit my fears and wonder at my lack of fear. In the first meeting with these trusted friends, my bravery fell away. My words came out through a swollen throat and shuddering body. Their response gathered me up and held me. It now seems clear how much we all long to have the walls and barriers down, to give all we can to each other, to recognize how much we have in common.

Early on, I had a dream in which I was driven along a winding mountain road by someone paying too little attention to the job at hand. All of a sudden we missed the curve and sailed off toward the valley far below, to my certain death. I woke hollering "Noooooooooo!" I do not want to go. It is too soon. I will miss the decades we assumed we would have together, to enjoy the dream house we built, the retirement I have earned. I will especially miss this peaceful, loving partnership.

And yet "I've been to the mountain and I've seen the other side" as King said. The blissful world of that mystical experience awaits me, and I am not afraid. No, it is Margaret and my other loved ones who have the harder path. They will be left behind to grieve.

And meanwhile, they, mostly she, bear the burden of my care. I see Margaret's life filled with my needs and what used to be my chores, at the same time that my life is emptying. It has been so hard to simplify my busy schedule, until now. I laid down everything and asked to be led to what I should do now, with my remaining time. My health has leveled off and allowed me to follow the quiet voice of my heart. I pause often to gaze out the window at this beautiful world, so grateful to be still here. I am content. It is Margaret's patient holding that allows me this special time.

I am also grateful for my computer, which collects my thoughts and connects me to my circle of friends. We send out health updates and receive such a wealth of blessings in return. I thought we would be bothering people, but instead, the circle keeps widening. More and more friends ask to be included. Our plight is held in people's hearts. Their prayers are holding us up. My health is not declining as quickly as expected.

I am filled to overflowing with these blessings, which do not stop with me. They cycle through to those I am with. They are something not of me or from me. Some friends have asked me to help them through their difficult times. And so I, or Margaret and I together, sit vigil through surgeries, difficult job interviews, and dying.

That long-ago promise, that I would be held in God's love throughout my life, has been fulfilled. I have felt it so many times, in private and through others' tender care, and now I feel it almost constantly. I fall asleep into a soft palm. The end will not be so very different.

In Sickness and In Health
Margaret Sorrel

When my partner Lynn was diagnosed with a terminal lung condition we shared the hard news with our far-flung community. Many dear friends responded by saying that they would hold us in the Light or pray for us or send healing energy in our direction. During a period of amelioration, when Lynn's health seemed to be improving against all the doctor's predictions, we wished we knew more about the nature of what our friends were doing on our behalf. We knew that the diversity of this ministry was great but we never could have imagined what we learned when we asked some of these dear friends to tell us about their own practice. It is through the hands and hearts and minds of people that the work of God is done. We feel the love of God through these friends in the harder times and in the times of greater hope.

Lansing, MI: I have Lynn's picture on my office computer wallpaper. So when I turn it on I get to see you laughing and pointing to yourself. I see that face and I tap the bell I have on my desk and listen to the sound of the energy, remember to center myself today, and am grateful for the two of you being in the world.

Corvallis, OR: Against my ache over the severe illness and daily struggle, I work to visualize you both in your full native strength and wholeness (which I believe was and is untouched by illness and death). Frequent flash visions come of you and your lives, flash memories of deep friendship and love for you, past, present, and future. I pray too for those who are present physically and spiritually more closely than I, giving you material and emotional and spiritual help in person. I pray for their hope and strength and love to keep steady. They stood and stand in place of all the rest of us who can't be there but who love you both. They are the channels for what flows from all of us everywhere. I count on them to carry my love in their hands and arms and bodies. Clearly they do that with grace, humor and hope! Life is such a miracle!

Pessac, France: Avec vous, et avec tous ceux qui vous aiment, je rends grâces au Seigneur pour cette amélioration de la santé et donc, de la vie quotidienne, de votre petite communauté insulaire. With you, and with all who love you, I give thanks to God for this improvement of your health and therefore of your daily life and for your small island community.

Tacoma, WA: I think of you two so often in my daily activity and each time bring forth thoughts of light and loving. There is a strong power within the Light and Love.

Salem, NJ: Our prayer content is now for rapid and continuous improvement with a long, long life ahead. For months your name has been lifted up at the end of Meeting each Sunday and more recently at the weekly healing sessions. We have no idea, do we, how effective this kind of prayer is. And because there were soooo many being sent to you from all over the country, perhaps a critical mass was reached.

Greenbank, WA: Each morning in my Theta meditation I 'see' you both surrounded in the Light and Love of Source, and the inner light of the wholeness of who you are shining and glowing brightly within you, supporting you and loving you.

Rossland, BC: I think miracles do happen because *we* make them happen, because we believe in the power of love. Which also might be God. Whatever is working, may it continue!

Hoboken, NJ: You have in the past and you are blessing me now. You're doing that for others too. Since the gift you called out in me is seeing the "divine core" as it expresses itself in others, then imagine me as your cheerleader. One household in Hoboken breathes a sigh of relief and gratitude—and I feel much of Jersey doing the same. Having written about holiness and embracing life even in suffering—there's also a lot of truth in my first response to your wonderful news: f*** suffering !!! What a gift to us, your friends, to see and know how God is answering our prayers in the two of you. Hooray! We'll keep praying and you keep drinking that turtle shell, mushroom, bark tea. Drink lots of it—okay? Nice to have something to say "thankyouthankyouthankyouthankyou…" to God about!

Langley, WA: I have lit a candle every night since hearing the news of Lynn's health issues. As I light the candle I say a prayer and as I blow it out I pray that the breath I blow out long and strong will give more breath to Lynn.

Mexico: I send you many "bendigas" as blessings are called here in Mexico and you are in my morning meditation.

Freeland, WA: I have kept a place for you both on my altar and I do believe strongly in prayer and intention. But you both are magical women and have called forth the love and prayers of those who are lucky enough to know you. That is indeed magic.

Vancouver, BC: The part of my daily practice that is directed toward helping Lynn build one of those mazes is a standing meditation, feeling my connection with the earth energies and opening myself up to the cosmic energies of love, courage, wisdom and healing. I invite that energy into myself and then send it out to others who need it…you dear ones to name two. The more I do this the more my heart opens up…

Soquel, CA: I affirm my faith in the unknowable possibilities of life each day. I acknowledge the intention of the life force itself and I make the space for it to express itself each day. You both are included in that great possibility of life expressing itself. I am always open and welcoming to the unexpected treats of life. I also know that they can't always express themselves and sometimes life loses its potent expression. In the meantime, let's revel in our love and connections with each other and celebrate!

Port Townsend, WA: You are in my daily prayers as well as called forth in my heart during Meeting for Worship each First Day.

Kennebunk, ME: I continue to take you both with me, in my heart and thoughts, every morning at dawning when I walk the ocean beach with Cady…I live in awe with the promise of each day's dawning…I have loved the story…when the Little Prince befriended the rose, giving it loving care, believing it would live. "It is only with the heart that one can see rightly; what is essential is invisible to the eye." I like to think that is the loving power of prayer.

Great Falls, MT: I have two intercessory prayer lists. One is an emergency one that holds just a few people in the light which I think or say every morning and night and several times during the day. Even though Lynn is better, I'm keeping you both on that list. I really hold you in the light as I do my daily 10 minutes of breathing exercises each morning.

Homer, AK: I have a meditation practice that revolves in circles of care…family, friends, clients and it ripples out to anyone who needs it in the world…Sometimes I wake up in the night, often with one of my mild or wild "heat flushes" and I go through that filled with the warmth of love and energy and friendship. Often then my attention goes to those who have health challenges. And the "ball of fire" helps dissolve pain and obstacles until I drift off again.

Wallingford, PA: In addition to spoken and silent prayer requests at Pendle Hill during Meeting for Worship, I write both of your names in my spiritual journal each week in a section I color in some way in shades of yellow—it's the spot where I hold people "in the light."

Wanaka, New Zealand: My favourite way to care for you is to run blue-green light through your lung and heart chakras, Lynn. Once, decades ago, in 1983, I was standing over the water at La Jolla and had a spiritual experience. The colour of the water was incredibly beautiful and had a "breath" to it! I knew (was told?) what to do. I ingested (for want of a better word) the light, energy, and colour of the sea for my own healing. …I inhale the colour of the sea and send it through my body and store it in my heart. With a never ending supply, I "will" it to you, by seeing it travel out my arm and hand and direct it to your lungs, Lynn. And Margaret I see you sitting in it near Lynn.

Seattle, WA: What I've been doing for Lynn all along is seeing you very, very, very old and Margaret, seeing you very, very, very old alongside her. I practice that visualization for people who are figuring out how to stick around on the planet and send that energy out in your direction—and will continue to do so. Jews don't do intercessory prayer to speak of, but one of our few is for healing, and I have put Lynn's name into the Mi Shebeyrach when I've been to services. L'chaim (to life).

Many in this worldwide community have told us that the blessings they receive from this ministry to us are returned to them many fold. I only wish that every person on this dear planet were the recipient of the love which continues to sustain us through this difficult time of our lives.

Held in the Light
By Rebecca Moyer

It was March 2003. I had been struggling with a chronic lung disease that had progressed since a 1991 hospitalization for bacterial pneumonia. Although I had been up and down physically since then, I had taken a real nose dive in 2000 when I moved from a rather isolated living situation to a community at 7000'. In addition, I had previously been self-employed and now I had a college teaching position. Both situations exposed me to a lot of illnesses and my immune system was not up to the task. I was sick about 9 months of the year and on oxygen whenever I was in my house or the car. Added to that stress, I loved the community and my teaching position, but knew I would have to leave both to lessen my exposure to illness and be in a lower altitude.

The community, concerned with my prognosis, graciously offered a second healing session for me, which I gratefully accepted. The first healing session had been about a year before and was filled with love. Although I did not magically get well, I felt comforted by the caring of the community. I expected an experience somewhat similar and was unprepared for what happened.

The day the healing circle was scheduled, I was quite ill and the short walk to the community house taxed my rattling lungs. Our community consisted of 70 members, both adults and children. Therefore, any of those people or others from outside of the community could come. Before I left my house. I wrote down the names of eleven adults and one child whom I knew would be in the circle. Out of those, I knew three would come from outside the community and who they would be. At the time, I seemed to be in an altered state of consciousness, so did not think it odd that I knew all these names.

Later, I remembered that detail.

The twelve healers gathered and I lay down on a pillowed bed on the floor of our community house. I closed my eyes and said to myself, "Help me, I don't know how to die." Immediately, dozens of friends and relations who had passed over came to me to give me their death experiences. There was no judgment about which way to die. I asked telepathically why I could see and hear them. They explained that although they had no bodies or voices, I in physical form put sound and sight into each of their spiritual energies, which made it possible for me to understand them.

At some point, I was asked why I wanted to die and I answered, "I have no quality of life. I am sick, in pain, exhausted and in bed most of the time. What's the point of staying?"

A collective voice said, "So you believe quality of life is related to health?"

"Yes, I do" I cried.

"But it is only what you believe that makes this so. We believe that quality of life is not related to health, financial wealth, the perfect mate, intelligence, power over others of the attainment of things," the voices continued.

"Then what will make me want to stay?" I asked in tears. There seemed to be a quiet pause at this point as if the spiritual energies present wanted me to pay close attention.

Then the answer came to my question came. "Being present to each moment. Seeing the perfection of *all* that *is* now."

I argued, "But how can I enjoy the moment when I am suffering all the time?"

"Most of your suffering is caused by the fears your mind plays with about the future, not the moment you are in right *now*. Remember this: you may ask for help and we will come immediately to guide you and alleviate your suffering."

Throughout the hour or so I was in this state, I cried. I was aware of being in the room with my friends, but the room seemed very far away compared to my contact with the spiritual world. I also saw the spirits of people who were still alive. One was my younger brother with whom I longed to connect, but who would have nothing to do with my family. He explained that we were deeply connected in spirit but that he could not be with me on the physical plane right now. (The longing went completely away and has never returned). Another brother, who had died shortly before I was born and with whom I saw and played with as a child (like an imaginary playmate), wandered in and out of my awareness seemingly lost. He didn't recognize me as the others had. I asked why; the voices explained that he was unaware that he had died and no longer in a physical body. I was horrified that he had been doing this for 60 years and was reassured that there is no time in their dimension. It was always "now". All that was needed was for me to tell him he was no longer in a body. When I did, he exploded into light.

At some point I asked why these twelve people, out of so many, volunteered to be with me. The explanation was very detailed and I heard such things like "The small child is here to hold the Light. His father is keeping you grounded; another is a receptacle for physical pain and still another for the emotional pain." No one person held any more importance than another. My job was simply to bring the knowledge back to all of them. Before I came fully back into the room, I was aware of the energies of the healers, how they looked and felt. I asked questions of several of them to confirm what I knew such as "How is your body?" to the person who was holding my physical illness. She burst into tears as she had gotten quite sick during the session. Then I saw a brilliant light to one side and recognized the child who was holding the light. I opened my eyes to see the lights and saw the three-year-old child looking right into my eyes. He came over and we hugged for a long time. The others said he never stopped looking at me during the entire healing. I began to explain what I had heard to the healers and a deep sense of joy came into the room.

I was in bliss for many months following this experience and find I can easily tap into this energy whenever I need it. I ask for and receive guidance daily and live my life with that trust. My illness is improved and I have learned so much about helping others. In fact, my new business is "Cutting Edge Health Guidance."

Resurrection Trees – Carolyn W. Treadway

While photographing the shoreline of Ruby Beach in Olympic National Park, I was suddenly swept into the ocean by a rogue wave, and nearly crushed by numerous giant logs crashing together around me. Then just as suddenly, the water deposited me back onto the beach, miraculously only bruised and scraped. The camera I had somehow kept on my shoulder was ruined. When I removed the film, part of the roll had become a gelatinous mass, but part had rewound into the canister and was able to be retrieved and developed. This photograph of the sun peeking through the costal forest fog was one of the prints from that very damaged roll. I call it "Resurrection Trees" because it too nearly died, and should have died, and yet somehow miraculously came back to life.

A Season When Jesus Carried Me
By Jonathan Holm

I discovered I was not like other boys when I was twelve. As the mysterious changes of puberty awoke a new and exciting interest in girls in my sixth grade male classmates, I was unique in developing an equally new and exciting interest in boys. But I knew I could never tell. I grew up in a rural corner of Texas, in a small town. We were poor, conservative, Republican, and Southern Baptist.

There seemed to be unanimous opinion among both my peers and the adults at home, at school, and at church: two men in love were disgusting and unacceptable. Gay men—no, "faggots"—were effeminate evildoers, flamboyant sinners who turned their backs on God. I identified as a man and a Christian; being gay was anathema to both.

And so I denied my feelings. I convinced myself I was just going through a phase. I told myself that some day my interest in guys would surely pass. Some day. But after a decade of inner turmoil, the "just a phase" logic wore thin. As a sophomore in college, I suddenly faced the horrifying reality of my orientation.

Terrified, I confessed my gay feelings to my pastor. He urged me to tell my parents, a conversation I was deeply afraid to have, fearing my parents would disown me or throw me out of the family. I waited until the last day of a Christmas holiday to talk with them. If they were going to turn me out of the house, the end of break would be the most opportune time, since I was already packed to return to school.

But they didn't throw me out. They reiterated their deep evangelical opposition to gay relationships, but they emphasized they loved me regardless. I cannot overstate my relief. My parents' unexpected words of unconditional love shone Light into a deep, profoundly lonely area of my soul—a decade of hiding and self-deception had allowed a monstrous fear of rejection to grow unchecked. I wept heavily the night of my conversation with my parents. In a wonderful, powerful way, their words ministered Light to me.

Our conversation didn't end there, however. My father, a child therapist, told me about a type of religious ministry that claimed ability to change gays and lesbians into heterosexual men and women. I had never before heard of "ex-gay" ministry, but my heart leapt that I could rid myself of my unwanted attraction to men. Eager to be normal, I asked my father to connect me with such a ministry. And so, one fateful day in February of 2000, I nervously walked into a ministry called "Living Hope," and so began my five-year involvement in ex-gay ministry.

I would summarize those next five years in three words: hope, confusion, and disillusionment. While in ex-gay ministry I met many wonderful, caring people, who loved God and genuinely believed being gay was against God's plan. They invested many hours trying to change my orientation through counseling, books, conferences, prayer, anointing with oil, fasting, worship services, and even two exorcisms. I trusted the ministry leaders. I did what they told me to do. I believed what they taught me. But as the years wore on, a painful reality became clear: neither I nor any of my friends in the ministries was actually changing. None of us lost attraction to the same sex. A few tried dating members of the opposite sex with varying results. Most of us did not.

Disillusionment overtook the lives of many friends in the ministries as they found their orientations to be unchangeable. I watched helplessly as several friends descended deep into depression. I, too, began to despair. I began intensive, additional counseling with a local evangelical counselor to battle the depression. Sadly, the intense sessions with the counselor only exacerbated the despair. Again and again I heard that God feverishly despised my orientation. I struggled harder and harder in my vain efforts to rid myself of my attractions. I hated myself.

Ultimately, I gave up. My wicked orientation was immutable; I must be a hopelessly worthless person in the eyes of God. I applied for and received a gun license. I made a plan.

A dear friend intervened the day I was going to end my life: June 12, 2005. He forced me to divulge my plan to my parents. That same day, my father flew from Texas to Illinois, where I was living for grad school. He encouraged me to resign my graduate work temporarily. I spent the balance of the summer living with my parents and painting houses in the Texas heat. Those sweltering hours of manual labor offered me ample time to ponder my struggle with my orientation. As the monotonous brush strokes gradually transferred paint from my can to the houses, I turned over the events of my life.

I came to an epiphany: perhaps my misery was not due to my orientation; perhaps my depression stemmed from a wrong understanding of being gay. I became consumed with Jesus' parable about discerning the nature of a tree by the fruit it bears: good trees produce good fruit; bad trees bad fruit. If my convictions about God and gay people were "good" (that is, accurate), why was the fruit they bore in my life so uniformly bad? Could the Spirit be using my profound depression and desire to end my life to diagnose errors in what I believed?

Deeply moved by this realization, I returned to graduate school in Illinois determined to reexamine my convictions. I decided to discontinue ex-gay ministry until I could determine whether my convictions about my orientation were right or wrong.

For nine months I spent my free time in the university libraries, reading every book I could find on orientation and faith. Also, for the first time in my life, I began to spend time with openly gay and lesbian people. I met many wonderful gay men and lesbians, people in happy, decades long, monogamous relationships, people raising healthy, playful children. I asked about their lives, observed their relationships, learned about their faith, and met their children. The ex-gay ministries taught there was no such thing as healthy, loving, monogamous gay relationships—they taught that gay people are all immature and promiscuous, and that most gay people are addicts. I discovered these teachings to be profoundly untrue—they were contradicted by the academic literature and the lives of the people around me. Gradually I realized I had been wrong.

And then I met Chris.

We were in the same church small groups and social functions. Outgoing, funny, and very attractive, it wasn't long before I sensed myself falling in love with Chris. However, unlike the other times I had crushes, this time I wasn't so sure I should ignore my feelings. I decided not to suppress my attraction, but rather to hold onto it and consider it carefully and prayerfully. Something wonderful and unexpected happened: my depression vanished completely. Then I noticed something even more wonderful and unexpected: Chris seemed to reciprocate my feelings for him. This never happened before.

Our friendship was forged and had been developing at the same time I was researching and discovering the errors in my former worldview. As months passed, I was coming to realize gay relationships could be every bit as healthy, loving, and mutually beneficial as heterosexual relationships. At the same time, not-so-subtle sparks were beginning to fly between Chris and me.

Then, on a frigid afternoon in January 2006, I finally broke the silence. Chris and I had met in a coffee shop downtown, ostensibly to study. I finally got up my nerve. Heart thudding in my chest, I explained to Chris my attraction to him and my desire to try dating. Although I wasn't completely certain of my convictions, I told him I wanted to explore the possibility of us growing old together. His response was precious: Chris laid his head on the table and wept quietly. I craned my neck to bring my face down near his. Between tears, he managed to say, "I'd like that, too."

That wonderful, thrilling conversation set off a whirlwind. Committed not to hide our affection for one another, that very same week Chris and I began sharing with our evangelical friends and my family this wonderful development. Only, as expected, the news was not wonderful to their ears. Turmoil ensued. I exchanged long letters with my parents and spent hours on the phone with them. There were many intense meetings with leadership of the church. The five evangelical men with whom I shared a house made it clear I was unwelcome if I pursued relationship with Chris.

At the end of the spring of 2006, Chris and I had yet to officially begin dating; we were still working through our convictions, reading books about faith and discussing them. We had fallen in love, but we continued to struggle for certainty about God's perfect will for us.

My openness with my family prompted one of my brothers to cut off all relationship. The church officially asked me to leave their fellowship. And my roommates asked me to move out of the house. I was without a church, without a home, struggling to come to grips with my brother's rejection, and still fighting to understand God's will for me and Chris.

Out of the blue, I learned of a student who needed someone to house sit with her pets for the summer. God had provided a place for me to stay; moreover, he had provided a temporary home where I was never alone. Unlike my family, my former church, and my evangelical friends, the feisty cat Mitya and eccentric dog Shasta were always welcoming and always happy to see me. They were the perfect companions for that tumultuous time. They were present yet silent, affording me hour upon hour to think and pray and sort things out with God.

It was also during that summer that I found my way into my first Quaker meeting for worship. I had been looking for a new spiritual community to call home, and after learning that the local Quaker meeting welcomed people like me and Chris, I made my way to the meetinghouse and settled into the silence of that first meeting for worship. I was immediately moved to tears in the quiet gathering. All my life I had been accustomed to someone else instructing me what God wanted. Here I found something entirely different, a reverent silence in which I could dialog directly with God.

If there were any time in my life that I should have felt rejected, it should have been that summer. Yet I look back on the summer months of 2006 with great fondness. Like the hard times in the life of the narrator of *Footprints in the Sand,* that was a season when Jesus carried me. Then, with the mischievous cat and eccentric dog, and in the stillness and silence of Quaker worship, I found calm within the storm. In spite of all the tumult, I felt the nearness and care of God.

In God's miraculous way, the complications were sorted out that summer. After much prayer and consideration, Chris and I both concluded that God was "for" our relationship. We began officially dating in July and have been together ever since.

Moreover, we discovered a wonderful spiritual home among the Quakers and have been befriended by many Friends.

The counsel of several wise Quakers and the ministry of the silent worship has led me through troubled emotional waters. My brother hasn't spoken to me in two long years, but the ministry of the Friends has helped me understand and release him. Finally, and perhaps most exciting, the Friends approved the marriage of Chris and me under their care! We were wed in a meeting for worship in June 2008, the two-year anniversary of that pivotal season of transition when Jesus carried me.

My Mother Holds Me
By Carol Clarke

My Mother holds me
And I feel softness and warmth and safety.
She is energy.
She is the moon, the mountains, the trees,
The movement of water in streambeds,
The flight of a bug, the call of a bird.
She is a candle burning on my altar.
She is the rock that watched over me during my VisionQuest.
She is in smoke and in every smell.
She is inside me: my instincts and my better judgment.
She gives me my dreams and speaks into my inner ear during my
morning prayer
And sometimes while I'm driving my car.
She rewards me when I ask for help or give her my problems.
She is spinning the world,
Guiding it in its journey around the sun.
She is the source of all balance, all knowledge,
All love and all life.
She loves me and protects me and shows me the way.

Sheltered Path – Carolyn W. Treadway

One Heart was in Charge All Along
By Doug Seeley

This is a story of a great healing of my heart-mind. It came in the middle of a 30-day retreat with Joanna Macy on the Oregon Coast in early October 2007, but actually had been building for some time. I knew that this retreat was something that I absolutely had to do in this lifetime. Joanna's work had already brought the scientific (systems) side of me together with my spiritual side. I wanted more of this work, and to be really grounded in it.

Report from the Field

I joined sixty talented adults of all ages in a wonderful abode called Westwind in early September 2007. It is a rustic, ecological resort that includes the realms of the Pacific Ocean, high bluffs and mountain meadows, and the rich delta land of the Salmon River. Early on, a challenge arose for me. Each of us was invited to give a fifteen-minute "Report from the Field" about what we had been doing to contribute to the Great Turning. Activists conceive this Turning as a tectonic shift of modern civilization away from the endless industrial growth that has been ruining our planet at a quickening pace, towards a much more life-sustaining and healthy Gaia. Resources and species are being depleted at alarming rates, and the energy infrastructure for our current industrial civilization is coming undone. This has been called the Great Unravelling.

Only in the last decade had I become an activist and teacher about this Great Unravelling. But other than an occasional activist rant, or teaching resistant students about the one earthly system called Gaia, what could I report that I had really done, especially when I started to hear courageous reports from others in our group? For example, some were nuclear activists confronting their opponents, or social workers immersed in the domestic violence in Brazil, bringing survival skills and hope to those in immediate need.

I went into a crisis of wondering what good had actually come from my spiritual and intellectual pursuits, and from my own company's work in industrial ecology, which attempted to foster a whole systems approach to business. After some pondering, I sketched out a bio of all the things I had done in my life that seemed to have any relevance. I hoped to discern some relevant contributions to the Great Turning.

First I noted my boyhood interests in deep, psychic connections with others, an interest that progressed over my early years to synchronicity—the startling coincidences (alignment) between our inner and outer worlds. Eventually, synchronicity had become an authentic spiritual path for me.

In my twenties and thirties this path led to experiencing several forms of parapsychology, including plant communication, remote medical readings, remote viewing (telepresence), as well presenting university courses on synchronicity. My drive to experience what was really going on included practising holographic art and in 1976, publishing an article in People's Computer Company called "The World As a Hologram in Your Heart."

In the 1980's, I followed a spiritual teacher to Australia. As a professor of computer science, I started a successful consulting /software company with an ecological approach. I also worked with this teacher on a theory called the Lila Paradigm, which "scientifically" describes how the material world emerges out of a game of hide-and-seek in the spiritual (but unmanifest) world, a game called by the Hindus rasa-lila.

As my bio progressed, it became clear that my overall theme or mission was deep synergy: the idea that at the base of the Totality of all that is there are only our deep connections. Moreover the world emerged or was co-created from the dynamics of these connections. In 1974, not only did deep synergy represent for me a forthcoming major shift in our world, it also strongly validated the core role that our deep connections played in it. In my whole story line, it became apparent that I was using my conceptual knowledge to understand how the world works, rather than fully immersing myself in Life.

Hence, when the Bodhisattva exercise came along in the third week of the 30-day, I was vaguely grasping that there had actually been a theme to my life, one that was coming from a very deep and directive place that my intellectual mind had not previously been willing to consider.

The Bodhisattva Check-In

Something really pulled me toward this exercise because it had been rewarding for me in the past. By chance my partner in this exercise was a woman whom I will call Wendy. Joanna explained the context roughly as follows:

The Bodhisattva perspective is that of choosing to incarnate, again and again and again for the sake of all beings, for the sake of helping to bring All Beings to liberation. If we are all at essence Bodhisattvas then we choose incarnation with such an intention. Hence, this mission will direct us to make decisions that move us towards fulfilling this purpose. The exercise is to review our lives and some of the key decisions that we made in choosing to incarnate as the beings we are, with our unique strengths and weaknesses, in the locations and situations that shaped us. The exercise helps people to notice the long-standing directions to their lives, and for some, creates a strong alignment to the Bodhisattva theme.

Wendy and I started by reviewing our choices for being born into the bodies, families, locations, time, and with the qualities and genetic propensities that we were. I was very moved to learn of her very large family and how early in life she had to take charge of parenting all her siblings.

As my story emerged of how my decisions had moved me into a supportive and loving extended family, a photo kept popping into my consciousness. It was of my cousin and myself standing in front of the pillars of the County Jail that was my family home for my years between three and six. There my single parent mum lived with her parents and siblings while my grandfather ran the jail. In the photo, I was a vivacious, skinny little boy offering a huge openhearted gesture with my arms, as my much bigger cousin stood by with a quite sullen face. The photo image reminded me of the joy that I experienced at that jail.

At age six I moved hundreds of miles away into a small nuclear family with my biological father whom I had not really known, but had longed for. After the initial enthusiasm of finally living with my father wore off, some difficult events and choices began to emerge for me. I had re-visited these before in meditation and in therapy, but this exercise provided a new context.

A key situation occurred when I was seven and a half, at a time when it seemed my parents were making lots of decisions that greatly affected me without consulting me or even giving me explanations. I felt very much on my own. I decided to take charge of my own life and my own upbringing. I was never going to share my feelings with them again, nor were they going to find out what I was really thinking.

So I stopped playing at home, and went everywhere else to play with others. Especially I went to the library and started reading voraciously. Encouraged by my third grade teacher Ms. Eisely, I started with astronomy. As the years went on, the subjects expanded to cosmology, modern physics and eventually psychology. I used all this to excel at school and to inform my success in the world.

However, as a child I gradually became aware of an unsettling feeling. It was as if I had killed a small boy! I felt like I had to hide from something that made me guilty. In my dark moments, there was an inner sense, a gnawing guilt of having killed a boy. At times I had a disturbing sensation that this victim was an innocent version of myself. As I described these feelings to Wendy, the sense of having selected "deep synergy" as a life mission persistently presented itself, and the photo of the openhearted little boy kept appearing in my mind.

At this moment in the exercise, all of the threads that had woven my fate untangled and I melted into a joyous torrent of tears. These tears of joy expressed my realization that my whole direction in life and my key decision points had been directed by the open heart of that little boy. The tears lifted the feelings and burden of guilt that I had been carrying for more than fifty-five years. The boy was the openhearted child standing in front of the Jail—obviously still very much alive!

It also was obvious that the openhearted boy was the One who had always been in charge; he was the one who was behind the scenes selecting choices, interests and activities. He was the one who chose and was still choosing Deep Synergy. That open heart was what was behind everything I ever did…The intellectual self that garnered so much self-attention was his creation. It was never in control. I melted.

The open heart of that "little boy" had enabled all of this to happen and had held me throughout my life. It had enabled the intellect to have its illusion of control, and had nurtured the wants of the child—the wants for being spoiled, getting love from others, and compulsively eating. Although the child had its being held in this open heart, a balancing act between the child and the growing intellectual had been made. In this balance was an accommodation for childish behaviour, especially the substitution of my mother's affection by food.

The impression of having killed a little boy was a construction of an intellect who wanted to be the real one in control, who made sure that I succeeded all through school and got my Ph.D., eventually making my living as a professor and intellectual. Thank God that someone like Wendy was there to receive me when all this emerged. We have since become fast friends.

In life I followed the illusion that insight could substitute for open experience in the Present. It has now become so entrenched in my behaviour and my being that I find it difficult to "turn it off." I always raced ahead to the next thing in order to avoid an awareness of the little boy's open presence. Still, the racing is a fierce guilt, a compulsive avoidance of the shame of turning my back on joy that keeps this vicious circle in place.

When it became time for all of us in the Bodhisattva exercise to share our experiences, I insisted on telling mine to the whole group in order to give me the courage to live it more fully. As the 30-day continued, this enabled me to receive the hearts of others more completely and more often. And I lost weight easily!

The Indigenous Ritual

A few days later all of us participated in a ritual honouring indigenous cultures and grieving the genocides that had devastated them in the name of progress and European civilization. It took awhile for me to actually feel something genuine within myself rather than just thinking. Finally I was able to recall the Tasmanian decimation of Aboriginals in a deeply meaningful way I presented this with a heavy heart to the ritual's "bowl of tears."

From that moment on I felt the pain of the atrocities that others brought to that bowl of tears. That pain was in me. For me, the pain in anyone's heart is a pain in our One Heart. Moreover, in each atrocity, the pain of the victim and the pain of the perpetrator were present together, inseparably. This pain exists in our One Heart. We ignore it at our peril. The end of the ritual, with all of us parading together to carry the bowl to the ocean to return the tears to the surf, was a very moving event for me.

For me, when we break our hearts open like this, allowing all of this pain to be present, we also allow all of our joy to be also present. This is our Joy of Being, our Joy of Inter-being. This Joy can hold us in all of the rough times now and ahead, especially when we live in concert with others. This joy emanates from the One Heart that we all share.

For me, this heart is where we are all deeply connected. Hence, it is the One Heart where each of us experiences the others, uniquely. Perhaps, it is All that actually is. In any case, this One Heart has held me all along in my life and mission. I ignore it at my own peril.

When I Do These Things, My Life Makes Sense
By Maria Schmeeckle

I do not normally think of my work to help global children as a project about love. It's not that it is *not* about love, it is just that love is not the main way I conceptualize what I am doing. Instead, I feel at a deep level that when I teach about street children and orphans and other vulnerable children worldwide, and work with students to try to help some of these children, and identify the large-scale causes of children lacking adequate care, when I do these things, my biography makes sense. And I marvel that at the soul level, maybe I even set things up this way so that I would come to this point.

To understand what I do today, it helps to have a window into my past. My upbringing can be characterized as filled with upheaval. Some major events included my mother's death, sibling separation, my father's remarriage, my stepmother's divorce from my father, more sibling separation, and my brothers being in foster care. These events affected me in important ways. I went through a long period of feeling worthless and unlovable. I felt a great deal of responsibility for my younger sisters and brothers, and eventually became a pseudo-guardian for my youngest brother during his last three years of high school. I became fascinated with sociology—family sociology, to be specific.

After finishing a Ph.D. and taking an academic position, I started to incorporate service learning into my teaching, focusing on local foster children. After a few years, the pressures of academic life and relationship upheaval caused me to start asking myself some **big** questions. *What would I do if money were no object?* I felt sure that the answer to that question would unlock a key to my future. Even though money *was* an object,

I felt I could *approximate* my dream somehow, if I knew what it was. As I explored my question, answers started to emerge. It had something to do with the world's orphans. I wanted to help orphans, and to develop a global perspective on their situation.

Teaching a course called Contemporary Social Problems in Global Perspective had broadened my focus from foster children to orphans. I had resonated with a global perspective while teaching that course, and asked myself, "What is the global equivalent of a foster child?" Realizing that many countries lack a system of care such as the one we have in the United States, I began to think about orphans, and later, about street children as well.

Awareness of my passion for orphans served to energize me, and I developed a renewed appreciation of how being a university professor gives me a platform for raising awareness. I began to work with a small group of students, then a larger one, to build a program called Global Children Outreach. In doing this work, I am retroactively healing that part of me that felt orphaned myself as a young girl. I can now see my past experiences as tools and reference points instead of wounds. I have a meaning and a purpose to my life that guides me, and many others are also responding to this calling. I trust in this. I will continue on this path. Perhaps one day, I will be able to say it was all about love. But for now, I will just say that when I do these things, my life makes sense.

Moments of Grace
on the Peace for Earth Walk
By Louis Cox and Ruah Swennerfelt

We were having lunch in the patio of a sandwich shop in northern California in March 2008 when a young man in worn and dirty work clothes walked past us to sit at a nearby table and noticed the banner on our two-wheeled cart announcing that we were on a 1,400-mile "Peace for Earth Walk" from Vancouver, British Columbia to San Diego, California.

"I think what you're doing is so great!" he said as he sat down to eat. He returned to our table to once again exclaim how appreciative he was of our efforts. A few minutes later, he came over to our table again and announced, "I am a poor, poor man, but I really want to give something to support what you're doing." He then reached into his pocket and handed us two dollars. We had learned by this time that true humility was to just say "thank you" and not the usual, "Oh, you don't have to do that." People wanted to be part of our journey in whatever ways they could.

This spontaneous gesture was one of the many ways that countless people gave us encouragement and comfort during our six-month pilgrimage to bring John Woolman's message about living in right relationship with all of God's creation to Quaker Meetings and community groups on the West Coast. We weren't really prepared for the abundance of love that we received. At times our hearts felt so big that they would burst!

We were always gratified when people came to our scheduled presentations and when we could tell they had understood our message about integrating the historic

Quaker testimonies of Peace, Simplicity, and Justice with the emerging Testimony on Earthcare. (In the end more than 1,000 people came to hear us at some 60 venues, mostly at Friends meetings and churches) But we had not expected to be on the receiving end of such an outpouring of care and assistance from the hundreds of people who served as local coordinators and overnight hosts for the Peace for Earth Walk, or from many people we happened to meet along the way. From donating financially to paying for our meals to tending to us when we were sick, people found a way that they could personally be part of the walk.

Here are a few of our favorite examples:

One day a man called out to us from his driveway as we walked along. He said he had read about us in the local newspaper, and since Ruah was on the cell phone, Louis walked across the street to talk with him. At the end of their conversation the man asked whether he could pray for us. Louis said, yes, of course. Then he put a hand on Louis's shoulder and said a simple prayer for our safety and the success of our journey. We had so many spontaneous encounters like this because people sensed that we were totally available for them. We could stop and listen and talk at any time and never felt rushed. People also sensed our vulnerability (being just two people walking along) and responded to that with love and kindness.

We started our trip on November 11, 2007, walking south out of Vancouver, British Columbia, knowing that winter in the Northwest would be typically very cool and wet. But despite our supposedly waterproof shoes and clothing, over many long hours of walking in the rain moisture still managed to find its way inside, so we were often soaked and chilled by the end of the day.

One day, after walking seventeen miles in a constant downpour, we reached our "tenting" site that was at an RV park. We stood before the owner (who had, in anticipation of our arrival, tried to figure out how we could keep a fire going on the little bit of green lawn where we were supposed to pitch our tent) and asked for a dry place just to prepare ourselves for the long, wet night. Taking pity on us, she reached in her drawer and gave us the keys to the community room, a heated room with kitchen and bathroom facilities where we could stay the night!

Another late-December day in southwestern Washington, we pitched our tent at yet another RV park/campground and after a continuous rain all night we woke up to a scratchy feeling in our throats that was a sure sign of a developing head cold. (Apparently we picked up the bug at a previous host home.)

For the next six hours, as we plodded along the narrow shoulder of a rural road in a cold drizzle, we began feeling worse and worse. Several miles from our destination, we decided that we ought to cancel our scheduled stay with an older couple in the next town and to check into a local motel instead, so we wouldn't be passing our colds on to them. But when we called the couple on our cell phone and shared our concerns, they said "no" that they wanted to "minister" to us and they insisted on coming to get us. (Although we tried to avoid using cars during our walk, we agreed since we were feeling so sick.) Ruah had been fanaticizing about some chicken soup and hot tea and it had become a mantra that day, so we were absolutely delighted to arrive at their home and find delicious hot chicken soup, grilled cheese sandwiches, and hot tea waiting for us! We felt like little children being cared for by our mother. They were so nurturing to us that we were able to resume our journey the next morning with renewed spirits and energy.

Several days later, because we were still fighting our colds we spent Christmas Eve at a motel, instead of at another RV park/campground. The next morning, we got a call on our cell phone from the couple who were to be our next hosts. They lived in a small town about two days' walk to the south. When they learned that we were "under the weather," they offered to pick us and drive us to their home and let us stay with them for several extra days to give us a chance to more fully recover. We readily accepted the offer, having decided that some R & R at their home would be much more healing than two more days of walking in the rain. During that time our hosts treated us royally, providing tasty home-cooked meals and engaging us in lively conversations.

On another occasion, we were the guests of a man who lived in a small hand-built cabin several miles up a beautiful redwood-lined canyon in northern California. After offering his best hospitality--home-cooked food, thoughtful conversation, and home-spun country dance music—our host announced that we would be sleeping in his bed in the loft, while he spent the night in the barn. We chuckled over this reversal of the story of John Woolman's visits to Quakers in the 18th century (a standard piece of our presentations), when he choose to stay in the barn rather than sleep under the roof of homes where slaves were kept. We were humbled by the number of people who offered their beds to us.

A story we love to tell is of the circulating $20. We were being hosted by someone who was so proud of us that she was introducing us to all her friends at a restaurant before heading to her home. One man reached into his pocket and gave us $20. The next day we met a man who was walking his bike up a large hill. He had all his belongings on the trailer attached to his bike and he spoke of being a free spirit with no home and that he was on his way to Alaska! We told him we had been gifted $20 the night before and wanted to give it to him. He laughed as he accepted it because he had gifted someone $3 earlier that day. Shortly after that we stopped in a little café for lunch and a man read our sign and reached into his pocket and gave us a $20 bill! (He later paid for our lunch as well.) It's such a wonderful lesson about giving and receiving.

We also received financial support from individual Friends and Meetings where we gave our presentations. After most of our speaking venues people put cash and checks into a donation basket, as they were led. (Other people sent money to our Friends Meeting for us.) The total of these contributions always seemed to be just enough to cover our expenses for food, lodging, and supplies for the upcoming legs of the journey.

We were especially pleased when people wanted to walk with us. The deepened conversations with people walking all day together were a special gift. Many times a small group of people would meet us in the morning as we headed out and bring their joy, laughter, and spirit to the day's walk. The day went by so much faster when we had company!

Why such an outpouring of care generosity from so many people? We think several factors may have been involved. People probably took us more seriously because we were dedicating a considerable amount of our life energy to do this walk. We received a certain amount of sympathy because we took in stride whatever changes in walk-ing conditions and weather we encountered. Also we touched people's lives because we were not just carrying a message. They knew we had a purpose because we had banners and carried a large Earth flag, but even more important was the way we were being the change we wished to see in the world, leaving behind non-essentials in order to focus on the serious social, political, and ecological crises that are looming for this and future generations.

In the beginning we felt embarrassed that we were being offered meals and a place to sleep just for the act of walking. Walking twelve to fifteen miles on level ground seemed like a walk around the block, after we were acclimated to it. Only when we had to go up and down hills or walk as far as twenty miles in a day did we feel particularly stressed. But when we walked in the door of a host home, regardless of how long we had walked, we were welcomed as heroes. After a few weeks we were less embarrassed and learned to accept each act of love as a gift of the Spirit.

When we first started out on this journey, we didn't realize how time-consuming some of the tasks of planning our walks and finding venues and hosts would turn out to be. We were both surprised and saddened to realize that many roads today are not safe for pedestrians. As a result, we and the coordinators had to spend a lot of time through e-mails and telephone calls to make judgment calls about routes that would be accept-able. Many of the coordinators personally drove over proposed routes to take note of walking conditions, while some even prepared annotated maps to show spots where we could stop for meals and bathroom breaks. Where safe alternate routes couldn't be found, we were sometimes given rides, although we tried to do this with buses and trains when possible.

We are so grateful to the loving and thoughtful support we received from our own Quaker community over the two years we spent planning for this journey. Our home Meeting, Burlington Friends Meeting of Burlington, Vermont, appointed a clearness committee to help us discern whether our intentions were grounded in the Spirit. Then the Meeting appointed an Oversight/Support committee that met with us for over a year to help us work out details of the walk and to help us stay spiritually grounded. Our Meeting members, as well as other Friends in New England and the Steering Committee of Quaker Earthcare Witness (for which we work), held us in prayer over the six months. We know our spirits were strengthened to help us complete the walk because of their care.

By the end of our trip, we came to understand that the Peace for Earth Walk was not just a tactical success that helped us meet and engage thousands of people along the West Coast and got us safely home again. It taught us an important lesson in how to be receivers and not just givers as we all work together for a peaceful and sustainable future. We learned that carrying a message with love opened unexpected doors. Many people don't get involved in important issues of the day, not because they don't care, but because they haven't found a meaningful personal role they can play. Our walk provided roles for countless people we met and helped most of them realize that they could be part of something bigger that could make a difference in the world.

As we reflected on our pilgrimage, the overwhelming conclusion is that it was a journey of love. We were held in love by so many people in a myriad of ways. It was more love than we could have imagined, for which we are most grateful.

The Evergreens and the Anchorites
By Hollister Knowlton

When my job was eliminated and I was offered early retirement, it seemed an answer to my prayers. Way had opened for me to devote my life to working for the earth—for calling Friends (Quakers) to live a life of right relationship with all creation and for lifting up the Truth that peace, justice, and ecological sustainability were all one issue, inextricably interconnected.

Without an income, I could no longer afford to keep my house, a 120-year-old fixer-upper I had been lovingly restoring, but selling it was to provide several other blessings.

First, it enabled me to pay off the mortgage on a small row house down the street and put enough money in the bank to live simply for a while.

Second, the need for its sale, and the fact that Marcelle had moved into my third floor several years before, led to formation of an extraordinary worship group, the Evergreens, thus named because we lived on Evergreen Avenue.

Wanting to stay in her third floor refuge, which had allowed her to follow a leading to write about women and spirituality and to teach part time at the Quaker study center Pendle Hill, Marcelle thought of Laura. A fellow Quaker, Laura was just finishing a year at Pendle Hill, and Marcelle knew she was looking to buy a house.

Laura was drawn to our village community with our Quaker meetinghouse down the hill and fellow Friends scattered throughout the neighborhood. She bought the house, and was happy to have Marcelle stay. When she asked if the Quakers in the area of Evergreen Avenue met for daily morning worship, we were surprised, but intrigued with the idea.

Soon we were meeting from 8 to 8:30 each morning for silent worship, and sharing our reflections afterwards. Our Catholic neighbor joined us, as did a Methodist, and I came too, from my smaller place on the same street. In time there were about 12 of us meeting regularly for worship and study, mostly Quaker, but greatly enriched by our friends of different faiths.

Over the last five years we have become a blessed community of support and caring for one another. We take turns leading our study together, celebrate birthdays and special occasions, share in the work of one member's large community garden plot, and provide prayers or clearness for one another as needed. With our "adjunct" members, some who can not join us in the mornings because of full time work, and others who have returned to homes as far away as Wales and India, we number perhaps twenty-five, all connected via an electronic list serve.

As if this loving group was not enough richness, a core group of five "anchorites" has also formed. Originally we were the spiritual care and support group for Laura's two years in the "School of the Spirit" program. We now serve similar roles for one another, supporting the endorsement for religious service that each of us has received from our local Quaker Meetings.

We hold one another in love. We also hold one another accountable.

Last fall, when I was invited to be a plenary speaker at the 2009 Friends General Conference Gathering (FGC) and also at Illinois Yearly Meeting, and then accidentally said "yes" to a third invitation that conflicted with my own yearly meeting, the anchorites were there for me.

These women have held me in love, sitting with me as I spoke of my apprehensions, my feelings of inadequacy, and my quandary about whether to prepare a written address or to simply prepare spiritually and then speak from the Silence. Two women listened to an early initial draft and offered gentle guidance. One recent morning, when I had awakened early and was moved to write, they listened through my tears, crying with me, as I read the first ten minutes of what seem to be the words I am being given. They have nudged and supported me in a way that has made me feel enormously cared for. Three of them will be sitting on the stage with me as I give the plenary at the FGC Gathering in Virginia this summer. I am blessed, indeed.

Wrestling In Truth-Love
By Ken and Katharine Jacobsen

We along with other faculty members of a small Quaker boarding school were in deep divide. It was three weeks before graduation. A charming and talented senior had just violated a major rule for the third time. According to the rules, he was to be expelled.

As frequently happens in matters of rule breaking in a residential teaching/learning community of teenagers, some faculty members took a strong stand on discipline without exception. Others spoke of the need for compassion, noting all the contributions the student had made to the academic and community life and pointing out that not to graduate would interfere profoundly with the student's plans to move on to college. The argument that the student was a citizen of another country was used both for and against compassion.

Weary and aching for vacation, the teachers grew more and more adamant in their opposition to each other, and the sense of community, so precious to all, especially at the end of a year together, was so severely shaken that the divide (and the cause of it) were obvious to other students. They too began to take sides.

The clerk of the Board of Trustees, a trusted Quaker elder, lived nearby. When hearing of the controversy, he smiled gently and said:

> The two angels…one of discipline, the other of compassion…are wrestling again. They often do in a learning community like this one. Both are agents of Love and they are wrestling for a loving answer to the problem, an answer that will come out of both discipline and compassion and transcend both. Go back into your faculty meeting, start with silent prayer, and see what rises out of the silence. Take

as long as you need—for this is God's work of Love you are finding yourselves in.

This advice was followed although there was resistance at first; end of year checklists made it hard to relax into silent prayer. Gradually teachers began to speak out of the silence and there was a new tone, a different, uplifting energy, an earnest questioning rather than expounding. The anger and opposition were gone. The student had been testing the limits of the community, yes, relying on wit and charm, and a serious lesson was needed—but permanent estrangement from the school was not the answer. What was? Gradually and collectively the answer came.

The student, whose parents had already made reservations to attend graduation, was allowed to participate in the commencement exercises but his diploma was withheld for two years. The situation was truthfully and tenderly explained to him, to his parents, and to the university in his home country that he planned to attend. All accepted the two year "stop-out" of formal education and the soul-searching that the decision implied, seemingly appreciating the way in which Truth and Love had come together.

The student ultimately received his diploma and has been in touch with the school since. Equally important, the faculty members of this little residential school, who will inevitably fail to see eye-to-eye on matters relating to students and their needs from time to time, learned that tension can be light and life-giving if hearts do not harden and differences in perspective are welcomed and not allowed to separate. The conscious act of holding one another in Love, if chosen and practiced by individuals and communities, is the first step in true reconciliation.

Opening – Carolyn W. Treadway

Bodh Gaya*
By Joanna Macy

Soon after sunrise, the marble is already warm under our bare feet. It is fresh-washed and wet, when we enter through the eastern gate and pause to take in the scene that opens out below us. It is a many-acred mandala of shrines and memorials, trees, flowering shrubs, with the towering temple in its center, almost yellow in the early sun. But we don't pause for long; like the other pilgrims, we have our circumambulations to make, and in another two hours the walkways not in shadow will be hot as a griddle. We won't descend the stairways yet, to walk the lower paths; we like to start out on the highest level. Opening our striped umbrella, whose shade can cover us both, we smile to each other and begin.

I have been to Bodh Gaya before and treasure each visit to this hub of the Buddhist world, this spot of Gautama, the Buddha's enlightenment. But I never came with Fran. I never thought he wanted to come. Now here we are, in the fifth decade of our marriage, on either side of seventy, giving ten whole days to the enjoyment of this place.

It is the bodhi tree, not the grand nine-story temple above it, that holds the center. In the course of the morning, Fran and I move ever closer to it, until its rustling heart-shaped leaves are overhead and we can touch the mammoth gold-flecked trunk. Here, two and a half millennia ago, under an ancestor tree to this one, Siddhartha Gautama sat in vigil, became the Buddha. Here the pilgrims cluster today, as they have through the ages, offering flowers, intoning prayers, sitting in closed-eyed silence. The reverence of centuries bathes us.

On our first morning, I tell Fran about the Buddhist practice of "transferring the merit." On a three-month vipassana retreat, I had adopted that practice, to dedicate each day to someone who mattered to me. When the long hours on the meditation cushion became hard, even scary, I discovered that the one to whose benefit I had offered the day buoyed me. Or at least my love for them did.

Fran likes the idea; it gives added purpose to our earnest pleasures. So here in Bodh Gaya we dedicate each day to those we hold in our hearts: friends with a teenage child in trouble, a couple struggling with their marriage, a neighbor in surgery, colleagues in Moscow caught in the collapse of the Russian economy. As we start out, clockwise from the eastern gate, we decide who it will be this day, then settle into the silence of mindful walking. It is such a luxury to be able to reflect at length on those who have graced our lives. Soon our concerns and intentions for them give way to thanksgiving for their existence; to see their qualities afresh is like opening a present on Christmas morning. Already on the first circuit, by the time we reach the sun-baked northern side, we are telling each other about the wonderfulness of our person of the day.

We give a day, of course, to each of our children—Peggy, Jack, Chris. And the same magic happens. We start out picturing their lives back Berkeley, focusing on the particular challenges they face. Soon they seem to walking beside us in the bright, green morning. I pretend they can see through my eyes the emerald parakeets swooping by the red hibiscus blossoms and feel through my soles how the marble cools in the shade.

I have grown accustomed, once again, to our children's company. There were years when we lived far apart—Peggy in Ecuador with the Peace Corps, then in Paris with her lover Gregoire; Jack in Boston, settled into his circle of friends from college and his environmental work for Massachusetts; Chris wandering around Oregon, in and out of touch with us. Our family seemed permanently scattered when Fran and I finally sold the Lowell Street house in Washington D.C. and moved to California, where work and colleagues beckoned us. We never dreamed that we would all live close together again. But then, over the last ten years, like those parakeets dropping into the taramind tree, our children settled around us.

The innermost walkway around the bodhi tree and its temple is enclosed by stone rail fence. It was built, they say, by King Ashoka, twenty-two hundred years ago. Each pillar is carved with medallions, and on this day dedicated to Peggy and her family, I see that most of the medallions are lotuses, that many of the lotuses enclose sculpted faces, and that all of the faces are smiling. I see Peggy's smile, and Mama's too, for whom she was named. They are a lot alike in their loveliness and laughter. Mama never lost that buoyancy, even in the hardest times with Papa, and Peggy never seems to lose it either, though many of her children, in the pediatric AIDS service of Children's Hospital, die.

My fingers caress the lightly eroded face in the stone lotus. I see her sitting in the backyard of the two-flat house that Fran and I bought with her and Gregoire. She is making a quilt for the thirty children she lost, a differently colored and patterned square for each one. It is an act of completion, and also an act of hope, because the quilt is for the child she hopes to conceive. After two years of struggling with infertility, she now seeks, in this ritual of her own design, the blessings of those who best know the kind of mother she can be.

Now the smile in the lotus becomes *her* smile as she holds her baby boy, and Gregoire's as he roars home on his motorcycle to greet his "petit poussin." And it is Julien's as he climbs the stairs to our flat and heads to the toy basket, as if he owns the place.

After sunset, when the heat is spent, we return to the mandala rising around the bodhi tree, walk through pools of darkness and lamplight. On the evening of the day that is Jack's, a tide of chanting Sri Lankan pilgrims sweeps around us, sets the banks of oil cups ablaze. He loves South Asia, too, that earnest blue-eyed son. I stop before a smoke-blackened deity in the temple wall, glinting in the glimmer of the candles below it. Who is this man, whose birth in Munich hung me on a turning wheel? Who forgave my maternal angers and outgrew his boyhood timidities, who has accompanied me into danger and discovery? As I stare into the stone's greasy glisten, I can almost see his face, grime-streaked at the encampment by the Seabrook reactor. And I'm crying a little, knowing, as I always have, how he impelled me to learn what I needed to learn about the state of our threatened world.

I move on to find Fran. He is on the temple's western side, watching the lines of Sri Lankan devotees; he is easy to discern, being so tall, with silver hair glistening in the light of their lamps. We take each other's arm for the one last go-round. We don't need to speak, for we know each other's gratitude: for Jack, for his decision to come west to direct San Francisco's recycling program and to settle in Berkeley close to our house; for beloved Charlotte who followed him from Boston; and for their child, year-old Eliza.

As Fran and I head out on our rounds on Christopher's day, we step into our old patterns of worry on his behalf. How deeply we want stability for Chris—a relationship he can commit to, a job that can last, even a steady place to live. But once again, as happens so repeatedly here, concerns give way to gratitude. Chris is no longer lost, drifted out of sight. When he came down from Oregon to paint the rooms of the house we bought with Peggy and Gregoire, he stayed on. We see him continually, hear his stories of the life of a handyman around Berkeley. The instant he opens the door, I know it's him because gorgeous wolf-dog Esther is already up the stairs and in the kitchen. Then, after finishing off our meal, we may go out with them for a walk in the hills or a ramble through the Ashby flea market or an evening of jazz.

Today Fran and I branch off the south side of the perimeter and walk around Muchilinda pond, where a carved Buddha sits amidst the water lilies. He is protected by the serpent king, whose hood spreads above him like a parasol. The scene fades into images of Christopher in Nigeria, with his royal pythons around his neck and shoulders; and then of him scuba-diving with me in Tunisia as we spiral and somersault down through schools of colored fish.

When I turn back toward the Mahabodhi temple, I can almost see on its high, intricate facade a boy-form climbing—as ten-year-old Chris climbed the sculpted temples of Khajuraho when we lived in India. It scared me then, just as it did when he disappeared into the inner scaffoldings of the National Cathedral. He always treated the monuments of our civilization as if they were his playground. Or as if the proud achievements of our culture already lay in rubble, to be turned to new, ingenious uses. In any city, he still heads into the alleyways, the flea markets, the encampments of the homeless—as if what is broken and discarded has some meaning for the future. Chris, the paradox, who stockpiles old clothes and cars with rusted transmissions, yet lives on nearly nothing.

Chris, the survivor, who may help us pick our way some day through the ruins of our civilization. Chris, who follows, in every local speech and interview I give, the work I have chosen to do, and whose brown eyes both support and forgive my ambitions.

In the Mahabodhi morning, I follow Fran down the steps toward the great tree and let go, once again, of my worries for Chris. As the once-great Bodh Gaya establishment crumbled and then revived in simpler, truer form, so have my hopes for our first-born son.

To the north side of the temple, halfway up toward the perimeter, stands a venerable cousin to the bodhi tree. Carved figures, black from lamp smoke, cluster in the folds of its huge, gnarly trunk, and its far-reaching branches shade living figures as well —meditating, reading, doing prostrations. Fran and I have adopted this great being as our "ancestor tree."

Here we take time every day to place a flower by its roots and sit a while on its broad stone terrace, offering thanks for those who gave us life. Silently we remember our parents, and their parents too; then, finding a spot to talk, we speak of them together.

I sense Fran's gratitude that I loved his mother and father so deeply, sharing more of myself with them than I could with my own family. They saw me—saw who I was—as no one in my own family ever seemed able to do. And they loved me as the daughter they never had.

I had always delighted in watching my mother with Fran, chatting about people and plays over their ritual bourbon. He relished her warmth and wit. Having loved Mama so, he shares the loss I feel at her going, and also my relief with the end of the long vigil—kept most closely by my brother Harty—as that elegant woman faded and shrank into Parkinsonism.

For my father I do a number of circumambulations around the ancestor tree and light a candle stub in the recesses of its trunk. Making my peace with that man has been a lifelong undertaking. Gazing up into the leaves, I recall the long-ago morning when I awoke in Fran's arms and realized that my terror of Papa had relinquished its grip on my heart. After that I let myself begin to appreciate the strengths he possessed, and summoned in me. Years after his death, I can acknowledge that I owe to him much of my stubborn intellect, my love of languages and poetry, my eloquence. Perhaps his most valuable gift to me was the most painful to acquire: in countless confrontations he was the noble adversary who forced me to find my own integrity—and the power to defend it.

Our last night in Bodh Gaya, and out of a clear sky there's a light rain. Fran is sitting right under the bodhi tree with a passel of pilgrims; he sits as quiet as they do, though he's not used to the posture and his knees stick up. I'm glad that Herb King, at that Greenwich Village supper forty-six years ago, told me to keep seeing him as a stranger. Mostly I have done that. And so do I now as I walk by and let my eyes fall on him. His hands hold the prayer beads that Choegyal Rinpoche blessed for him two weeks ago; his eyes are closed. I imagine him hearing the rain on the leaves as we used to hear it on the walls of our tent when we camped in the Adirondacks. As I walk on round the temple, I seem to be dedicating these last rounds to him—to us. I let myself be thankful, once again, that we never turned our marriage into a prison, from which I would need to escape. It never became that bride-suffocating trunk I had feared as a child.

Tired, I sit on a low ledge in view of the tree. All the ones in many places, for whom we have walked, come again to my mind, and others around the world as well. They hover so close I can almost see their faces, hear their voices in the patter of rain on leaves. Rilke's poem murmurs in my mind, "I live my life in widening circles."

The young poet went on to say, "I circle around God." Whatever that meant to Rainer Maria Rilke, the widening circles of my life have not had as their center the Big Papa God of my preacher forebears. I walked out on that belief when I was twenty. What authority now holds me in orbit?

The soft rain has ceased. Above the bodhi tree, the moon appears, lopsided, almost full, and I am thinking: no, it is not Fran around whom I circle, nor my children, or even Julien and Eliza. It is not Khamttul Rinpoche or Choegyal Rinpoche or Mummy, my honored Sister Karma Khechog Palma, who brought me into Dharma practice. Nor is it Adekimba or Ocean of Wisdom, showing me, as they did, my heart's capacity; nor my dear colleagues in Germany, Australia, Japan, Chernobyl, showing me, as they do, the promise of our work together.

Is it my love for them all that holds me in orbit? Or is it the fate awaiting my planet's people in this harsh, momentous time?

The tall Tibetan monk strides by me, his lined face catching the lamplight. And there sits the young Japanese woman, eyes closed, still as a stone, and the Sri Lankan bhikkhu rearranging his robe, his sheaf of texts. For ten days their devotions have enriched my own. I want to say good-bye to them, to tell them that tomorrow I will be gone. But I don't. I only thank them, silently, for their company.

* Excerpt from Joanna Macy, 2000. *Widening Circles*. Gabriola Island, BC: New Society Publishers, pp. 271-277.
Editors' Note: On a visit in December, 2008, Fran Macy suggested that we use this story in *Held In Love*. Fran died suddenly one month later, on Inauguration Day, 2009.

Held By this Love*
By Georgina Chambers

You are the star of the morning
You are the dust of all birth
Emptiness always unfolding
Heart breaking over the Earth

Mystery cries out in the darkness
Circling the vastness of Space
Naming the child of my longing
Ancient One come take your place

Now in this moment, forever
Here in this place, everywhere
Under one moon, all light streaming
Within this breath, every life

You are the dance of creation
Music that wakens each soul
Wisdom of ages unfolding
Making the broken ones whole

Loneliness older than mountains
Moves us to open beyond
What we had thought was protection
What we believed made us strong

One tear, a part of an ocean
One grain, the essence of stone
Each holding true to the memory
Calling us home, to our home

We are a ribbon of brilliance
Crossing the vastness of Space
We are Love singing her sadness

Held in a moment of grace

We are Love singing her sadness
Held by this Love, we embrace

* Explanation for these lyrics:

In the summer of 2006, Carolyn McDade, songwriter, spiritual feminist and social activist, invited women from 12 communities across Canada and the US to collaborate in the *My Heart Is Moved Project*. Hundreds of women enthusiastically joined together to spend the next year reflecting on The Earth Charter while learning a body of music relating to the essence of this UN document. This experience was to shape and change our lives and challenge us to find ways to move what we were learning into and beyond the widening circles of our home communities.

The following June, 85 women gathered in Boston to record *My Heart Is Moved*. Though many of us had never met before, the moment we began to sing we were brought into one sense of heart and purpose. Over the course of the week, moved by laughter and tears, we sank into what Carolyn describes as "music that guides us through the narrows to a deeper understanding of who we are as planetary and cosmic beings."

In Boston, we women of Atlantic Canada also represented the collective heart and voice of those who remained at home holding the energy and supporting us. We were asked to describe what it meant to be carrying the intention of our entire community of singing women to this recording. Each piece of writing was an eloquent and heart full expression of honour and joyful responsibility. Each woman spoke of the deep sense of being held lovingly by those at home who would be supporting our recording across the lands and waters of this continent.

But try as I might, I could not make myself sit at the computer and put what I was feeling into words, as the others had so beautifully done. Then one day as I was playing with a new melody on my guitar, words began to arrive and I realized my response was to take the form of a song.

Held By This Love speaks from the deeply held knowledge, so often buried or forgotten, of how connected we humans are to each life form of the universe that has breathed us here and that continues to sustain us beyond time and space, until we can once again open to its creative gesture.

Defending Mother Earth
By Kevin Kamps

I have been an anti-nuclear activist for sixteen long years now. Although I've met some fellow activists who have been at it for over forty years, I know from experience how hard it can be. This story is difficult for me to write, because it forces me to look closely at something I struggle with every day—how to continue with this work, to sustain it for so long, to hold onto hope and not succumb to despair? I take inspiration from Native American activists I have met, torchbearers of a "resistance movement" that has lasted not decades, but centuries.

My introduction to anti-nuclear activism came in 1992 on the Walk Across America for Mother Earth, which cured my paralyzing despair and has sustained my work through the years.

The Long Road to the Walk

The threat of global nuclear annihilation has long troubled my heart and mind, even since childhood. It can feel very lonely in this society, which largely treats such concerns as taboo. It has been essential to connect with others who recognize the risks, and more importantly, do something about them.

My junior high science teacher probably had no idea how much the article he posted on his bulletin board would impact me back in the early 1980s. It was a short op/ed in the Kalamazoo Gazette, written by a physics professor at Western Michigan University. I think it was part of a national campaign, coordinated by Physicians for Social Responsibility. The article described what would happen to my hometown in the event of a nuclear war. Because a local factory manufactured a part for atomic missile engines, chances were good that the Soviets had targeted my hometown with a 20 megaton warhead, a thousand times more powerful than the atomic bomb that devastated Hiroshima in 1945. Suffice it to say, my entire world would have been obliterated. It made quite an impression on me. I tried to bury my healthy fears, without knowing what to do about them.

By college, I felt miserable about the state of things. I thought a Quaker school would be an oasis of sanity in a world gone mad, but I felt the craziness had established a beachhead right on campus. My grand plan had been to major in biology and work for Greenpeace someday, to save the planet and its diverse, precious species. So I was disconcerted to confront "genetic engineering 101" in my classes, with little to no talk of ethics. Dabbling with billions of years of evolution didn't smack of wisdom to me. And how it comported with Quaker simplicity, I couldn't figure.

The first Persian Gulf War didn't help me emotionally either. I wish I could have had the clarity and the courage to involve myself more deeply in the peace studies program and its community, but I was still held back by fear—perhaps of learning how deep the abyss really is that humankind has dug for itself and the rest of the planet. Instead, I felt more and more isolated as the war rushed forward. I felt lost when the college president announced his neutrality on the war, and when a small group of drunken students disrupted a silent candlelight peace vigil on campus by singing the Star Spangled Banner at the top of their lungs. I did not know how to respond. When the war erupted, I felt so isolated all I could think to do was watch Apocalypse Now, alone.

I was at this point so full of despair something had to change, despite my fears. The Great Mystery, a name for "God" used by certain Native American peoples, was about to guide my steps with some powerful "road signs" that would dramatically change the direction of my life.

Somehow *Bury My Heart at Wounded Knee* came into my hands. It really shattered me. I learned the 1991 "Highway of Death" in Kuwait and Iraq wasn't the first massacre carried out by the U.S. Armed Forces. In fact, Columbus's landing 499 years earlier had begun the ravages right here in North America, perpetrated on the indigenous peoples of this hemisphere. I felt the urge to do something, lest the despair and shame of such a violent—and very often hidden and denied—history would undo me.

Greenpeace showed up in our student union. Their poster read "Scene of the Crime," and depicted the nuclear weapons testing sites around the world. From the Nevada desert to French Polynesia, Novaya Zemlya in the Russian Arctic, and China's Lop Nor Desert, these places were beautiful, but lethally contaminated. And the bomb "tests," often on indigenous peoples' lands, amounted to "target practice" for vaporizing cities. I had to do something.

Theologian Rosemary Radford Ruether came to our campus, on a tour for her book *Gaia and God.* I remember the story she told about Native Americans in Maine resisting "development" of their traditional forests. An indigenous woman elder had said to the developers, why don't they take off their shoes, walk barefoot on Mother Earth, and get to know Her, rather than pave Her under? I wanted to take off my shoes and walk upon the Earth.

The Walk

The Lakota translation for "Great Mystery" is Wakan Tanka. The Anishinaabe (Potawatomi, Ojibwe, and Odawa) in Michigan where I come from say it Gitchi Minidoo. How else to explain the Walk finding me, curing me of my spiritual paralysis? It showed up right at my very doorstep. The Walk Across America for Mother Earth was traveling, by foot, from New York City to the Nevada Test Site. Over the course of nine and a half months and 3,500 miles, the walkers strove to end nuclear weapons testing. Comprised of a few hundred people, mostly Belgians and Native Americans, the Walk sought to commemorate the 500th anniversary of Columbus's invasion of Native America by ending exploitation of indigenous peoples, specifically focusing on nuclear oppression.

I was terrified to drop out of college and join the walk, but knew I had to. Being so young and inexperienced, I did not realize I could negotiate a leave of absence from college and return later. I certainly was not calm enough emotionally to wait any longer, to postpone joining the Walk till summer vacation, after classes ended. I felt too desperate for such patient deliberations. Less than a week later, I was a "peace pilgrim," marching westward twenty miles per day, toward a rendezvous with my "heart of darkness" at the Nevada nuclear weapons test site.

I was very fortunate to find myself amongst a courageous and determined community of hopeful activists. The Walk was far from a perfect utopia, but we did our best to create a non-violent community based on consensus as an alternative to the violent "might-makes-right" worldview we saw ravaging the planet. Given the intense stress of life in a tight-knit village that each day changed location twenty miles further west, by foot, with few resources other than our own passion and the kindness of others, it is a miracle we made it. The beauty of the North American continent and its living beings helped a lot. The experience inspired me sufficiently that sixteen years later I am still engaged in full time anti-nuclear activism. It changed me forever.

A Belgian group, For Mother Earth, conceived of and organized the Walk. Belgian anti-nuclear activists, including Pol D'Huyvetter of Gent, had traveled to the Nevada Test Site (NTS) for protests. Pol was part of the widespread European movement against deployment of U.S. intermediate range nuclear missiles in Western Europe. It made a lot of sense for Belgians to "give peace a chance"—Belgium had been overrun by two world wars in the space of a single generation.

In Nevada, Pol met Bill Rosse, Sr., a Western Shoshone Indian traditional elder. Besides his beloved sense of humor, and the heartfelt renditions of Johnny Cash songs he played on his guitar under many a starry sky, Bill Rosse had devoted himself to shutting down the NTS. Over 1,000 full-scale nuclear blasts were carried out at the NTS between 1951 and 1992, including a hundred above ground that directly spewed deadly radioactivity downwind. This gave the Western Shoshone's homeland (which they call Newe Sogobia, for the land of "the people of the Earth Mother") the dubious distinction of being the most bombed nation on Earth, with all the consequent radioactive fallout and contamination of the air, land, and water. In fact, the Western Shoshone National Council, especially its spiritual leader Corbin Harney, had led protests against nuclear weapons testing for decades. When Pol asked "What will we name the Walk?" Bill Rosse suggested "For Mother Earth, because you're doing it for Mother Earth."

The traditional Native American ceremonies were the most powerful part of the Walk for me. They were devoted to global healing, but they were also helping me heal. The name of a grassroots group that formed after the Walk, not far from NTS, captures it well: "Healing Ourselves and Mother Earth". Even its acronym carries power: HOME. These sacred ceremonies included Lakota sweat lodges on the Great Plains; "Wiping Away the Tears of 500 Years" in Independence, Missouri (at an ancient sacred site, in the hometown of President Truman, who presided over the atomic bombings of Hiroshima and Nagasaki); a heart-rending commemoration of the shameful Sand Creek Massacre of hundreds of defenseless Cheyenne and Arapaho Indian women, children, and elderly men by a white Colorado militia under the command of Colonel John Chivington in 1864; and the culminating "Healing Global Wounds" ceremony, with 3,000 participants, led by Western Shoshone elders in the Great Basin desert at the front gate of the NTS. It was a tremendous, life-changing honor and privilege to be a part of it all.

I learned at the feet of people, mostly Native Americans, who had devoted their lives to defending their communities, the land, and the "winged ones, the four-leggeds, the rooted ones," even the "stone people, and creepy crawly ones"—that is, the entire sacred Creation, all plants, animals, even rocks. For example, take the Western Shoshone leaders I met on the Walk. Corbin Harney, who passed away in 2006, often spoke of "one Water...one Air...one Mother Earth," and for decades led efforts against nuclear weapons testing and radioactive waste dumping in Nevada. The Dann Sisters, Carrie and Mary, have defended their land rights all the way to the Supreme Court. Despite the utter disregard of the U.S. government for the "peace and friendship" treaty it signed with the Western Shoshone in 1863, they have won major victories—recognition of their land and human rights—from the Organization of American States and the United Nations Committee on the Elimination of Racial Discrimination. The Timbisha Band of Shoshone Indians, including elder Pauline Estevez and young leader Joe Kennedy (now tribal chairman), won federal recognition for their land rights in Death Valley after decades of struggle. They now are challenging the proposed federal high-level radioactive waste dump targeted at their sacred Yucca Mountain, which would eventually spew deadly radioactivity into their drinking water supply, the lifeblood of their entire, most fragile ecosystem. The young leader Ian Zabarte, Secretary of State for the Western Shoshone National Council, nearly twenty years later still now actively watchdogs the Nevada Test Site and Yucca Mountain, leading the Native Community Action Council. Former Western Shoshone National Council Chief Raymond Yowell has kept the U.S. Congress on its toes for many years, reminding it of its constitutional obligations under the Treaty of Ruby Valley of 1863.

These extraordinary, courageous people continue to stand up against the most powerful companies, government agencies, even the military—non-violently, with little to no monetary resources, but with a deep connection to ancestors past, and generations yet to be born. Their deep connection to the land, its plants and animals and sacred sites, astounds me still.

Keep on Walking Forward

I had learned about "Winter Counts" from Lakota Indians on the Walk—pictorial accounts of significant events from the past year, depicted on buffalo skins during the "down time" each winter to record the tribe's history. After the Walk, I drew a Winter Count of my experiences, so I wouldn't forget them. It remains important to me, and is available to view. *

I have had the honor, privilege, and challenge of doing anti-nuclear power and nuclear weapons work at the national and even international level for the past decade. Living in Washington, D.C., I am still inspired by Native American leadership defending Mother Earth. Native American grassroots activists—Navajo, Chippewa (Ojibwa), Ontario First Nations, Sauk and Fox, Apache, Goshute and others—continue to fend off environmentally racist radioactive waste dumps targeted at their communities by the nuclear cabal in industry and government.

Whatever "Great Mystery" inspires indigenous peoples to survive and continue their resistance—after so many decades and even centuries of violence and abuse—inspires me too. They are the leaders in defending Mother Earth. They urgently need and deserve as much support as the rest of us can muster.

* To view the Winter Counts poster, click on 'About' then on 'Kevin Kamps' at www.beyondnuclear.org

The Power of Many:
Linking Arms to Build Sustainability and Justice in South Africa
Third Story of "A Trilogy at 5 AM"*
By M. Paloma Pavel

It is 5 o'clock in the morning. I wake up to the heavy breathing and snorting of zebras outside my tent. I can feel the presence of these large bodies through the thin membrane of canvas tent and I hear them munching on the thick Bermuda grass. I gather my camera and passport and step out in the moonlight to a silver haze hovering over the grass. The frost on the tough green "carpet" supporting our tent village crunches as I slip into the crisp pre-dawn air. My eyes scan our tent village for signs of life stirring: a kerosene lamp illuminates the silhouette of one human moving, someone coughs in the dark a few rows down; now three more green canvas structures glow like large lanterns. As I walk about, more shelters begin to flicker with candlelight.

Hundreds of travelers are living under canvas at the "Cradle of Humankind." We are in Johannesburg, South Africa, in 2002, ten years after the first United Nations Summit for Sustainable Development in Rio de Janeiro. NGO leaders from our various habitats spread across the metropolitan region commute into the meetings, exchanging strategy, and sharing concerns. I tuck passport and toilet paper in my vest, along with my video camera and extra tape, small notebook, and a spirit of flexibility, readiness for anything. We will meet on the highroad where trucks will be coming by from the townships. Hitchhiking of rides should be available to Alexandria ("Alex"), about 30 minutes towards town. The plan is to gather in Alex, the closest township to the heart of Johannesburg, still without electricity and water in most of the one-story cement block homes, and walk to Sandton, one of the wealthy commercial centers in the continent of Africa. There the financial transactions of empire take place, with cosmopolitan shops, many banks, and office buildings. This is the center for the official delegate meetings of the World Summit on Sustainable Development.

There is some tension, for word has gotten out that community leaders have been arrested in hopes of discouraging today's Landless People's March. I can feel my own heart beating quickly as I wind my way through the tents. I see many new friends emerging, grabbing their ponchos and jackets, in a quiet scurry to reach the main road in time.

At this early hour, there is purposeful motion, but little sound. But it is clear from the hum of humanity gathering here that this day is important. The official proceedings are becoming stalled, and the thousands gathering in the NGO groups are becoming agitated and aware that their message and voices are not part of the central conversation.

Winding through the labyrinth of Johannesburg in buses, cars, and trucks, we see the history of the land emblazoned in the landscape: racial geography that has become a worldwide symbol for spatial racism—pilings from mining, roads used as divides.

It is sunrise when we begin assembling on the high hill at one end of town. There have been some leaflets, a few handmade signs. Mostly, word has traveled through the grapevine. We are surprised by tanks and machine guns in place where four nights ago 10,000 people convened under the full moon to share rising concerns about threats to privatize water, aspirations for self-governance in post-apartheid South Africa, the need for land ownership and distribution, and access to transportation throughout metropolitan Johannesburg. And now, a call to action has this day buzzing, heating up. Buses and cars arrive at the dirt lots beside the primary school.

There has long been both a racial and spatial apartheid between the official representatives and community leaders. This is a moment of great tension. The main road has been blocked by tanks. Images of Tiananmen Square cannot be far from the memory of many who are here. It is painful that some of these police are black South Africans, and that they were called here by black mayors.

I am here as part of the Cradle of Humankind group, the location of Leakey's first discoveries of hominids, the Rift Valley. With my camera, I pull away from the organizing instructions on civil disobedience and arrest procedures to notice what is happening in between the clusters of humanity this morning. There are prayer groups buzzing, songs and chants in other clusters, growing sparks. The South African anthem arises. I am moved by the electricity in the air, a current you can feel as it erupts here and there in gestures of solidarity.

There are emblematic moments that burn in my memory. One of them is watching the villagers of Alex who are *not* in the march today, the too young and too old, all curious, on the porches. My eye is caught by a young girl who has been weaving through the crowd on her bicycle. She has found a red armband and tied it to the handlebars. I see her father with her now, about to leave the house, trying to un-peel from his daughter. But the girl is insistent, like a crowbar wedging in the small crack of perfunctory attention; she leverages the split-second contact into a monumental moment.

I did not notice how quickly she had untied the armband from her bike, but now her father has stopped, is crouching low on one knee and paying exquisite attention as his child is struggling to wrap the red fabric on her forehead. She lifts both spindly arms and works on securing a tie at the back of her head. Is she seven, maybe eight, I wonder? Her father sees her struggling and seems horrified by the sight of his daughter joining in the activity of the day. Her insistence wins out, and as she closes the gate, about to join the march, he runs out to catch up with her. At first he shoos her back, then sees it is impossible, inevitable, and surrenders. There is a moment of embrace; he sucks his child in deep, like oxygen. Then he looks into her eyes, says words I cannot hear, and lifts his daughter up on his shoulders as the two go on together.

It all happens quickly, but it is inscribed in my mind. I feel embarrassed to be witnessing this moment, personal business out in the street, then honored to see such a transformative and raw shift happen just like that, a kind of initiatory moment.

Light is now pouring over the rolling partially paved streets of Alex, with the heat of the day rising, with the hum of many South Africans, African Americans for whom this is the first journey to Mother Africa, Europeans, Asians, Brazilians, and others now gathering in the face of the mounted horses and tanks. Homemade signs and banners begin to unfurl.

There is a turbulence arising as we hear that the tanks have blocked the main street in an effort to stop the march. More guns appear. I catch sight of the small girl still mounted on her father's shoulders a block away. This tension mounts as we wonder: will the tanks advance, will the phalanx in riot gear move in, will arms be used against this crowd? It is now clear the military are intending to stop the march. For an hour people continue to stream into the dirt street, packing in. The outcome is uncertain. There is a chance that the group will be stopped, or that violence will erupt.

Then a slow hum starts, a rhythm begins to grow, and then a wave of song starts with a slow pulse. This Swahili chant soothes and mellows out the group, easing the tension. Slowly, there is a wave-like motion from the periphery of the crowd, and a message is passed through the entire assembly. Some scouts at the tail end of the march have charted an alternate route. The entire group, now tens of thousands, slowly reverses and the march is now led from what was originally the end of the line. With minimal words, instructions, or even effort, thousands and thousands of people reverse direction and continue slowly, rhythmically, like a giant swarm. The march proceeds. The detour adds about an hour to our total march from Alexandria into Sandton. There is no firing of arms, no one is injured, and the tanks have no need to advance, avoiding a violent confrontation. Instead, the military become a force at the rear of the procession for about a mile, more like an honor guard than a menacing opponent.

Throughout the day, we continue walking, chanting, and singing. Townspeople serve us free food and water along the route, and many cheer us on as we pass through the township and poorer suburbs of Joburg. Ten hours later, the first wave lands at Sandton with peaceful assembly, a victorious demonstration of collective imagination, trust, and capacity to innovate under pressure. As the sun sets in the brick and sandstone square, the sound of global music interweaves with presentations by community leaders from all corners of the world. A petition is drawn up and reaches the main assembly that is now heard, backed by the power of collective action.

I know I will never forget the visceral experience of that day: the hair on my arms and the back of my neck rising in the face of the armored tanks and guns in the early morning, the palpable joy and relief in my gut as a collective intelligence emerged just in time to provide a way out of 'no way.' We were individuals but also a group working in collective non-violent, compassionate action, a swarm-like organism, with an innate intelligence that cared for the whole—thousands of people from throughout the world united across barriers of color, language and ethnicity. All arrived safely together, and found a voice. We learned that between 40,000 and 50,000 people had come together for what became known as the "Landless People's March".

Lying in my tent again at the end of a long day I remember the young girl on her bike, the red scarf her father reluctantly tied, and the threshold they both crossed together as he lifted her on his shoulders and joined together in the march. I see that my own participation in the Landless People's March from Alex to Sandton has also been an initiatory experience for me. I reflect on the many layers of the day's learning: that being held in love means being an *I* in the midst of an ever expanding *we*. We as Americans, we as landless people, we as advocates, we as fearful townspeople, we including the police and the official delegates, and we as the land, long mined for gold and diamonds. As these thoughts stream through my consciousness, I hear the snorting of zebras through my tent, bringing me back to the ancient journey of humanity from its earliest roots in this part of the world, a kind of homecoming, and seeing with new eyes.

Since that experience in Africa, my sense of *we* continues to expand and to challenge my sense of kinship and identity. In the months and years that have followed, demonstrations have increased in number around the world. I now see that our march is also part of a larger rising tide of social movements organizing around the world in the early 21st century, an uprising to preserve and sustain the conditions which support life in the face of global extinction, climate change, and worldwide economic meltdown. I now see this blessed unrest as part of a Great Turning.

*This trilogy is composed of three stories of my own waking up, to the experience of being held in love that has provided grounding for my life and for my work as an activist for sustainability and social justice. These stories represent three transformative experiences that have provided the soil out of which my life and work have grown.

Solstice Waters*
By Duncan Berry

come away with me
while our world tips
its farthest
from the sun
come away
to this place
of waters
which has called us home

to the flanks
of a headland
where we sit
in the company of
bare alders
staring straight
down the throat
of a storm
whose winds
are given shape
by the water they bear.

to walk elk trails
punctuated with squat spears
of sitka spruce
driven deep into the land
the air reverberating
with sounds
from the black head of the raven
and the white head of the eagle
everything above
and below us
fed

by the now fallen water
running in darkness
just under the skin of the land
in a liquid
tithing to each living being
it encounters
on its gravitational
migration

to this land of
never quiet
where converging
these waters feed
the great reverberating
bowl of the pacific
who sends one swell
after another
to break
into white noise
below us
that ancient duet
moving
the tiny drum
inside our ears
every hour of
the day
and night
gently
endlessly
in the
dull rhythm of
their meeting

and we
are inseparably

of these same waters
you and i
the vessel of our skin
containing them
briefly
in a currency of blood
giving life
to love
fueling
and bathing
bringing and taking away

you and i are
different expressions
of the same orbit
around this simple
unifying
liquid
benevolence

come away with me
while our world tips
its farthest
from the sun
come away
to this place
of waters
which has called us home

* for Melany

Atmosphere
By Melany Berry

Estuary
a place where land and water embrace.

Land, River, Ocean, Air
breathing together
creating pine forest, salt marsh,
sandy beach, rocky shores.

Estuary
the sphere that has inspired
Unconditional Love all my life.

As a child
Sung
to sleep by its songs
Embraced
Walking on land and swimming in water
Nurtured
creating imaginary worlds in the sand
Weaving together resilience.

As a youth
friends riding bareback horses,
Nighttime bonfires
of songs and dreams.
Generosity of Spirit for land and each other

As an adult
Center of my universe
Integrating new cultures
into present moment Homecomings

Creating joy of service

touching the landscape
breathing in this atmosphere,
listening and learning these songs

Estuary
a place where land and water embrace

WE
By Carolyn W. Treadway

We crossed the tidal river on a small raft, taking us far from the frenzy and cacophony of the "civilized" world. Behind us, beyond the reach of usual methods of communication, we left our loved ones, our vocations, and all the concerns and tasks of our daily lives. Ahead of us in a new and different world was the unknown. What we found and created was a crucible of distilled experience, and an unexpected laboratory for learning how to hold each other in love.

Sixty of us from four continents gathered at Westwind, a camp and nature preserve of indescribable beauty on the Oregon coast where mountains and a great river meet the mighty ocean. We came together for Seeds For The Future II, a thirty day Intensive to train us in deep ecology and deep time with Joanna Macy, creator of The Work That Reconnects. (See www.joannamacy.net.) Even as we walked through the soft sand from river crossing to lodge, we were already walking back in time. Back to a time of living in harmony with and reverence for the land that so powerfully held us in love the whole time we were there. First, foremost, and always, there was the "land"—the whole magnificent bioregion of land, river, and sea. On our first training day, we were privileged to hear a member of the Siletz tribe describe the ways of his ancestors who had lived for hundreds of years in this very place. The old growth forests, beaches and tidal marshes that they had preserved now welcomed and sheltered us. His sharing evoked not only our reverence for this sacred land, but our longing to know the wisdom of our indigenous elders and our pain at the travesties which have happened to indigenous peoples the world over.

It was amazing how quickly how so many of us settled into natural rhythms, as if our cells and psyches already knew them and could relax into them once again. We put away our calendars and watches to live by natural cycles of day and night, moon, tide, and weather. Every moment of time for thirty days we heard the powerful roar of the ocean surf. I came to feel held by the very sound of the sea.

One full day each week, in solitude and in silence, we went onto the land to connect deeply with it and let it teach us. We let the land give us our verb-names, telling us who we are and what we are called to do for the Earth. In times of distress, there was always the refuge of the land to hold us. As we ever more profoundly loved this land, it loved us back through many messengers. Wild animals that never came close to camp came near, and stayed around longer in the season than they usually remain. Many of us had remarkable encounters with various creatures: deer, elk, bear, beaver, porcupine, salamander, various birds, and the inquisitive seals which would follow our kayaks or come to swim with our few hardy ocean swimmers.

Ever more deeply the blessings of this wondrous, abundant land filled us until gradually we came to realize the land itself was holding us in love, just as surely as a foundation holds up a building. In this hologram of creation, nature constantly offered us her bounties. How could it be anything but love? It was *all* sacred, *all* blessing, *all* love. Living in this level of synchrony with the land led many of us to feel this reverence, this love. This realization alone would have been sufficient learning for the month. But there was so much more. Being held in love by the land provided the larger foundation (or container) that held us as we worked to learn to hold each other in love as well.

Each of us came to Seeds II because of our pain about what is happening to our Earth, and to all the support systems of the Earth, and with great desire and intention to learn what we could do toward preserving and healing our Earth Home. Together, we set our goals, such as acquiring conceptual tools, cultivating resources, enlarging our vision and capacities, expanding our temporal context, realizing our mutual belonging in the web of life, and deepening our spiritual life. Then we got to work, courageous work not for the faint of heart or the uncommitted! Joanna called our month a "basic training" in being warriors with weapons of compassion and insight (into the radical interdependence of all phenomena) that will be much needed in our world to come. A basic training for our times it was, and an Intensive indeed.

We opened each day by dancing The Elm Dance in unity with our sisters and brothers in Novozybkov, the downwind city that received the largest dosage of radiation from the Chernobyl disaster. Through teachings from Joanna and sometimes others, plus sharing and processing in large and small groups, we cognitively, emotionally, and spiritually dived into some of the most difficult problems of these times: destruction of environment and biosphere; accelerating climate change; shortages of water, arable soil, food, oil, and mineral resources; nuclear power and nuclear weapons; political repression; war; and so much more. We tried to prepare ourselves for the Great Unraveling—the breakdown of economic and social structures as we currently know them—that may well come as humans learn to shift from the Industrial Growth Society to a Life Sustaining Society. Sometimes the pain was far too great to bear. We would then come together in powerful modes of grieving and mourning. New rituals would emerge spontaneously, and often we would drum or dance our way back toward life and hope and deepening commitment to the healing of our world.

Week by week, we followed the spiral of the Work That Reconnects: first gratitude, then honoring our pain, then learning to see with new eyes, and finally preparing to go forth. We delved into the types of actions needed for the Great Turning, each one necessary and mutually reinforcing: actions to slow damage to Earth and its beings, analysis of structural causes and creation of structural alternatives, plus a fundamental shift in worldview and values. We also learned to dwell as much as possible in the Fourth Time, a larger temporal context that simultaneously holds past, present, and future. We learned to access Fourth Time through present time whenever we chose, doing so through mindfulness. Along with the creatures of other species, the ancestors and future beings were increasingly present for us at Westwind.

Pain and fear began to transform into great energy for learning and creating. Many activities arose, and many small groups pursued various topics. All the while, people shared with, learned from, and supported and held one another in love. Connections among us deepened as sixty separate people increasingly became one community, one whole, in spite of differences. Our sense of unity galvanized on our eleventh day together, during a mini-drama about war. In it, as "we, ours" turned into "me, mine", we powerfully saw and felt the genesis and impact of divisions and of war. Suddenly, "we, we, WE" became *our* name, the name for something greater than the sum of our individual parts. Each of us was a small part of "WE", but together we were one "WE." It seemed to me that our WE-ness carried through the remainder of our time together, and far beyond. We even had shirts made with "WE" stenciled on them. When it came time to leave, I felt I was leaving fifty-nine parts of myself behind. For quite a while, I felt incomplete without them.

Not that all was harmonious, far from it. Differences between us were sometimes obvious, and upon a few occasions even erupted. As we could express and resolve these differences, by listening and very carefully holding each other in love, our learning and our regard for each other deepened. At the times this healing did not happen, we all paid the cost of what might have been but could not arise. This too was powerful learning, most relevant to the work we do in the world.

More than any ideas or any practices, it was the *experience* of living in a community truly seeking to hold each other in love, through thick and thin, which held the most impact for me. This cannot be adequately described, only felt. To feel it, to live within it for thirty days, was life changing for me. It opened a whole new vision for me, a vision of *how* all of us together will need to learn to live if we are going to be able to transform the Industrial Growth Society into a Society That Can Sustain Life.

Individual discords seemed to be ripples or storms carried along on the surface of a much deeper flow of care for each other and reverence for life. When I was too tired, which happened often, I would want to seclude myself and take a nap. Instead, I learned to let the energy of the whole group carry me along. All I had to do was to stay in the flow (not get off into an eddy), and rest in the larger energy. It was powerful learning for me to realize that at times, even without expending my own effort, I could be part of the community and the flow. I could rest and still truly be held in love! I felt it deeply; what a gift this was!

All too soon the thirty days passed, and we had to prepare to return to the frenzied outer world. Even the thought of this was jarring for me. Many people had new and specific ideas of what they would go forth to do. I did not. I could only think of how I wanted to *be*. I profoundly felt the qualities of *being* so vibrantly lived out in our deep community: love, kindness, tenderness, respect, appreciation, attention, deep listening, care for one another, generosity, gratitude, tenacity, fortitude, courage, fearlessness, wisdom, brilliance, synthesis, openness, trust, hope, phenomenal energy, joy, laughter, grief, shared sorrow and mourning, creativity, invention, brain-storming, heart-storming, problem solving, strategizing, preciousness of each other and all that is. Reverence for and sacredness of *everything*. Enormous gratitude. Celebration of life. Claiming our gifts, making our contributions. The list could go on and on. Gift after gift after gift given and received into the deepest levels of our *being*.

Each of these qualities, these gifts, arose as so many of us held each other in love and were held by the community as a whole, and by the land itself. These were the gifts of nature, of Earth herself. Also, these were the fruits of our intentions and our efforts, made possible by our deliberate choices in the ways we perceived each other and treated each other with respect, care, and reverence. I experienced in the core of my being what it means to hold each other in love.

These are the lessons I learned, and that humans must learn. Only if we can practice such qualities in the ways we perceive and treat each other will the species survive...

Living out these qualities is the bedrock of the tools and the practices we need to transform our world. Who knew that Seeds II could create such guidelines for the future of life on this planet? But, in some ways, I believe we did. Hafiz summed it up very well centuries ago in his poem "It Happens All The Time In Heaven": *

> It happens all the time in heaven,
>
> And someday it will happen here too on Earth,
>
> Where men and men who are lovers

And women and women who give each other light
And men and women who are married
Will get down on one knee
And while so gently taking the other's hand in theirs
Look them in the eye and say:
My dear, how can I be more loving to you?
How can I be more kind?

On our answer to this tender and gentle question, the fate of our world depends.

May each of us hold this two-part question deeply in our heart every day, letting it guide all we are and all we do. This is my ongoing prayer. This is the essential core of being held in love, and holding in love, that I learned experientially by living for thirty days in profound community—and becoming part of "WE."

* Hafiz, translated by Daniel Ladinsky, 1996/2003. *The Subject Tonight is Love: 60 Wild and Sweet Poems of Hafiz*. New York: Penguin, p. 45.

The Whole Year 'Round
By Jim Brown

The whole year 'round, from my front porch
(except for days-on-end of snow clouds, rain clouds)
I watch the sun set behind every bump and dip
of the mountain skyline, from north of Mt. Eddy
to south of Castle Crags.

Tonight, a few hours before summer solstice,
I stand just outside my front door and note once more
the sun's intersection with the skyline, hidden
behind the slender trunk of our neighbor's cherry tree.

The door and the tree establish themselves
as cardinal points of observation
for this annual event.

After I am gone, my successor
might continue the observance, and so on
until the cherry tree, the house, are gone.

Long after the age of human observers
the Eddies and the Crags will shift and crumble
and be gone, but the planet will continue
tipping one way, then another, as it circles
the sun, the ancient one that subsumes
all we are and all we know.

The earth, the sun, in far off temporal frames
we cannot imagine,

will themselves be gone.

But what of this joy?

Held By Past And Future
By Maggie Ziegler

Dear One,

    We, the past and the future, greet you with open arms and with gratitude that you are eagerly opening this letter, because most of the time you are so forgetful of us. It is we who widen your present moment and rise through your body until you are enveloped in a spacious lightness that expands outward until there is no separation of time and space. It confuses us that you have such difficulty remembering.

Dear one, moving fully into the present moment is the only way to find us and so we write to remind you of the breath door, the in and out door that is never closed, the life door that always says yes.

How silly to think that all you are is flesh and bone and muscle, to believe you are separate from all the atoms reeling through the universe, independent from the planet's continuing evolutionary journey. How painful it must be to be so alone and so that is why we are grateful that this afternoon you have opened the breath door that is never closed so you can see the present and the past and the future flowing every which way until all there is the now which is forever and you become an expanse so enormous that you are everything that ever was and ever will be. You are the lizards of history, the ancestors who created those great pools under the earth that are now being emptied, the mutations in the Chernobyl forests, the uranium traveling so far into the future. You are the stars and the sun and the endless galaxies.

We write now because you have let us in and we don't know when you will give us another opportunity. That saddens us. We encourage you to give up forgetting and fall through the door of the present moment into the deep flow of time, fall through the door that is always open and then, dear earth piece, you will not be so alienated from yourself. We are always here but you must give up this fast time trap, this nowness that has nothing to do with the present, in order to come home to your full time, to come home to a land of verbs where everything loosens and flows.

We invite you to let go of false constructions that constrict the breath door that is always open in a way that makes us invisible. We invite you to let go of narrowing identities that grieve us and make you a hungry ghost who cannot see us. Stop forgetting and walk into that wondrous place of deep time and then you will be all you are. Then you can sustain an open gaze and your compassionate heart will be boundless and wise.

We hold you, always.

Past and Future

Crop Circle Lotus - Janaia Donaldson

Epiphany*
By Angela Manno

Out of the depths I cry unto you,
Oh Presence, Maker of this perfect world
Out of this silence but for my own breath

Out of the darkness and weightlessness
The black infinite night
Encrusted with countless stars, cool, distant, white.

I turn my gaze, not ready fully to take in
The Spectacle below:

A slow procession of green and earthen landmasses
Mountains undulating
Grazed by gentle, drifting clouds
A miraculous harmony of soft and brilliant hues
Vast oceans
Shining with sunlight

From a well of tears
Come flooding...a sense of Being,
Connection, and yes *Love*
It's all alive, life within Life.

Garden of Eden
Suspended in space,
Nothing holding it up
No fulcrum upon which it spins

But wait...
Two new continents have come into view
And now, suddenly
The other side of the world is before me!

I must think:
Have I some special right to gaze upon such Beauty,
The living host of all we know: all of history and music and poetry
And art and birth and death and love and tears?

What have I done to merit this moment?
This glimpse of Divinity,
Devastating Beauty,
Mother of us all?

Though I float miles above,
I am a part of that Life,
Tied to her through her breath
Which I take with me
In a tank on my back

I am afloat in the infinite sea
My heart races
There is no up or down…

But there is worship
There is the bursting of my heart
There is the cry from the most profound depths:

See where you live, Humanity!
See your own Self!
This tiny, miraculous island of life
Adrift in the vast cosmos

We are so alone, so fragile.
There is nothing more glorious

So said the Saint:

"Because the divine could not image itself forth in any one being, it created the great diversity of things so that what was lacking in one would be supplied by the others and the whole universe together would participate in and manifest the divine more than any single being."

And the writer of Hindu texts: "I am Beauty among beautiful things."

For all eternity there is but one Earth.
I will tell them, I will make them understand…

Plunging back into you in a ball of fire,
I will not forget your face,
I will remember you, Jewel of the Universe,
Most Holy Ground, Home.

* In beginning a new body of artwork, I looked for inspiration in the ever-expanding file of quotations I had gathered over decades from numerous sources: world literature, spiritual traditions, physics, cosmology, indigenous wisdom, and ecology. In my search, a quote from Michael Collins, pilot of Apollo 11 (the first lunar landing) command module, struck me to the core:

"I think a future flight should include a poet, a priest, and a philosopher…we might get a much better idea of what we saw."

Sensing a new urgency to Collins' point, particularly as we continue to unravel the biosphere at an ever-increasing rate, and realizing that such a flight crew would probably not be forthcoming any time soon, I thought to myself: *I will try my hand at it.* After all, as a visual artist, I interpret and condense experience into images like a poet, I approach my art as a form of ministry/service, and I am a natural philosopher, prone to the pursuit of wisdom. Plus I have spent many hours in conversation with the astronauts and in reading what they have written and absorbing what they witnessed. Their accounts have been a deep and abiding source of inspiration to my art and have an urgent message for the world.

The Force Field of Love
By Carolyn W. Treadway

We are held in love
By the universe itself
Expressed in myriad ways
Through manifestations huge and tiny:
The orderly movement of stars
In the night heavens,
The communication of the honeybees,
The blooming of a flower,
The flow of the seasons,
Dolphins caring for wounded humans.
The patterns of the universe
From unfathomable vastness
To subatomic particles
These convey the glue that holds
Emptiness and motion
Together.

Some may call it gravity—
this pull we have on each other—
but I call it Love.
Love is the glue that holds us together.
How we treat each other
How we treat the Earth, our only home,
Depends on Love.
If we can't learn to act from love
We will not survive.
Love is our anchor, our core,
The force field that pulls us toward each other
To create the interconnected web
of life.

We are held in love
We are loved
We are love
We hold each other in love.

Biographical Information

Carl Anthony is cofounder (with M. Paloma Pavel) of Breakthrough Communities, an initiative to promote multi-class and multi-racial leadership for sustainable metropolitan communities in the United States. He is author of the forthcoming book *The Earth, the City, and the Hidden Narrative of Race: Discovering New Foundations for Just Sustainability in the 21st Century*.

Renate Baier lives near Innsbruck, Austria. She has three adult children and works with psychosynthesis and Nonviolent Communication. Her main areas of interest are: the search for healing and wholeness in every form of existence; the secrets and the intelligence of our heart; and witnessing and assisting the evolution of the immeasurable human potential.

Jennifer Berezan is a singer/songwriter, teacher, and activist. She explores environmental, women's, and other justice issues in her music, as well as Buddhism and earth-based spirituality. She teaches at the California Institute of Integral Studies, and produces multi-cultural musical events. Her albums include: *In the Eye of The Storm*, *Borderlines*, *Refuge*, *She Carries Me*, *Returning*, *Praises for the World*, and *End of Desire*. www.edgeofwonder.com.

Duncan Berry has founded and run a number of sustainable businesses around the world. Currently he spends much of his time conserving lands with monies generated from carbon offsets. He finds poetic inspiration at the edge of the wild continent, where the Oregon Coast meets the Pacific, and in his constantly evolving relationship with his dearest life mate Melany.

Melany Berry has enjoyed the blessings of a living relationship with the Salmon River Estuary on Oregon's mid coast since her early childhood. Her interests center around sustainable stewardship practices stemming from the generosity of spirit she has learned from this beautiful land.

Beth Beurkens is a poet and teacher of shamanism. Her first collection of poetry, *Shaman's Eye*, has just been released. She is on the faculty of the College of the Siskiyous and the Foundation for Shamanic Studies, and is also a poet-teacher with California Poets in the Schools. She leads the innovative writing program, "The Courage to Write," in Mount Shasta.

Joana Blaney is a teacher and Maryknoll missioner who lives in São Paulo, Brazil. She works in the area of restorative justice at a human and environmental rights center. Joana's passion is popular education. She appreciates the diversity, life, and challenges of this mega-city as we move forward in the Great Turning!

Shepherd Bliss has run the organic Kokopelli Farm since 1992. He teaches psychology part-time at Sonoma State University in Northern California. Dr. Bliss has contributed to two dozen books and in recent years has been writing about agropsychology and agrotherapy—farms as healing places, especially from trauma. sbliss@hawaii.edu; www.vowvop.org

Jim Brown is held in love and guided by love through all the aspects of his life: husband, father, grandfather, elder, consciousness theorist and researcher, counselor, teacher, poet, deep ecologist, and more he has no name for yet.

Molly Young Brown is a teacher and writer in the fields of psychosynthesis and ecopsychology, offering phone coaching and on-line training. Her four published books include *Growing Whole: Self-realization for the Great Turning* and *Coming Back to Life* (coauthored with Joanna Macy). Mother and grandmother, she lives with husband Jim Brown in the lap of Mount Shasta in northern California. www.MollyYoungBrown.com.

Elizabeth J. Buckley most deeply feels connection with the Life Force through engaging in the creative process as tapestry artist, writer, teacher, singer, and modern dancer. She lives in New Mexico.

Cindy Caldwell lives in Lexington, Illinois. She received her art degree in 1977, and since then has been has done acrylic painting for clients across the U.S.A. She emphasizes the sacredness of nature. Art for her is a process of distilling a visual representation on canvas, mixing reality and imagination, and searching for the essence of beauty and inspiration.

Janine Canan, Sonoma, California author and psychiatrist, devotes herself to planting, patients, poems and prayers. Her books include *Goddesses, Goddesses; Walk Now in Beauty: The Legend of Changing Woman; Journeys with Justine; Messages from Amma; In the Palace of Creation; Changing Woman* (poems); *She Rises like the Sun: Invocations of the Goddess*; and translations of the poets Else Lasker-Schüler and Francis Jammes. www.JanineCanan.com.

Dorothy Carroll is a Pennsylvania octogenarian and mother of five who lives a rewarding and interesting life. She is deeply involved in her Quaker Meeting, a leader in Re-Evaluation Counseling and its Elders Workshops, a community activist, and a loving human being. Her goals are to continue to follow leadings of the Spirit and to live each moment well.

Georgina Chambers lives in Halifax, Nova Scotia with her dog Daemon. Daily, he invites her to discover the seasonal wonders of the lands and waters where her family settled many generations ago. Neither urban nor rural, they reside on the boundary ~ a familiar place, inspiring contemplation, songwriting, and the sheer joy of embodied experience.

Carol Clarke is currently an organic farmer in New York State. She was a Marxist-Leninist organizer, and then a Business Systems Analyst in a large corporation. Shortly after leaving her corporate job in 2005 she encountered the Work That Reconnects led by Joanna Macy, and began her new life farming and promoting life-sustaining systems.

Lynn Clemmons is a Southern California native who now calls the San Francisco Bay area home. She holds a degree in political science and has worked in the professional insurance industry since graduating from college. Although she proclaims herself a dog person, she shares her home with two kitties, Basil and Sybil.

Louis Cox: See Ruah Swennerfelt

Paula D was born in Indiana but grew up in northern New Mexico where she was exposed to both the Indian and Spanish cultures as well as the scientific culture of Los Alamos. This mixture gave her both the awareness of spirit and the skepticism of science that keeps her levelheaded and open to the spiritual experience.

Barbara Darling grew up amongst lakes and waterfalls. After college, she volunteered two years in Germany with the American Friends Service Committee. Master's Degrees in both Special Education and Social Work have led her to fulfilling work in a variety of social service settings. She is captivated by the high desert, clear light, and red rock mesas of New Mexico, where she lives with her husband.

Abigail DeSoto is a transformational coach and trainer who lives in France with her four-footed companion Brownie. American by birth and education, she finds resonance in the peace and simple living of rural France, where the flow of life reminds her to live from the heart. She adores walking, swimming, teaching yoga, and accompanying clients on internal voyages of personal discovery. www.inner-discovery.com

Janaia Donaldson, a layerist painter, is also the producer and host, with her partner Robyn Mallgren, of Peak Moment Television conversations about communities building local reliance. www.peakmoment.tv. They live in the Sierra Nevada foothills near Nevada City, California. Their off-grid home is on a 160 acre, forested wildlife sanctuary they have protected with conservation easements.

Hannah Mariah Dube lives in the mountains of Vermont with her husband and two sons. These people and this place (and all the beings that cohabit) continue to teach her about life, dark depths, joy and all that love entails. She hopes to return some of the learning and loving.

Dina Emser has ten years experience as a Certified Professional Coach. She trains groups and organizations in teambuilding, communication, and cooperation. She loves public speaking and speaks nationally and internationally. Individually she works with professionals in leadership positions, educators, and parents to be more effective and happy by using their strengths to reach their goals. She lives in Eureka, Illinois.

Mariellen Gilpin from Champaign, Illinois, helps edit *What Canst Thou Say?*—a quarterly newsletter for people who have mystical experiences or pray contemplatively. She edited *Discovering God as Companion: Real Life Stories from What Canst Thou Say?* She wrote *God's Healing Grace: Reflections on a Journey with Mental and Spiritual Illness.*

Lyn Goldberg has remained curious and is first and foremost a student of life. Currently she lives in an intentional community and is a practicing Professional Astrologer. She has been married for over thirty years, and proud to say there is still passion and growing love in the partnership. One grown son still brings much joy in her life.

Linda Gunter worked as a print and broadcast journalist for twenty years before turning her attention to her true passion—the environment. In 2007, she founded Beyond Nuclear, an international non-profit advocacy group. She lives in Takoma Park, Maryland with her husband Paul, and her treasured adopted family including her two daughters, two cats and a dog.

Rebekah Hart is a poet, environmentalist, and a facilitator of the Work that Reconnects. She is a practitioner of meditation and of Hakomi Mindfulness Psychotherapy. In Montreal, she founded Earth Dialogue, an ongoing eco-spiritual forum. Rebekah feels called to support humans to experience their interbeing with all life as a gateway to personal and planetary transformation. Her writing has received several prizes. (dancingpine@gmail.com)

Barbara Sherman Heyl grew up in California and attended Stanford University for her BA in Sociology. Obtaining advanced degrees in the Midwest, she taught sociology at Illinois State University for thirty years. She especially enjoyed teaching qualitative research methods, helping students learn how to hear and document life-history stories. She lives in Bloomington, Illinois.

Jonathan Holm now works as an engineer in Illinois, where he and Chris attend the Urbana-Champaign Friends Meeting. He experiences God most clearly during quiet, unhurried time set aside for "listening". He and Chris happily celebrated their first wedding anniversary in June 2009.

Carol Hwoschinsky is a peacemaker by nature and has been fortunate to spend her career and her life bringing peaceful solutions to conflict in the US and abroad as a licensed counselor in private practice, an educator, and a mediator. The root of her work has been her training in Psychosynthesis. She lives in Oregon where she loves the out of doors.

Ken and Katharine Jacobsen attend Beloit Monthly Meeting of Friends (Quakers). Katharine is an elder for Stillwater Monthly Meeting, Ohio, and serves on Ohio Yearly Meeting's Committee for Friends Center in Barnesville, Ohio. Ken is in a doctoral program in theology, ethics, and human science at Chicago Theological Seminary. After years of serving as administrators at Quaker schools and a retreat center, they enjoy welcoming visitors at their modest retreat house in southeastern Wisconsin.

Ruthann Knechel Johansen, author and teacher, is currently president of Bethany Theological Seminary in Richmond, Indiana. Prior to her 2007 appointment to Bethany, she was a professor at the University of Notre Dame. Her books include *Listening in the Silence, Seeing in the Dark: Reconstructing Life After Brain Injury*; *The Narrative Secret of Flannery O'Connor*; and *Coming Together: Male and Female in a Renamed Garden*.

Catherine Johnson now lives, writes, and farms on thirty acres outside of Portland, Oregon. For seventeen years she taught graduate education. Her essays have appeared in *Face to Face, Teaching with Fire*, and *The Nature of an Island*. Currently she is working on a memoir and raising pigs.

Kevin Kamps has been an anti-nuclear activist since 1992. He serves as Radioactive Waste Watchdog at Beyond Nuclear in Takoma Park, Maryland. Beyond Nuclear aims to educate and activate the public about the connections between nuclear power and nuclear weapons and the need to abandon both to safeguard our future. www.beyond-nuclear.org

Hollister Knowlton clerks Quaker Earthcare Witness and Philadelphia Yearly Meeting's Earthcare Working Group, and also serves Friends Committee on National Legislation. Long concerned for the earth, in 1994 she gave up her car and became vegan, for reasons of conscience. She is now becoming a non-dairy "localvore" to further shrink her ecological footprint. She took early retirement in 2004 to devote her life to Quaker service for the earth.

Catherine Jane Larkin has 26 years experience as a midwife to the human soul. She facilitates the Hellinger Family Constellation work as well as individual sessions done in person or by phone. Her work of "Calling Dinah's Daughters" helps to heal the collective pain body of women and to remember our deep connection with the world soul. Catherine lives in Ashland, Oregon. catherinejanelarkin@yahoo.com, www.healingthefamilytree.com.

Karen Latvala helps people make conscious choices, move from inner conflict to inner peace, and manifest their deepest desires and visions. As a Life Coach and a Vessel of Peace she works with individuals and groups to consciously transform their lives, thereby helping the world. She lives in Colorado. www.consciouslifequest.com

Joanna Macy's writings and workshops blend East and West, and open us to other life forms as well as past and future generations. She lives in Berkeley CA near her children and grandchildren. Her books include *Coming Back to Life* with Molly Young Brown, *World as Lover World as Self*, and three volumes of translations of Rilke.

Angela Manno is an internationally exhibited artist whose works reside in many private collections and in major public collections including those of NASA and the Smithsonian Institution. She facilitates courses in ecological spirituality and is the founder and director of the School of Living Arts for Creativity & Ecological Culture. She is based in New York City and maintains her studio in the upper Hudson Valley.

Jennifer Mathews currently focuses on social transformation from the perspective of healing, after over a decade as an activist for economic equality. She considers herself a "spiritual cheerleader," encouraging hope, laughter, and non-judgment in the world by offering retreats and presentations across the U.S. Her home base is Mount Shasta, CA. www.optimysticinstitute.com.

Rebecca Moyer presently lives in Sedona, AZ where she has a business guiding people to cutting edge healing options.

Ulla-Madelaine Neurath is a therapist using psychosynthesis in Stockholm. She was raised in Sweden and Germany. Her companions in life are: humour, kindness, spirituality and the healing energies of music. Her motto is: "Never give up; there is always a solution." She aspires to be part of creating a more loving and peaceful world.

Tom Nylund has degrees in both chemistry and psychology. His has worked two years in the Peace Corps, twelve years in research, fifteen years in counseling youth, and currently tutors math students at a community college. He lives with his second wife, Linda, in Normal, Illinois. His story describes a dream/experience he had in his mid-forties while re-creating his life after divorce and a major career change.

Coleen O'Connell lives in a small intentional community, Ravenwood Collective, in midcoast Maine—the site for Lesley University's undergraduate Practices for Sustainability each fall semester. Coleen co-created, directs, and teaches in a unique ecological Master's program that helps teachers integrate systems thinking and ecology across their curricula. She is thrilled and grateful to get paid to do her life's soul work in this program.

Jill Pangman lives in the Yukon Territory of Canada's far north. Her passion is in exploring wild landscapes and sharing these experiences with others. She expresses her own love of nature and her commitment to the healing of our world through her wilderness guiding, parenting, writing, photography and conservation work. www.silasojourns.com

M. Paloma Pavel is president of Earth House Inc. of Oakland, California. She is editor of *Breakthrough Communities: Sustainability and Justice in the Next American Metropolis*, and co-edits Sustainable Metropolitan Communities Books. She is a frequent national and international lecturer and keynote presenter on the theory of living systems and urban sustainability, and consults with individuals, communities, and organizations on strategic planning, strategic communications, and leadership development.

Maurine Pyle is a Quaker traveling minister from Southern Illinois Friends Meeting. She has traveled extensively in the mid-western United States providing spiritual and pastoral support to Quaker communities. Ever since her Louisiana childhood Maurine has been a storyteller, and today she calls herself a story-listener.

Dennis Rivers is a communication skills trainer, ecology activist, writer and online publisher who lives in Northern California. He has, at various times in his life, been a graduate student in religious studies, sociology, counseling, theology, and communication studies. His books include *The Seven Challenges Workbook*, *The Geometry of Dialogue*, *Prayer Evolving*, and *Turning Toward Life*, which are available free as e-books at www.KarunaBooks.net.

Ellise Rossen, a retired marriage and family counselor, has taught courses in psychology, human services, parapsychology, and dreams. She has published a short vignette ("Good Night" in *I Thought My Father Was God*), a poem ("Circadian Rhythms" in *Avocet*, a journal of nature poems), and "Miguel" (in the journal *In The Family*). She currently lives with her cat, Samantha, in Mt. Shasta, CA.

Ruey Ryburn is a healer living in Honolulu, Hawaii, a professor emeritus of nursing from the University of Hawaii, a certified advanced practice holistic nurse, and a private practitioner. Upon retirement, she started her three-year Sacred Path Healing School. She has two sons and a grandson, and lives with her two dogs and cat on a mountain, with a sweeping view of the Pacific Ocean.

Maria Schmeeckle is an Associate Professor of Sociology at Illinois State University in Normal, Illinois. With her students, she has created a program called Global Children Outreach. Maria is currently collaborating with other scholars and practitioners to develop a global action agenda to help street children and orphans. www.globalchildrenoutreach.ilstu.edu.

Anne Scott is a national speaker, founder of DreamWeather Foundation, and leader of workshops and retreats around the country. Her work restores the link between feminine spirituality, everyday life, and social change. Her books include *Women, Wisdom & Dreams: The light of the feminine soul*. Anne has trained in dreamwork for 19 years in the Naqshbandi Sufi tradition, and lives with her husband in northern California. www.dreamweather.org

Susan Scott has lived in the Northwest for the past twenty-six years where her writing and photography have flourished alongside her work as a counselor in private practice. Living close to water, forest, and wildlife on Whidbey Island inspires much of her creative process. For publications and presentations see www/susanscottphd.com.

Doug Seeley is Dean of a Chinese Medicine College in Victoria, British Columbia. A Sufi, he practices Tai Chi, biofeedback, and coordinates (Bohm) Dialogues and Learning Circles. He was a professor of Software Design and a Whole Systems consultant. In 1976 he published "The World As a Hologram in Your Heart" with People's Computer Company.

Linda Seeley lives in San Luis Obispo, CA. A midwife for 30 years, she now is a full-time activist, serving on the boards of the San Luis Obispo Mothers for Peace, Sierra Club, and the Terra Foundation. She is a facilitator of Joanna Macy's Work that Reconnects, grandmother, and community elder. www.terrafoundation.org

Margaret Sorrel, a lesbian mother and grandmother and a lifelong Quaker, lives on Whidbey Island, Washington. She has practiced osteopathic manual medicine for thirty years, bringing hope and better health to children with chronic health problems and developmental disabilities. Bearing witness to Lynn's joyful spirit through this illness has been a great blessing.

Judy Young Smith lives in Santa Maria California with her feline companion, Lucy. A retired nurse, she works part-time at the library, reads voraciously, and enjoys crossword & jigsaw puzzles. She has two daughters and two grandchildren.

Ruah Swennerfelt serves as general secretary for Quaker Earthcare Witness (QEW), and Louis Cox is QEW's publications coordinator, newsletter editor, and webmaster. They live in a hand-built solar-powered house in rural Vermont, where they grow a lot of their own food and try to reduce their ecological footprints through frugality and simple living.

Kathleen Maia Tapp's involvement with story is life-long. She is the author of several children's novels and has also published spiritual poetry. She is a former editor of the Quaker newsletter *What Canst Thou Say?* She now travels as pilgrim-poet and listens and writes.

Pollianna Townsend is a branch manager of two Bank of America branches, mother of a blended family of four, grandmother of two, and a rider of a Harley Davidson Softail. She resides in the Quad Cities of Illinois and feels very blessed to have had the breath of God present throughout her entire life, always with her.

Carole Edgerton Treadway is a retired librarian and archivist, currently teaching in the two-year program "On Being a Spiritual Nurturer" of the School of the Spirit Ministry. She is a life-long Quaker, wife of Ray, mother of Eric and Annemarie, and grandmother of Braeden! She lives in Greensboro, North Carolina.

Carolyn Wilbur Treadway has been a social worker, psychotherapist, or pastoral counselor for fifty years. She advocates for Earth however she can—through being a climate messenger trained by Al Gore and an anti-nuclear activist, facilitating workshops and The Work That Reconnects, writing, speaking, and photography. She is a wife, parent, grandparent, and Quaker from Normal, IL. She offers personal life and sustainability coaching by phone: see www.GraceFullLife.com.

Laura Treadway is a Northwest-based artist and photographer. Her photography is the record of her search for beauty in the world. She earned a Certificate in Photography from the University of Washington in 2008 and works in non-profit management. More information and images at: www.lauratreadway.com.

Lynn Waddington is a retired Quaker teacher and active artist living on Whidbey Island, Washington. She has spent her life attempting to capture and express deep archetypal truths through theater, writing, video, and now sculpture. She is finding this time of illness to be an unexpected gift of grace.

Demaris Wehr is a Jungian psychotherapist living on Martha's Vineyard. She is currently writing a book provisionally entitled: *Making it Through: Stories of Courage and Connection in post-war Bosnia*, with a projected publication date of 2010.

Sarah J. Wolcott studies international development in England while working as chief editor for JustMeans.com. An entrepreneur, she wonders: how we can enhance our humanity in the face of ongoing global crises? She admires Michael Sandell, Wangari Matthai and Bill Moyers. She loves coastlines, public speaking, humanity's development, and poetry.

America Worden is a psychotherapist, gardener and artist in love with the world. She has an MA in Integral Counseling Psychology from the California Institute of Integral Studies and an MS in Holistic Science from Schumacher College. She lives on a farm on the San Francisco Bay.

Anne Yeomans is a psychotherapist and group facilitator living in Massachusetts. About four years ago, poems began to arrive in her mind. This was a complete and wonderful surprise! Since that time, writing, both poetry and prose, has become a central part of her life. She is also a grandmother and gardener—both sources of poetic inspiration and great joy.

Tom Yeomans, Ph.D., has been involved in the Human Consciousness Movement for close to forty years. He studied psychosynthesis with Roberto Assagioli in the early '70's, and has trained professionals in psychosynthesis and spiritual psychology throughout North America, Europe, and in Russia. He has published writing on psychosynthesis and spiritual psychology as well as three volumes of poetry and a children's book.

Maggie Ziegler, MA, is a writer, facilitator, educator and psychotherapist. She has a keen interest in exploring ways to support each other to engage with the social and environmental justice challenges of our troubled times from a steady and loving place. She lives on Salt Spring Island, British Columbia.

About the Editors

Molly Young Brown, M.A., M.Div, studied psychosynthesis with Dr. Roberto Assagioli in Italy in 1973, and deep ecology and systems theory with Joanna Macy, Ph.D in the 1990's. Molly currently teaches on-line training programs in psychosynthesis and ecopsychology, offers counseling and coaching by phone, writes essays and books, and presents workshops internationally. She also performs weddings and gives occasional sermons and talks in her vicinity.

Molly and her husband Jim have two grown sons and two grandchildren. They have lived in Northern New Mexico, the San Francisco Bay Area, and southwestern Colorado, finding different sources of fulfillment in each locale. In 2004, they moved to Mount Shasta, California to live in the lap of that powerful Being.

Other Books By Molly Young Brown

Growing Whole: Self-realization for the Great Turning (Psychosynthesis Press, 2009).

Unfolding Self: The Practice of Psychosynthesis (Allworth Press, 2004)

Growing Whole: Exploring the Wilderness Within CD, audiotape, and journal (Psychosynthesis Press, 1995)

Coming Back to Life: Practices to Reconnect Our Lives, Our World. Co-authored with Joanna Macy (New Society Publishers, 1998)

Consensus in the Classroom: Creating a Lively Learning Community. Co-authored with Linda Sartor (Psychosynthesis Press, 2004)

Available in bookstores and on-line at www.PsychosynthesisPress.com

Carolyn Wilbur Treadway, LCSW, ACSW, is a psychotherapist, pastoral counselor, and personal life coach. She has two private practices: Connections Counseling (live) and GraceFull Life Coaching (by phone). Currently she "speaks for Earth" however she can—as a climate presenter (trained by Al Gore and The Climate Project since 2007), workshop facilitator, anti-nuclear activist, speaker, writer, and photographer. She began her deep ecology training in The Work That Reconnects with Joanna Macy in the mid-1980's.

Carolyn and her husband Roy have three adult children (one son, two daughters) and one grandson. Since 1977 they have made their home in Normal, Illinois. Previously they have lived in Iowa, Indiana, Pennsylvania, Connecticut, New Jersey, Japan, France, and Turkey.

Selected other publications by Carolyn Wilbur Treadway
Book chapters in:

Discovering God as Companion, Mariellen Gilpin, editor, AuthorHouse, 2007

Out of the Silence: Quaker Perspectives on Pastoral Care and Counseling, J. Bill Ratliff, editor, Pendle Hill Publications, 2001

In Her Own Time: Women and Developmental Issues in Pastoral Care, Jeanne Stevenson-Moessner, editor, Fortress Press, 2000

When Children Suffer: A Sourcebook for Ministry with Children in Crisis, Andrew D. Lester, editor, Westminster Press, 1987

Photography in:

Images: Sights and Insights, Mary Kay Himens, editor, Golden Apple Press, 1996 (Available from Carolyn@GraceFullLife.com)

Articles:

"Nuclear Energy and the Care of the Earth", in *Quaker Eco-Bulletin* 5:4, July-August 2005 (See http:// tinyurl.com/f5rq4)

"Awakening to a Sustainable Future", in *BeFriending Creation* 22:3, May-June 2009

Artists' Statements about Cover Art

Front Cover

Cherishing the Earth by America Worden

This image was created as a flag for the sea cave designated as women's space during the Seeds for the Future II training at Westwind on the Oregon Coast. It depicts a woman cherishing, comforting, and protecting the Earth in her embrace.

Back Cover

Life Becoming by Cindy Caldwell

"Life Becoming" is an expression of joy of the Source, the vortex from where all comes. It is the mother of the energy that enthusiastically expands into further form and diversity of life. This is the spiral dance that brings into being the miracle of the world of which we are a part. This tree holds immense love for all of its creations, filled with potential, possibility, and passion."

Breinigsville, PA USA
14 October 2009
225873BV00003B/1/P